Islam and Liberty
The Historical Misunderstanding

Mohamed Charfi

Translated by
Patrick Camiller

Zed Books
LONDON & NEW YORK

Islam and Liberty: The Historical Misunderstanding
was first published in 2005 by
Zed Books Ltd, 7 Cynthia Street, London N1 9JF, UK and
Room 400, 175 Fifth Avenue, New York, NY 10010, USA.
www.zedbooks.co.uk

This book is a revised and updated edition of the title first published
in French as *Islam et Liberté* by Albin Michel in 1998.

First published in Lebanon, Bahrain, Egypt, Jordan, Kuwait, Qatar, Saudi Arabia
and United Arab Emirates by World Book Publishing,
282 Emile Eddeh Street, Ben Salem Bldg, PO Box 3176, Beirut, Lebanon
www.wbpbooks.com

First published in Malaysia by
Strategic Information Research Department (SIRD),
No. 11/4E, Petaling Jaya, 46200
Selangor

Cover designed by Andrew Corbett
Set in 10.5/13 pt Bembo
by Long House, Cumbria, UK
Printed and bound in the United Kingdom
by Biddles Ltd, King's Lynn

Distributed exclusively in the USA by Palgrave Macmillan, a division of
St Martin's Press, LLC, 175 Fifth Avenue, New York, NY 10010

A catalogue record for this book
is available from the British Library

US Cataloging-in-Publication Data
is available from the Library of Congress

ISBN   983 2535 59 X Malaysia
ISBN   9953 14 069 3 Lebanon
ISBN   1 84277 510 3 Hb rest of the world
       1 84277 511 1 Pb

Contents

Introduction[1]

Future generations will remember 11 September 2001 as the dark day of an unprecedented tragedy, when more than three thousand people died as a result of terrorist actions so terrifying in scale that they marked a watershed in international relations. Until that day, relations among states seemed to be growing calmer following the fall of the Berlin Wall, the collapse of communism and the end of the Cold War. Free enterprise as an economic system of production, together with democracy as a political system of government, seemed to have triumphed all over the world – a situation that led Fukuyama to imagine the end of history. To be sure, Huntington already envisaged a major conflict between the West and the Muslim world, but his shock scenario, though sometimes triggering heated debate, remained almost marginal. Most states in Europe and North America maintained relations of friendly cooperation with the countries of the most traditional form of Islamism and, like most Western intellectuals and humanitarian organizations, were very critical of Islamic countries whose modernization efforts brought them into conflict with religious extremism. Criticism was justified when it referred to human rights violations, but it was marked by a complete failure to understand the danger of Islamic fundamentalism. Having applauded the Iranian Revolution, Third Worldist intellectuals downplayed Islamist violence, pointed to a legitimate identity claim in fundamentalist positions, and argued that progressive democrats were actually deracinated supporters of Western schemas inappropriate to their own society, as if it were not legitimate for a Muslim to campaign for freedom and democracy in his or her country.

Islamic societies were the first to suffer the effects of fundamentalist violence, at a time when leaders of even the most violent Islamist movements were being fêted in US universities and English debating circles. After 9/11, things went from one extreme to the other. First, the United States declared war on Afghanistan, overthrew the Taliban and established a new regime there. This was a legitimate response, because it has been shown that the 9/11 attackers were part of al-Qaida and that the Taliban were refusing to close its training camps and to expel the terrorists from Afghanistan. It was also a legal response, precisely because it was accepted as legitimate by the United Nations.

With the invasion of Iraq, however, the United States and certain of its allies have taken things considerably further. At the same time, the Palestinian tragedy continues without any solution on the horizon, and there is cause to deplore the inhumane treatment at Abu Ghraib prison and the holding of detainees in Guantánamo in conditions that are outside the law. In fact, people in the Muslim world have the impression that Islamophobia has assumed disturbing proportions in the West.

Islamism today poses a problem for the whole of humanity; it is the main cause for concern in the field of international relations and security. Western countries have a perfect right to defend themselves against any risk of terrorism, or hostage taking, but the Islamists do not constitute an army that can be destroyed by another army, and the West cannot wage war on one and a half billion Muslims. To find the best way of confronting the Islamist phenomenon, it will therefore be necessary to understand it correctly.

The occupation of foreign lands cannot help in the finding of a solution. Ideas cannot be exported like a commodity. Towards the end of the nineteenth century France did indeed colonize certain Muslim countries, officially with the aim of bringing them its Enlightenment philosophy. But it turned out to be an injustice doomed to failure: the development of a people's ideas cannot be achieved by anyone other than its own elite; foreign powers cannot serve as a substitute but can at most provide various forms of assistance. And the precondition for any assistance is an understanding of the societies in question.

The first essential task is to differentiate between Islam and Islamism. Often the two are confused with each other because Islamists demand the application of the sharia (classical Muslim law). Laid down by the ulema (doctors of religion) more than a thousand years ago, the sharia contains a number of anachronistic laws, and today its underwriting of corporal punishment and sexual inequality conflicts with a consciousness shaped by the Universal Declaration of Human Rights. But that is no reason to criticize Islam as a religion. We should not forget that respect for the physical integrity of human beings is a new principle in the history of humanity, and that sexual inequality has been an experience in all civilizations. The characteristic attitudes of patriarchal society have existed almost everywhere in the world; they are no more Muslim than they are Christian, Jewish or Hindu. In Europe, female emancipation was the result of a long struggle against traditionalists attached to male privilege. The right of women to vote was accepted in France only at the end of the Second World War, and in Switzerland only thirty years ago. The reproaches laid at the door of Islam are therefore not specific to it. The simple fact is that ideas have developed among the Jewish and Christian peoples and are in the course of developing among Muslims.

All civilizations and all religious conceptions evolve. The Greco-Roman legacy is no longer visible in state organization or the citizens' way of life in Europe and the Americas, and nothing about contemporary Christian thought reminds us of the ideas that prevailed at the time of the Crusades, the Inquisition or the trial of Galileo. Since the Second Vatican Council, the Catholic Church has bid farewell to the Middle Ages and closed the parenthesis of the Counter-Reformation. In fact, it has opened wide its door and windows. From time to time it may take a questionable position on some matter, but the road it has travelled over the past century remains impressive. Even in Israel, where the state is based on religion, the emancipation of women means that Mosaic law is no longer observed in its entirety.

The prohibition of divorce in Christianity and the allowance of polygamy in Mosaic law[2] have become museum pieces, and this no longer causes any dissension among the great majority of believers in the two religions. Indeed, the new situation is so much part of collective Christian or Jewish thinking that no major popular current in Europe or Israel demands a return to those old laws in the name of identity or authenticity or another vision of immobility. The existence here and there of fanatical sects or tendencies concerns only a small minority that has no influence on mainstream Judaism or Christianity.

There is nothing surprising in this metamorphosis of the other two monotheistic religions over the last few centuries. For evolution is the law of life itself, and it also applies to religious conceptions.

Islam is no less capable of evolution than Christianity or Judaism. But whereas, over the past few centuries, Europeans have undergone profound technological, economic, cultural and political changes, often amid considerable suffering and with major ebbs and flows, the Muslim peoples have fallen greatly behind in all spheres. This is not a fate to which they are doomed for ever; it is possible for them to close the gap. Corporal punishment, for example, has long since disappeared in most Muslim countries. And in Tunisia the sharia laws punishing theft with amputation of the fist or adultery with death by stoning have been obsolete for several hundred years. The banking system – which can promote development if it is properly organized and managed – functions normally in almost all Muslim countries in spite of the religious ban on interest-bearing loans. Muslim women have escaped from their threefold prison: they are no longer confined at home; they have broken down the invisible barriers of ignorance; and they have torn the veil to become fully fledged citizens.

These various changes have not happened without difficulty and sometimes heated debate. When slavery was abolished in Tunisia between 1842 and 1846, some 'narrow-minded' religious leaders – the fundamentalists of the time – declared that Islam was being scandalously betrayed since the Koran tolerated that institution. Claiming that no one had the right to forbid what the sacred texts permitted, they went even further and claimed that the people behind the moves were seeking to 'please the West'. The reformers, for their part, vigorously and courageously defended themselves from attack.[3] When we read the articles of Bayram (a Tunisian thinker of the mid-nineteenth century), we have the feeling that they could have been written by a present-day democrat. He showed that it was the abolition of slavery rather than its continuation that was in the true spirit of religion, and that it would allow the master to avoid the numerous sins he committed by mistreating his slaves. Later, when Kacem Amin in Egypt and Abdelaziz Thaalbi in Tunisia campaigned for the education of girls and the elimination of the veil, they used the same method of justifying reforms by the spirit of religion and its founding texts.

A number of factors made this evolution possible. First, enlightened thinkers and reformers were often the inspirational force for state action when it functioned as an engine of change. Second, the great majority of the (often illiterate) peasant population had no trouble following them; the country had never been especially noted for fanatical religiosity or scrupulous respect for the sacred precepts, and Bedouin women, for example, had never worn the veil. Finally, the only real resistance to change came from within the religious universities (Zituna in Tunisia or Al Azhar in Egypt), which did not play a decisive role in shaping public opinion or the course of state policy.

In view of these important changes, it is tempting to say that the Muslim peoples have already left behind the Middle Ages and fully entered the modern world, that they have known how to adjust to new exigencies while remaining faithful to their religion. But recent events obviously demonstrate that the changes remain fragile. The reason for this is that, although political, juridical, economic and social structures have undergone significant evolution, political discourse and the system of cultural references have continued to lag behind.

All over the Muslim world, a policy of general education has been introduced along with other measures of modernization and development. However, nearly all the thinking in this regard has been quantitative; there has been no mature reflection or serious debate about the content and methods of education. It has usually been thought sufficient to add on science teaching and foreign languages to the syllabus of the traditional schools, which not only taught Islam as religion but presented it as an identity and a political–legal system. But the truth is that the rising entity of the Nation is not the same as the *Umma* (the community of Muslims): the new political regime, theoretically grounded upon sovereignty of the people, has nothing to do with the caliphate; and the modern juridical system has neither the same origins nor the same content as sharia law. Whereas the new law was adopted by a parliament theoretically issuing from universal suffrage, the sharia was the work of theologians. Whereas the new penology is designed to rehabilitate offenders, or at least to remove them as a threat to the public, the sharia, like all ancient systems of criminal justice, contains provisions for corporal punishment and penalties such as stoning whose aim is the infliction of pain.

All these major innovations have never been properly explained or justified to the public. Year after year the gulf has been widening between an idealized ancestral system, which is held sacred and disseminated through school, and a new system that is ever more widely regarded as an alien import contrary to Islam. This is a grave discrepancy that tears people apart and brings them to the verge of schizophrenia.[4] For they do not wish to sacrifice either Islam or modernity. They are as attached to the Islamic religion as they are to the structures of the modern state, which they insist should be genuinely democratic and representative. At the same time, they vaguely feel the contradiction or even incompatibility between the two. The dysfunctionality of the modern Muslim system is such that the existing situation becomes precarious.

Islamists are part of a minority of the population who want Islam to prevail over modernity. Theirs is a seemingly logical and coherent discourse: we are Muslims; we should therefore apply Islam as we inherited and learned it. Their discourse has such currency today because they sound like uncompromising militants in the face of regimes eaten away by corruption and failure to deliver on promises of development. Above all, they enjoy the huge advantage that there is no credible counter-discourse. For, in most Muslim countries, attitudes on the ground as well as government discourse express a hesitant modernity, one that is neither fully accepted nor reconciled with Islam. In these crucial respects, we may say that Tunisia is a little more coherent than the others.

Hesitant modernity

In the late 1950s and throughout the 1960s, the Arab world was torn among a number of political discourses. In the East, in the lands of the Fertile Crescent, the Baath Party ruled as undisputed master; while in Egypt and the Maghreb three men of great stature – Nasser, Boumedienne and Bourguiba – developed their distinctive sets of ideas. One party and three men, each with his own strategy and style: it would be useful today to compare their results.

The Baath was originally a modern secular party. Formed by a core of Christians and Muslims, who therefore could not agree on a religious foundation, it developed a project independent of all religions. But the modernization of society was secondary to its main goal: unification of the Arab world, for which the models, so often held up as an example, were the unification of Italy and of Germany in the nineteenth century. The need to act quickly meant that all means could be used, including military force and the unifying power of a state. Efforts were therefore concentrated on the armed forces. Instead of creating more and more activist branches and intellectual discussion clubs, the Baathists lined up tank battalions. Hence the repeated putsch attempts, and hence too the eventual split between the Syrian and Iraqi Baath.

It would be futile to look for any real ideological divergence to explain this split. In fact, the conflict between the two factions – or two armies – can only be understood if we remember that the dream was to return to the golden age of the Arabs, which for Syrians meant the age of the Umayyad dynasty with its capital in Damascus, and for Iraqis meant the age of the Abbasid dynasty with its capital in Baghdad. Pan-Arabism was no longer anything but a façade for expansionist micro-nationalism, as the two regimes became more and more authoritarian. Each silenced its Islamist rivals (who believed in a different way of transcending frontiers) and tried to reduce their influence by playing up to their base among traditional social layers. That spelled the end of modernization projects. The Syrian regime allied itself with Iranian radical Islam and the Lebanese Hezbollah, while its counterpart in Baghdad went so far as to claim that Michel Aflak, the founder president of the Iraqi Baath, had converted to Islam on his deathbed to erase the original sin of having been born a Christian. On the day after the invasion of Kuwait, Saddam Hussein had the words *Allah Akbar* (Allah Is Great) inscribed on the Iraqi flag.

Today, it is enough to go for a walk in the streets of Middle Eastern cities to see that, after the interlude of the 1950s and 1960s, the great majority of women have taken back the veil. We can conclude that secularization and modernization projects have been sacrificed to the failed cause of unification. The Baath party is no more than a shadow of its former self.

As to the three men – Nasser, Boumedienne and Bourguiba – a sometimes muffled, often open conflict came between them. Nuances separated the first two, but there was a profound divergence between them on the one side and Bourguiba on the other.

Nasser was a great tribune and mobilizer of the masses, a sincerely modernist leader much admired for his honesty and integrity. However, his was a hesitant modernism because it took second place to objectives he considered more important: Arab unity and the liberation of Palestine. And, in order to attain those goals, it was necessary to mobilize the people, to humour public opinion without neglecting any sector of it. This quest for massive popular support led Nasser to make huge concessions to traditional layers; it is true that he opposed the Muslim Brotherhood and had its chief ideologue Sayed Kotb executed, but this by no means affected the heart of the matter. In reality it was a fratricidal conflict. For Islamism and pan-Arabism, being two sides of the identity strategy, were sometimes enemies but always brothers. To further his struggle against the Islamists (who had tried to assassinate him), Nasser handled very gently the ulema religious scholars – that is, the official Islam that has been the nursery for militant popular Islam. He developed the theological university of Al Azhar (which by 1995 had more than a hundred thousand students) and reined in anything that might vex the Islamists. The women's liberation movement, which until 1952 had been the strongest in the Arab world, dried up after the seizure of power by the so-called Free Officers. No significant steps were made towards a codification of family law. In 1955 Nasser abolished the religious courts,[5] which were generally thought of as archaic institutions, but he then transferred their powers to ordinary courts whose traditionally formed magistrates applied the sharia whenever one party to a dispute was a Muslim – with the result that the situation of Egyptian Copts grew worse instead of better.[6] No family planning was tried for fear of antagonizing the Al Azhar ulema. Thus, while proving unable to achieve Arab unity or the liberation of Palestine, Nasser also failed to modernize Egyptian society and even took a few steps back.

Boumedienne's policy was similar to Nasser's, though with certain peculiarities. Apart from his Arabism, he was a fervent supporter of scientific socialism and the anti-imperialist struggle; he dreamed that his country would assume the leading role for Africa and even the Third World. For this he needed a larger Algeria, more populous than it was at the time and much stronger than its neighbours – hence his rejection of any family planning, his creation of the Western Sahara problem to weaken Morocco, and his sabotage of the planned unification with Libya that would have strengthened Tunisia. Like Nasser, he thought that unanimity was essential for his grandiose projects. And so, although he was a modernist, he did what was necessary to placate traditional layers of the population. He offered the ulema a magnificent gift by handing over the educational sector. He followed in Ben Bella's footsteps by calling on the services of large numbers of Egyptian voluntary workers – a policy that allowed Nasser for a time to pack his fundamentalists off abroad as teachers,[7] who then helped to train the future cadre of the Algerian Islamic Salvation Front (FIS) and Armed Islamic Group (GIA). At the same time, Boumedienne set up a number of Islamic studies institutes, where the most classical theories were on the teaching syllabus. As regards family law, he wavered until his death between a traditionalist project and a code that would have modernized family structures and promoted the emancipation of women. In the end, it was the former project that prevailed under his successor, Ben Jedid, so that by the time of the 1991 elections many voters could see no difference between the candidates of the FIS and the ruling National Liberation Front (FLN) candidates and stayed away in droves.

As to Bourguiba, despite a substantial body of opinion to the contrary, he was neither anti-Muslim nor anti-Arab; he simply had a degree of contempt for the Arab leaders of the time. His historic and well-considered speech in Jericho in 1965, which took the calculated risk of calling for talks with Israel at a time when east Jerusalem, the West Bank and Gaza were still in Arab hands, proves his attachment to the Palestinian cause. And the torrent of abuse he received from sectors of Arab public opinion stoked up by their leaders, as well as the resultant stir among the Tunisian public, prove that he paid a higher price for his Arab-Muslim feelings than did most other Arab leaders.

For Nasser, colonialism was the source of our ills: it exploited and oppressed us, and had imposed artificial borders that we needed to abolish. In a series of fiery speeches, he therefore flattered the pride of citizens and sought to mobilize their nationalist feelings against imperialism. Bourguiba stirred up no one's passions, but he did arouse everyone's interest. He calmly addressed people's reason as he explained that, since independence, the causes of our underdevelopment had been inside ourselves. He also indicated the ways in which we might escape it. We should emancipate our women so that they can participate in the work of building a new society – hence the Tunisian Code of Personal Status. We should control the number of births so that economic growth is not cancelled by demographic growth – hence the major efforts in family planning. We should reflect on the reasons why we lag behind. We should get down to work and modernize our attitudes and social structures, in order to 'join the train of civilization'. It was an analysis based more on self-criticism than on criticism of others, with objectives that, though appearing more modest, were in the end both more feasible and more important. Today, Tunisia is bearing the fruit of this policy.

This is not to deny that Bourguiba was a megalomaniac dictator with an inflated opinion of himself, who ruled through a single party, torture and a state security court. These violations of public liberties were neither legitimate nor even useful for his policy. Bourguiba's legacy is a real modernity which, because of the lack of democracy, nevertheless remains notably inadequate. Even less have the authorities in other Arab and Muslim countries taken up the task of modernizing the state and society; they do not think of these as priorities.

Modernity not accepted

Olivier Carré has written that the main problem for the Muslim world is not to invent secularism (which already exists) but to conceptualize a secular reality that it has hitherto denied.[8] This is rather an optimistic view, however. For the countries that maintain, in their laws and social practice, such institutions as polygamy, repudiation of wives or the marriage of pre-pubescent girls merely with paternal consent cannot be described as secular countries. And such institutions exist throughout the Muslim world, with the exception of Turkey and Tunisia. To gauge the extent to which female inferiority is, despite certain appearances, a social and legal reality, we may recall one incident that was widely discussed a few years ago. In Egypt, which for a long time played a vanguard role in the emancipation of women, social affairs minister Aisha Rateb had difficulties with her husband and lived apart from him while awaiting a divorce. But on one occasion, when she was waiting to catch a flight on official business, her husband managed for some time to prevent the aeroplane from leaving, on the grounds that he had not given her permission to travel.[9]

When an intellectual makes some points tending to reconcile Islam and modernity, the ulema call for the terrible infidel to be struck down, and the rulers – whether out of fear or demagogy – add their voices to the chorus. Sadly, this is a practice of long standing. In 1925, for instance, when the liberal Muslim Ali Abderrazak published *Islam and the Foundations of Power* (a major attempt to reconcile Islam and modernity at the level of the political system), the ulema forcefully denounced him and, with Egyptian government approval, expelled him from the University of Al Azhar. Saad Zaghlul (head of the supposedly secular Wafd, then the most prominent party fighting for independence) denounced both book and author with the same vigour.[10] And, still today, the Egyptian authorities have not seriously changed their policy on the matter. It is true that Abderrazak's work has been published at government expense in tens of thousands of copies,[11] but this has done nothing to alter the fact that it is ignored in Egyptian schools.

Also in the mid-1920s, in Tunisia, Tahar Haddad's *Our Women in Sharia Law and in Society* called for the emancipation of women and sought to show that Islam, properly understood, was not opposed to it. Although he was supported by enlightened sections of the intelligentsia and the general population, the ulema of Zituna university decided that he should be driven from their ranks. The colonial administration implemented this decision by preventing Haddad from assuming the position of judge. Immediately after independence, however, he was rehabilitated by the government and often referred to in official speeches. A cultural club bearing his name was created, and his works were taught in schools. Moreover, nearly everyone agrees that, despite Bourguiba's major role in its adoption, the Code of Personal Status is based on the theories of Tahar Haddad.

In this respect, however, Tunisia remains the exception in an Arab-Muslim world that has not generally achieved a successful reconciliation of religion and modernity.

Making peace with modernity

The enthusiasm for Arab unity has died away since one Arab state (Iraq) invaded another (Kuwait) and a number of other Arab states allied themselves with foreign powers to wage war on Iraq during the first Gulf War. Moreover, non-fanatical Islamists have lost their illusions as a result of the barbaric actions of the GIA in Algeria, as well as the crimes committed in the name of Islam in the United States, France, Spain, Kenya and elsewhere. The time has probably come for the Arab masses to give up their pipe dreams and to adopt more useful and realistic goals of modernization and development. Such a reorientation can take place only if there is internal peace and calm, through a reconciliation of being and becoming, between Arab civilization and Islamic religion, on the one hand, and modernity on the other.

Paradoxically, the obstacle to such a new awareness is nothing other than the policies of leaders who describe themselves as modernizers. Authoritarianism practised in the name of modernity makes modernity itself appear suspect or even loathsome; the Muslim countries will be able to advance only through democratic debate in which all tendencies, including the Islamists, can freely participate. At the same time, however, many political leaders share with ordinary citizens a diffuse feeling that Islam and modernity are incompatible. Riven by what they feel is an elemental contradiction, they have a kind of guilty conscience that they are both Muslim and modern; this prevents them from clarifying their discourse, defending their policies and adopting a more consistent standpoint. Eager to remain in power at any price, they opt for demagogy in their speech and attitudes – a course that leads them to combat fundamentalism with fundamentalism, and gives rise to a confused, indefensible and sterile form of politics.

At this level too, Tunisia is an exception. After pointing this out, the well-informed expert on the Arab-Muslim world, Jean Daniel, writes: 'Tunisians are in the course of becoming sincerely Muslim and sincerely secular. Since the mid-nineteenth century, the country that houses one of the three oldest mosques in the Islamic world (ninth century) has also been a country of reformers of Islam.'[12]

This specificity is inscribed in the Tunisian Constitution, which was adopted in 1959.[13] Article One states that 'Tunisia is a free state, independent and sovereign; its religion is Islam, its language is Arabic, and its form is the Republic.' One could discuss at some length whether the words 'its religion' refer to the state or to Tunisia. But despite the apparent ambiguity – the writers of the Constitution did not want to show their whole hand at that time – the words actually refer to the country. This becomes clear from the other articles of the Constitution and from the legislative and political course taken by Tunisia since independence. Thus, Article One states that the Tunisian people are in their great majority Muslim, and asserts that, unlike Turkey (whose constitution establishes a French-style principle of secularism), the

Tunisian state does not ignore the sociological reality or certain peculiarities of Islam. This means that the state must take responsibility for
the running of mosques and for religious education. But, on the other
hand, unlike most of its counterparts in Muslim countries, the Tunisian
Constitution does not say that 'the state is Islamic' or that 'Islam is the
state religion'; nor does it claim that 'sharia is the source of the law', or
its 'main source' or 'one of its sources', or even a source of 'interpretation' for the judiciary or 'inspiration' for the legislature. Indeed,
Article Five affirms the principle of 'freedom of conscience' and Article
Six the principle that 'all citizens have the same rights and duties' –
which, as we shall see, is contrary to sharia law.

'Sincerely Muslim and sincerely secular': Tunisians are both because,
in their reading of it, Islam can perfectly well go together with democracy and human rights; it is not incompatible with modernity.[14] These
assertions, so often repeated but rarely explained, will require a closer
study of the relationship between Islam and law (Chapter 2) and
between Islam and the state (Chapter 3). We shall see not only that such
a reconciliation is possible and desirable, but that it corresponds to the
most faithful reading of the religion and the most accurate reading of
history. If things have been otherwise up to now, it is because of a series
of events that have nothing to do with the essence of Islam and the text
of the Koran. These events have led to a truly deplorable historical
misunderstanding. For the past century and a half, numerous Muslim
reformist thinkers have tirelessly shown this to be the case, in
demonstrations that remain convincing even if they are only partial or
fragmentary. In most Muslim countries, the voices of modern Muslims
have not been heard. Whether out of fear, demagogy or ignorance,
governments exclude their ideas from school syllabuses and teach
instead various anachronistic theories whose main effect is to disorient
young people. It is high time to introduce a radical change in
educational policy and to teach modern theories that reconcile Islam
with modernity (Chapter 4). First of all, it will be useful to recall the
origins, nature and objectives of the international fundamentalist
movement, and to assess some of the damage it has caused so far in
Muslim countries (Chapter 1). This will show how urgent it has
become to find more just and appropriate solutions to this grave
problem.

1

Islamic Fundamentalism

Nothing is more terrifying than ignorance that has an effect.

Goethe

Violence and obscurantism

Between 1992 and 1995, Islamist terrorism in Egypt caused the death of 984 persons,[1] mostly Copts but also democratic activists, intellectuals and foreign tourists. In Algeria, during the three years between the suspension of the electoral process and its resumption with the election of President Liamine Zeroual in 1995, Islamist terrorism and reactions by the forces of order are commonly estimated to have caused 40,000 deaths, perhaps as many as 50,000 or 60,000. According to Amnesty International, the total number had risen to 80,000 by the beginning of 1998.

Paradoxically, this wave of violence initially met with a degree of understanding among the European and American political class, on the grounds that it reflected popular demands that were not being met by the rulers. Moreover, most of the regimes in Muslim countries can be rightly blamed for their non-democratic character – which may be why many Islamist leaders were able to find refuge, sometimes even an open welcome, in the West, in the name of humanitarian principles and the right to political asylum for freedom fighters and people suffering oppression. Such leaders had considerable scope to hold meetings, to print and distribute their propaganda, and to organize all the operations that sowed terror and death in their countries of origin.

Subsequently, Egyptian Islamists inspired by their ideologue Abderrahman staged the first attempt to destroy the World Trade Center in New York, and Algerian Islamists attempted to export their violence to Europe. A wave of terror that began in France in July 1995 killed or wounded dozens of people, all of them innocent victims of a blind ideology and a conflict to which they were completely alien. In Algeria itself, a number of murderous attacks were directed against foreigners, especially members of Christian orders, some of whom had been active in the struggle for independence.

As political Islamism showed its true face as a source of violence, terror and injustice, the favour it had enjoyed in the West began seriously to decline. This evolution of attitudes among Europeans and Americans mirrored that which had occurred a few years earlier in relation to the Iranian Revolution. As the reader will remember, that revolution initially aroused enthusiastic admiration for a people who had toppled a bloody dictatorship with their bare hands, it being forgotten that it had taken place in the name of religion and therefore promised nothing good. Politicians in the West pretended to be unaware of the large body of historical experience around the world showing that a religious government cannot be democratic, and that, while any dictatorship must be condemned, a religious dictatorship is the worst of all. For such a regime claims to dictate not only political and social relations but also individual attitudes, not only people's behaviour but also the workings of their conscience. The policies pursued by the Islamic Republic of Iran therefore soon led to disillusionment among its early supporters.

In 1985 Massoud Rajavi, chairman of the Iranian National Council of Resistance, issued a list of 10,300 executions carried out by the Khomeini regime, which included 18 pregnant women, 430 adolescents and 54 candidates in the first parliamentary elections after the fall of the Shah.[2] Since 1985 the number of victims has continued to grow. One notable directive issued by Ayatollah Khalkhali, when he was head of the Judicial Authority, instructed policemen and others guardians of the Iranian Revolution to 'finish off' wounded demonstrators rather than arrest them, because they would anyway be sentenced to death and executed the following day. Shah Reza Pahlavi, himself anything but a democrat, never went as far as that. In fact, after ruling for a long time with an iron fist, after years of torture and killing of communist, democratic and Islamist militants that gave Savak (his secret police organization) international notoriety, after a period at the beginning of the revolution when he gave orders for the police to fire on demonstrators, the Shah eventually recoiled from the scale of the horrors, went into exile and allowed the revolution to succeed. A modernizer who engages in repression does so with a trembling hand, going against some of his convictions in the belief that he is choosing the lesser evil (which is a mistake, because unjust repression is always reprehensible). But a religious extremist who oppresses others does so with a clear conscience; his mental structures are devoid of such braking mechanisms; his culture induces him to go further and further.

Islamists think they are acting in accordance with God's will. This is why an Algerian terrorist who kills a missionary of Algerian nationality – with a background of fighting for the country's independence – simply because he is a Christian, or who slits a young girl's throat simply because she does not wear the veil, or who kills a baby simply because its father is a policeman, does not feel the horror of what he does. He genuinely believes, as a rank-and-file militant, that his action will reserve a place for him in Paradise.

It makes little difference whether a fundamentalist is in power or in opposition, whether he is fighting against an authoritarian or a democratic regime: violence is for him a normal means of action, legitimated by the noble goal of establishing the Kingdom of God, especially as it reminds him of the *jihad* that he has heard praised so much. For reasons and with methods that we shall examine later, he has been taught that violence is the best of prayers, the finest act of devotion, and that it was the means whereby the Prophet himself triumphed over wicked infidels. Such a rank-and-file militant is the product of a culture and a history, and above all of a particular kind of education. As for the leaders, who have resulted from the same factors, they have enough intelligence and presence of mind to gauge the effects of their misdeeds and to dress up their ideology accordingly.

Islamist leaders have learnt to speak to the West in the language it understands and rightly treasures: the language of democracy and human rights. It is a profitable approach, a good cover, but it is not able to cover everything. It cannot cover up the terrorist attacks, ambushes and murders resulting from the conflict between Sunni and Shiite extremists in Karachi in 1995,[3] or the 'major technological advance' in Iran, which is how the Supreme Council of Justice described in February 1985 the development by doctors and technicians of an electrical machine to cut off the hands of thieves.[4] This was doubtless the device used on five occasions in April of that year, at the same time that two people accused of adultery were stoned to death and 160 others were flogged for various illicit acts.

Since then, such practices have gone beyond the experimental stage and received widespread application. The new Iranian penal code, which came into force on 9 July 1996, officially established flogging as the 'normal' penalty for various political or ordinary offences: to be precise, 74 strokes of the lash for women found uncovered in a public place, 99 strokes for people guilty of extramarital sexual relations, and death by stoning for those guilty of adultery. Moreover, capital punishment is prescribed for any display of contempt towards the founder of the Islamic Republic, Ayatollah Khomeini, who died in June 1989, or towards his successor, Ayatollah Ali Khamenei.

In Sudan, during the few months that he served as justice minister in the Nimeiri government, Hassan al-Turabi enforced amputation of the fist in 96 cases of theft.[5] This same man, who for several years was the ideologue of the Islamist regime in Sudan and claimed to be head of a kind of Islamist International, was often interviewed on Western television. Turabi spoke of science, progress, democracy, modernity and human rights, and aided by the pleasant aspect imparted by his little white beard, his smiling face and his polished English, he struck certain Westerners as the epitome of a moderate Islamist intellectual. Nevertheless, he shows no regret for the crimes he committed as justice minister; he has never uttered a word of self-criticism over the execution of his political opponent, Mahmud Mohamed Taha, on the pretext of apostasy; and he referred to those who tried to assassinate Hosni Mubarak in Addis Ababa on 26 June 1995 as a 'group of mujahedeen' (fighters for the faith) who had been 'hunting the Pharaoh of Egypt'. He added: 'Allah's wish is that Islam should begin its rebirth in Sudan and travel up the Nile to cleanse Egypt of its stain.'[6]

The fate that Islamists reserve for the female sex is by now well known: numerous books have exposed the suffering inflicted on women, both in militant Islamist countries such as Iran and in the lands of traditional Islamist rule. Fundamentalists are less than persuasive in their criticism of 'Western propaganda' on this issue, especially when the authors who make such attacks go on to describe the ill-treatment of foreign wives in certain Muslim countries, or, worse still, the use of stoning as a form of punishment.[7]

The new Iranian penal code affords impunity to a husband who catches his wife with her lover and kills her. Since the lovers are supposed to be put to death anyway, a bullet or even a knife is evidently less painful than stoning. (According to the ulema – the doctors of law – only pebbles and small stones should be thrown because they prolong the suffering as much as possible; there is a risk that large stones might cause death too quickly.) A wife who catches her husband with a lover, however, does not have the same right to kill him – after all, she is only a woman. Her husband can also be unfaithful to her in complete legality, by taking a second, third or fourth wife. And if he already has the maximum of four, he can always tell the one who catches him *in flagrante* that he repudiated her five minutes earlier and agreed to marry his current mistress, as no formality is required to do this, and the repudiated spouse does not even need to be informed.

Khomeini's *fatwa* that sentenced Salman Rushdie to death for his authorship of *The Satanic Verses*, and promised a high reward to anyone carrying out the sentence, has considerably enlightened international public opinion about how fundamentalists conceive of the freedom of opinion and expression.[8] And the fate of the Bahai minority in Iran, hunted, repressed and subjected to all manner of abuses, has given us an idea of how fundamentalists conceive of the freedom of conscience. In his report for the year 1995 Abdelfattah Amor, the UN special rapporteur on religious tolerance, noted that since 1979 approximately ten thousand Bahai had been removed from the Iranian civil service and denied the pension rights for which they had paid contributions, and that at least 201 Bahai had been killed.[9] To liquidate this minority in the future, the Supreme Cultural Council issued an order that children of Bahai families should only be allowed to attend primary and secondary schools 'with a strong and impressive religious [that is, Islamic] ideology'.[10] With regard to higher education, access to university is virtually denied to Bahai since it is conditional on the passing of an exam in religious knowledge;[11] this exam, introduced in the early days of the Revolution, indeed excluded the one-third of students who had been unwise enough not to espouse militant Islamism.

In the case of Algeria, fundamentalist leader Ali Belhaj stated during the 1991 election campaign that democracy was a sinful (*haram*) Western invention alien to Islam, and that the legislative elections (which he expected to win) would be 'the last in Algeria'. This made Islamist propagandists very uncomfortable, because it exposed the carefully disguised roots of their thinking and spelled out the content of their doctrine.

Like Khalkhali in Iran, Belhaj has the great quality of frankness and clarity, which reveals to us his complete obscurantism and naked primitivism. By contrast, Turabi in Sudan or Ghannouchi in Tunisia have for many years sought to disguise exactly the same totalitarian ideas beneath a veneer of democracy, and their discourse has indeed tended to throw inadequately informed observers off the scent. This makes it necessary for democratic activists, feminists and republicans to engage in a long labour of elucidation, using infinite pedagogic skills to unmask the double-speak and to strip away the undergrowth of obfuscation. The large number of democrats and feminists in Algeria who have been murdered for this ideological critique shows the extent to which it embarrasses the fundamentalists.

Today things are becoming fairly clear. The social project that the fundamentalists are struggling to achieve is one of religious totalitarianism in which all collective and individual liberties are suppressed, the impetus for literary or artistic creation is stifled, intellectual debates are forbidden, minds are bound and chained, and free rein is given to the oppression of women. In short, it would be a return to the Middle Ages, or to our 'dark centuries', with the addition of cars and computers – as if it were possible for a backward society genuinely to assimilate technological advances while remaining frozen at the level of lifestyle, ideas and behaviour.

One of the errors of analysis committed by fundamentalists is to believe that Muslim societies lag behind only technologically. In reality, a technological lag cannot be isolated from political, economic, social and cultural factors; it is the interdependence of all these factors which makes the lag general. Reformers have never ceased to make this point, and conservatives to deny it, since the early days of the Muslim renaissance.

Conservatives and reformers

There is no disgrace in admitting this lag. It is an evident fact, which is proved by the fact that we were colonized.

Of course we were colonized because there were colonizers – that is, stronger countries which, in pursuit of domination and profits, took the liberty of occupying our lands and enslaving our peoples. But the spirit of domination and profit was not the main cause of colonization. For unfortunately it is a law of human history that, whenever the balance of forces between two neighbours is broken in one way or another, the stronger always ends up dominating the weaker. Did we not for a long time occupy Spain and Sicily?

The chief cause of colonization, the most interesting to study and the most fruitful to criticize, derives from the fact that we had become *colonizable*. The key question, therefore, is why Muslim societies, after their golden age, entered into a period of decline. Or, to quote the thinkers of the Arab-Muslim renaissance of the nineteenth and early-twentieth centuries, 'Why did they [Europeans] progress while we regressed?' It is a fundamental question, but one so painful that people rarely ask it nowadays. For, whether the answer is given in terms of economic, social, religious, cultural or educational factors, it will be bound up with our own culture and attitudes – and self-criticism, self-reproach always hurts a lot. It is so much easier to place the blame on others, especially if they actually happen not to be innocent.

Nevertheless, since the time of the nineteenth-century reformers (Rifa'ah al-Tahtawi in Egypt, Khereddine in Tunisia) and those who succeeded them, since the modernization movements such as the Young Turks and the national liberation parties, ways have been found of posing the problem correctly. For the thinkers and movements that have done so, the task is to grapple with the lag that has accumulated since the fifteenth century, to learn foreign languages, to open up to nations that have outstripped us in science and technology as well as at the level of ideas and political systems, and to advance our culture and philosophical conceptions through an effort of reflection, *ijtihad*, that enables us to adapt to the new times while still remaining ourselves. There is no harm in drawing inspiration from what other countries have done. Did Europeans not do the same when their situation required it?

We should not forget that one of the main factors in the European Renaissance was the discovery of the heritage of antiquity, and that this discovery was made through Arabs who had translated and enriched Greek philosophy and science. Arabic numerals, for example, which are today used all over the world (except by Arabs in the Mashriq[12]), were introduced into Europe in the tenth century by Sylvester II, the first French pope and an 'admirer of Arab-Islamic civilization'.[13] This is just one important example among many others. The contribution of Averroës to the emergence of rationalism is rarely disputed, and in the late Middle Ages the direction of scientific translation (especially in mathematics, astronomy and medicine) was mainly from Arabic into Latin.

Unfortunately, Averroës (Ibn Rushd in Arabic) fell victim to the obscurantists of his age. But, although he was reduced to silence and his books were burned, the seeds of his thought sprouted elsewhere. This is why he is known today as Averroës, rather than Ibn Rushd.[14] It was he who developed the idea that human reason has an essential role to play alongside revealed texts and in the interpretation of those texts. This cornerstone of modern thought may strike us today as obvious enough, but at that time, when religion everywhere dominated and held back the sciences and thought in general, the ideas of Averroës were nothing short of revolutionary. There is an evident affinity between, on the one hand, the theories of Averroës and his contemporary, the Jewish thinker Maimonides, and, on the other hand, the theories later developed by Thomas Aquinas in the realm of Christian thought.

It is a constant feature of history that civilizations borrow from one another; human progress is the synthetic fruit of different contributions. If we have thus lent in the past, why should we not borrow today? There is no reason to have a complex about it. But we do need to recognize our backwardness, to question and overturn our traditional habits, to disturb our certainties and our intellectual complacency. Change is usually achieved at the cost of suffering and wrenching splits.

In Tunisia – probably as elsewhere – political life for the last century and a half has been a to-and-fro movement between two poles, a constant and sometimes fierce battle between two major forces: the force of action and progress, and the force of conservatism and immobility.

When Khereddine, the founder of modern Tunisia, woke up to our backwardness and decided to take action, he wrote a book in 1868 that described all the scientific, economic, social, cultural and political progress in Europe and called upon Tunisians to open up to the world by learning foreign languages and the new sciences.[15] At the same time, he pointed out that Tunisia lacked a political and intellectual life because it had only one centre, the religious university or Zituna, which lived outside time in a shell where the only subjects taught, with content and methods that had not changed for centuries, were sharia law, the history of the Prophet, and Arabic grammar.

In 1873, when Khereddine assumed the post of prime minister, he undertook a number of reforms, the most important of which was the creation of the Sadiki college for the teaching of foreign languages and the exact sciences. At the same time, he did not give up on the Zituna but set out to reform it through changes to its syllabus and mode of operation. But, while the decision to create Sadiki took effect, the Zituna reform programme remained a dead letter because of inertia among the people teaching there.[16]

During the further eighty years until independence, therefore, educated Tunisians fell into two broad categories: Sadiki graduates possessing a dual culture and open to modernity; and Zituna graduates enclosed in Arabness and a conservative mentality. In 1905, when Abdelaziz Thaalbi wrote his first book, *The Liberal Spirit of the Koran*,[17] calling for the education of girls and abolition of the traditional women's veil, it received a warm welcome from Sadikians and fierce opposition from the Zituna, especially its teaching staff. And in 1929, when Tahar Haddad published his book calling for female emancipation, *Our Woman in the Sharia and in Society*,[18] it aroused enthusiasm among Sadikians and anger among Zitunians,[19] to the extent that the academic staff at the author's alma mater met and decided to revoke his degree.

The Sadikian-led Tunisian national movement, which built the new state after independence, pursued a general policy of social modernization, especially through the abolition of sharia courts and *waafs* (widespread religious property-holdings) and the adoption of a code of personal status ending the practices of polygamy and conjugal repudiation. These measures were opposed by most of the Zituna leaders and the religious courts, but this opposition, expressing the age-old conservatism of the Zituna, had little impact among the wider population.

Today, the fundamentalist movement is taking up the flame of the old Zitunian conservatism, with the same references to religion as it was understood a thousand years ago, the same slogans of opposition to women's emancipation and social modernization, and the same attachment to a closed Arab culture. It is the type of leaders that has changed, and their methods of action.

The old Zitunian leaders came from well-off aristocratic milieux, and it was with the appropriate refinement of speech and manners that their erudition was imparted to their students. Always close to the government of the day, they tried to influence it to act in line with their cultural tradition. But they did this with less and less conviction, since in the end they were not taken in by it. They could see the writing on the wall, and they all tried to salvage something by sending their children to a modern school that would prepare them for future life. Knowing themselves to be doomed, they lost the battle in advance without really engaging in it. By contrast, today's fundamentalist leaders mostly come from popular layers, with personal and occupational horizons that are considerably less promising. They address the most disadvantaged sections of the population and do not shrink from strong-arm tactics.

We have lost on the exchange because good manners, velvet tactics and erudition have given way to frustration, violence and shallow knowledge. But the ideological references and social–political objectives are exactly the same. From scholarly conservatism to popular conservatism, the line of descent is perfectly clear. And for progressive forces, now that we have certain gains to defend, it is more necessary than ever to continue the struggle.

In essence, it has remained the same struggle: between patriots and collaborators in the early twentieth century, between progressives and conservatives in the middle of the century, between modernists and fundamentalists today. It is a struggle of openness against closure, of action against immobility. But it has taken different forms depending on the circumstances, each time crystallizing around a number of precise issues.

In the early twentieth century, the main issue was the position that should be taken towards the colonizing power. The Tunisian national movement was founded and led by people who were called patriots or nationalists at the time, but who would today be called modernizers by virtue of their formation and their political or social ideas. The seventeen founder members of the militant newspaper *Al Hadhira* created in 1888, seven years after the establishment of a French protectorate in Tunisia, were nearly all Sadikians who had received a modern education.[20] This newspaper, which continued publication until 1911, was the mouthpiece of a transitional elite that devised a policy for the Tunisian intelligentsia *vis-à-vis* the colonial authority and formulated the first demands on political, economic, cultural and educational matters.

Beki Harmassi, a student of the formation and role of the Tunisian elite under the protectorate, has taken a special interest in the type of 'leader' who emerged in the national movement. He shows that, out of the 39 principal leaders, 38 had had a modern education and only 1 came from a traditional Zituna background.[21] These leaders had to fight on two fronts throughout the colonial period: against the colonizer to assert their national identity and to defend the interests of the Tunisian people; and against the forces of tradition to assert the necessity of opening up to the world and profiting from the knowledge and experience of others.

Today's Islamists are therefore heirs of the forces that have resisted progress all through the recent history of Tunisia.

Militant conservatism

Already in 1904 in Cairo, when Mohamed Abdu and Rashid Ridha began to call for limited reforms in their journal *El Manar*, the Zituna ulema petitioned the Tunisian government of the time – ultimately, the authorities of the French protectorate – to ban distribution of the journal inside Tunisia, on the grounds that it attacked maraboutism, sought to revive *ijtihad* and expressed views different from those of the four orthodox rites. '*El Manar*,' they added, 'finds readers among the young students at the Great Mosque of Tunis, and unless due care is taken it will instil in them ideas that are totally contrary to holy orthodox doctrine.'[22]

In the same petition, they demanded the right to censor any article with a religious character that was scheduled for publication in Tunisia. The same sheikhs, who also wrote articles in Tunisian newspapers criticizing *El Manar*, insisted that the earth was not round and did not circle the sun – for that would be contrary to the Koran.[23]

Fortunately, an intelligent and open-minded Zitunian occasionally appeared who had the courage to explore new directions, but anyone guilty of such foolhardy behaviour soon incurred the wrath of the Zitunian aristocracy. Thus, in 1902 the Sharaa Council in Sfax secured the removal of the reformist professor Mohamed Shaker and even got the Great Mosque to withdraw his graduation diploma. The accusation was that, like his friend and mentor the Egyptian Mohamed Abdu, he had attacked the cult of saints and the veneration of holy relics.[24]

Later, when Tahar Haddad began to call for the emancipation of women, the Zituna reacted by condemning his theses and publishing a book against them by one of the orthodox professors.[25] The Egyptian Al Azhar university did exactly the same in relation to Ali Abderrazak, whose *Islam and the Foundations of Power* has since established itself as one of the key works of Muslim reformism, probably the most important in the twentieth century. The Zituna joined in the chorus of denunciation with a book by one of its people.[26]

The sharpest attacks, however, were directed against the future founder of the Destour Party, Abdelaziz Thaalbi, who began to develop his ideas in 1895 in his journal *Sabil Errashad*. When it was banned the following year under pressure from Zituna notables,[27] he made do with spreading his ideas orally, in the souks and cafés. But he did not hesitate to criticize the saints, especially the most popular one at the time, Sidi Abdelkader; to challenge the Zituna's idealized version of history, by pointing out such home truths as that 'the caliph Uthman was the first to introduce despotism and arbitrary rule into Islamic government'; and to denounce both the methods and content of Zituna education, by arguing that its 'ineffectiveness' and 'hollow erudition' created 'an intellectual proletariat' or 'pseudo-intellectuals', whereas it would be better 'to train craftsmen with a minimum of knowledge, whose trade enabled them to earn a living'.[28] Above all, he ventured to denounce the Zituna aristocracy, whose teaching 'distorted the mind instead of enriching it with knowledge',[29] and which was itself marked by 'corruption' and 'lack of culture'.[30] In 1904 an alliance was formed between the heads of the brotherhoods (especially the Issawa) and the Zituna sheikhs – hence, between the leaders of popular Islam and official Islam.[31] The former organized demonstrations that attempted to lynch Thaalbi, while the latter – the people of the Sharaa – called a meeting of the two chambers, Malekite and Hanafite, to examine his case and to bring him to judgement.[32] In fact, they were prepared to send him to his death for blasphemy and apostasy;[33] it is even said that they actually passed sentence,[34] although this is not certain. The French authorities then intervened to transfer the case away from the sharia court to a non-religious court in Driba, which tried to calm things down by sentencing Thaalbi to two months' imprisonment.

Before this court, Thaalbi declared: 'The opinions I profess are not at all in contradiction with religious principles. The only concern behind them is to clear the Muslim religion of everything that ignorance, fanaticism and the lure of riches have added to it, and to restore the original purity that was its strength.'[35] Or again: 'May I be the last victim sacrificed on the altar of fanaticism.'[36] It could be the voice of a democrat today locked in struggle with fundamentalists in any country of the Muslim world.

Not by chance was it the leader of the colonialists, V. de Carnière, who ratified the judgement against Thaalbi so much desired by the religious authorities.[37] The Zitunians were conservative, but that did not mean they could not show a little understanding when the colonial administration demanded it. Under the land ownership decree that had been issued in 1885, which was designed to make it easier for farmers to settle in Tunisia, the status of land and the various forms of appropriation were governed by Muslim law; however, a number of legal problems of a more or less religious nature were posed in relation to its implementation. Theology professors, muftis and Al-Islam sheikhs therefore obligingly delivered the fatwas that the colonial authorities needed to allow French settlers to occupy lands falling under the category of *enzel*, *kerdar*, and so on.[38]

Likewise, during the First World War, when the authorities of the protectorate mobilized young Tunisians to fight and, above all, to fill the need for agricultural labour in France created by the departure of young Frenchmen for the front, the Hanafite Al-Islam sheikhs issued the fatwa that made such replacement feasible during the month of Ramadan, by dispensing Muslim workers from the duty to observe the fast.[39] At the beginning of the Second World War, the Malekite Al-Islam sheikh gave a similar dispensation to Tunisians serving in the French army.[40]

In the early 1930s, when leaders of the national movement waged a campaign against the French naturalization of Tunisian managerial personnel, one of the top Zituna notables suggested that the colonial authorities might like to request a special fatwa on the matter – which the two councils of the Sharaa (Hanafite and Malekite) then duly provided.[41] They did this even though it was a highly fraught issue at the time. We may gauge just how fraught it was from the fact that the first post-independence code regulating nationality expressly stipulated (Article 30, para. 3) that 'any Tunisian who acquires foreign nationality of his or her own free will … shall be obliged to leave Tunisian territory.' Only in 1975, when passions had calmed, was this clause revoked.

Of course, any generalization can be misleading. A good many

Zitunians were active patriots and a good many Sadikians served and collaborated with the colonial administration. Zitunian students were always a considerable force in opposition to the colonial power, and through their numerous strikes, demonstrations and other actions they wrote glorious pages in the struggle for independence.

As to the institution itself, the Zituna is one of the oldest universities in the world, going back more than a thousand years. Its time of glory was during the first half of its existence, when its influence radiated throughout the Arab world, especially the Maghreb. In the course of the last few centuries, however, it grew dull and sclerotic and turned into the main centre of conservatism, closed in on itself, proudly ignorant of everything happening in the world and of everything that did not concern Muslim law and history or Arabic grammar. Even in relation to Islam, it clung to the most dogmatic conceptions and swiftly ejected the occasional reformer who emerged in its ranks. Its course corresponded to the general tendency of decline in the whole of the society.

Was it victim or instigator of this decline? It is hard to say. But when we think that the elite has always played a decisive role in the evolution of society, and that Zitunians long constituted the country's elite, we cannot absolve it of all responsibility.

It is anyway undeniable that, by and large, the section of the elite with a modern education led the struggle for progress and independence, while the ulema, who may be described as the Tunisian Muslim clergy, remained on good terms with the colonial power.[42] According to one Tunisian historian, the Zituna was both an 'accomplice' that accepted and collaborated with the colonial order and an 'obstacle' that stood in the way of any progressive evolution.[43] As a general rule – which does not exclude some exceptions – the ulema sought to protect their personal interests; they actively opposed any change or innovation and upheld the writ of the sharia courts. As fervent supporters of conservatism, who also demand a return to sharia law, today's fundamentalists are their worthy successors.

The programme of the fundamentalists

Today's social, economic and cultural context, both within individual countries and internationally, has little in common with the situation of Muslim countries in the nineteenth and early twentieth centuries. Yet, now as then, the only real demand of Islamist movements is that the state should have a religious character and that sharia law should be enforced. Human liberation, especially in respect of freedom of conscience, as well as female emancipation and the social-economic development so badly needed by Muslim peoples, are goals completely alien to them.

Economically, the Iranian Revolution has been a real catastrophe for the Iranian people. The brain drain has assumed alarming proportions, as more than a million managerial staff have fled the hell imposed by the 'revolutionary guards'. The flight of capital is no less substantial: total Iranian assets abroad have been estimated at some $180 billion. Per capita income stands at half its pre-revolutionary level.[44] Between 1979 and 1989 the population rose from 38 million to 53 million, GDP fell by 50 per cent, the rial lost 1,800 per cent of its value against hard currencies, investment fell by 35 per cent, and the unemployment rate soared to 48 per cent of the active population.[45]

The Afghan case is equally eloquent. In its struggle against communism, the United States made the strategic error of funding and arming the fundamentalists in Afghanistan, in a holy war that caused more than a million deaths,[46] and it is highly significant that the fighting did not end with the Soviet withdrawal in 1989 or the fall of the communist regime in 1992 but effectively continued right up to the US military intervention following 11 September 2001. Against the ethnic background of a tribal society, it was religious questions that drove the combatants in the various camps. Massoud, the fighter in God's name and slayer of the Red Army, was challenged as soon as he took power by the even more fundamentalist Hakmatyar, and both these leaders were subsequently overshadowed by the ultra-intransigent Taliban. The infighting and clanlike feuds were characteristic of people who had no programme and no plan for the future.

Once the Taliban had carried the day, they imposed on the Afghan population the strictest religious regime ever seen in the history of Islam. To convince ourselves of this, we have only to read the 'sixteen Taliban commandments':[47] for example, 'women are forbidden to work [with the exception of medical personnel] and to go in the street without being covered by the *chadri* from head to foot'; 'the Iranian chador is not sufficient' – the reason being that it allows the face to be seen. It was 'forbidden to own video cassettes and to listen to music'.

The Taliban were not content to announce the new laws but took enforcement action from the earliest days of their rule. Afghans caught listening to 'profane music' were sentenced to flogging and terms of imprisonment.[48] The only entertainment in Afghanistan was to be the 'festivals' at which adulterous women and their accomplices were stoned to death. For, as the *New York Times* put it, 'this too seems to be a festival, or anyway a show to which thousands of people are invited'.[49]

Other than the application of sharia law, the Taliban had no political, economic or social project. This was also true of those who staged the military coup in Sudan, the third country of militant Islamism, which has the sad record of being among the poorest in the world, despite its huge potential for, especially, agricultural development. Its leaders preferred for many years (before finally initiating a political turn) to devote their meagre revenue to the waging of war against non-Muslim Sudanese in the south, and to support for terrorists in the hope of unleashing civil wars in other Muslim countries. The fundamentalists who head opposition movements elsewhere in the Muslim world march to the same tune: their literature contains no reference to a social programme; they simply mobilize their rank and file (usually gullible people with no education other than simplistic political–religious indoc-trination) to sow discord and terror, to kill women, to slit children's throats and to oppress society – without even knowing the reason, except that a system must be established in which thieves' hands are cut off.

The founder of the Muslim Brotherhood in Egypt, Hasan al-Banna, had this to say when he was asked about his social programme: 'People gather around general principles, not around finer points of detail. If we spelled out the details, we would grow divided and come to an unhappy end.'[50] The Tunisian Islamist Hachemi Handi, who describes himself as a moderate, was more forthcoming: 'We in Tunisia do not claim to have an Islamic programme. I am not embarrassed to say that such a pro-gramme remains to be worked out.'[51] And his colleague Abdelwahab El Kefi added: 'Our movement does not have an alternative policy.'[52] Let's just act today – then we'll see!

Such statements are typical of Tunisia's Islamists. They know that they are operating in a country that began to evolve a century and a half ago, where modernity has already begun to sink deep roots. It is therefore difficult for them to admit in public that they are building a political party that does not and will not have a political project. Their talk of working one out in the future ignores the basic rule that reflection must come before action. Their only project, if we can call it that, is the application of sharia law. But they know it is unpopular, and so they try hard to cover it up.

In this respect, the Egyptian fundamentalists are less prudent. Omar Tlemceni, the guide of Egypt's Muslim Brotherhood, prefers to conceal his personal ambitions and to clarify the project so that he appears more sincere. 'It matters little who actually governs,' he says. 'The key thing is the rules of government. We will always remain loyal to our principles. We will ask successive governments in our country to apply the sharia. The foundations of state power are spelled out in the Koran and the Sunna. We demand their immediate implementation.'[53] Before Tlemceni, another fundamentalist doctrinarian, Abdelkader Auda, who was executed for his part in a plot to assassinate Nasser, wrote that it was necessary to fight against the 'positive' system of 'modern laws'. 'It displeases God that Muslims should obey these idols of the contemporary era, since it is through them that the rulers of Muslim countries forbid what God has permitted and permit what God has forbidden.' From this, Hmida Ennifar concluded that 'for a number of Islamists, the application of sharia law has become the philosophy of change, the project capable of leading Islamic societies from the impasse in which they find themselves'.[54]

This was already the Islamist philosophy when the Muslim Brotherhood was founded in Egypt in the late 1920s, and it is still the Islamist philosophy today. Hassan al-Turabi does not hesitate to argue that application of the sharia is 'one of the signs of real independence' that makes it possible 'to escape the vicious circle of poverty, debt and economic impotence'.[55] And, once the Sudanese dictatorship was up and running, he justified it on the grounds that 'the regime cannot grant freedoms which will be used to demolish it'.[56]

In reality, then, the Islamist demand is for application of the sharia, and the two central phobias are the West and women. To appreciate the intensity of this aversion to the West and 'Westernized minds', we can do no better than read the review *Al Maarifa* that Tunisian fundamentalists freely published between 1972 and 1979, at a time when Bourguiba and his regime were encouraging them as a means to beat down the left, trade unionists and democrats.[57] These Islamists had not yet learned the art of disguise and double talk; they wrote what they thought. For them, freedom and democracy were 'idols', and the West had invented the Christianity and communism that were now being used by Zionism for its own purposes.[58] It was to serve the Zionist plot that Freud, Darwin, Marx and Durkheim had developed psychoanalysis, psychology and sociology.[59] *Al Maarifa* quoted at random such thinkers as Descartes, Kant, Locke, Bachelard, Bergson, Sartre, Gide or Nietzsche, caricatured their ideas in a single sentence, or even a couple of words, and then quickly moved on to denounce them in no uncertain terms.[60] It rejected *en bloc* the human sciences. Sowing hatred and contempt for the West, the Tunisian Islamists of the 1970s deluded themselves with the apocalyptic fancy that it was heading for ruin, especially because of its moral laxity.[61]

As to the second devil, Ghannouchi's *Al Maarifa* in its final years reduced the social role of women to housekeeping[62] and directed at them a torrent of hatred that one would scarcely have thought possible at the close of the twentieth century. To take one little example, it quoted an ostensible hadith from the life of the Prophet, to the effect that 'women are the only source of conflict and disorder [*fitna*] for men that I leave behind me'.[63] Or again: 'I have been shown Hell, and I found a majority of women there…. You can do good to a woman all your life, but if you once do something she dislikes she will say that you have never been good to her.'[64] *Al Maarifa* considered Sayid Kotb and Al-Mawdudi to be the chief theoreticians of the modern Islamist movement.[65]

For the Egyptian Sayid Kotb: '… all the currents of philosophy, all the currents of psychology … all the social doctrines … are part of *jahilia*[66] thinking, that is, non-Islamic thought both past and present, thought that is directly influenced by pre-Islamic beliefs. Whether explicitly or deviously, most of these theories, probably all of these theories, are based on methodological roots hostile to the religious vision in general and the Islamic vision in particular. The myth of the cultural heritage of a humanity that has no fatherland, race or religion is valid only for the exact and applied sciences; it cannot be extended beyond them to philosophical explanations of the nature, activity and history of human beings, nor to literature, art and all the poetic expressions. Those are some of the traps of world Jewry.'[67] It follows that everything non-Islamic must be rejected.

Caution is required even within the Islamic heritage, however. For the Pakistani Mawdudi, after the four wise caliphs (that is, some thirty years after the death of the Prophet):

the land of Islam saw the introduction of a mixture of philosophy, literature and sciences from Greece, Iran and India. This brought into being Mutazilite conceptions, currents tending to foster doubt and atheism ... and therefore discord and factions, as well as the non-Islamic arts of dance, music and painting, which were encouraged by those to whom it was forbidden to engage in these vile arts.[68]

This dismissal of everything produced by the human mind outside the sphere of Islam, and even of any elements within it later than the age of the Prophet and the four wise caliphs, leads to a rejection of democracy and democratic attitudes.

It is worth recalling the foundations on which Mawdudi and Sayid Kotb built up contemporary political Islamism. In their view, Islam has freed man by replacing the submission of man to man with the submission of man to God. (In fact, the word 'submission' is not strong enough to translate *obudia*, which conveys a sense of servitude.) There is no submission except to God, who alone has power. If that were not so, there would be a 'deification of man'.

Sayid Kotb is clear on this point:

> To say that there is no god but God for the whole universe means a global revolution against any attribution of power to human beings, under any form or regime whatsoever, a total revolt all over the earth against any situation in which power belongs in any way whatever to human beings. In other words, it is necessary to rise up against any situation where man is deified in any way. Any regime that bases sovereignty on the will of men is a regime that deifies man instead of God.[69]

Man is free only if he is a slave of God. 'Submission to God is the summit of liberation.'[70] In the political arena, there is 'the party of God ... a single party, as there cannot be more than one ... the other parties are all parties of the devil or of evil despots.'[71]

Although Tunisian fundamentalist leaders claim these authors as the main thinkers of the Islamic revival, and although they feed their followers on the works in question, they refrain in public from endorsing such clear-cut assertions. Only a minority dare to take the doctrine to its logical conclusion. These are the members of the PLI (Islamic Liberation Party), which avoids double talk and has the 'merit' of clarity and consistency.

In 1990, this party published and distributed widely among students, both in higher education and in a number of lycées, a short work under the pseudonym Abdelkadim Zalloum. The cover of this book, which mentions the PLI as its publisher, bears the title *Democracy: a Regime of Atheism* and the sub-title 'It is a sin to adopt, apply or call for its introduction'.

Instead of a summary, a few quotations will suffice: 'Democracy is an invention of the infidel West.... It has no relationship, either close or distant, to Islam.... It contradicts the essence and the rules of Islam' (p. 1). It spells 'the separation of religion and life' (p. 8). It was 'dreamed up by the human brain, not revealed by God in any religion' (p. 12). 'The representative system of elections and popular sovereignty is a pure lie, a falsification of reality' (p. 16). 'The greatest catastrophe to afflict the world is the invention of the theory of public liberties, for it brings a slide into licence, sexual freedom and homosexuality … humanity is thereby degraded to a level lower than the animals, which do not engage in the same degree of sexual licence' (p. 20). 'Western society is a society of homosexuals and lesbians' (p. 22). 'It is foul-smelling' (p. 23). It has hatched a plot against Islam by seeking to spread the germs of its culture among us (p. 25) by means of 'our Westernized intellectuals' (p. 28) who claim that 'Islam also contains democracy and human rights … whereas Islam is totally incompatible with them'. In Islam, sovereignty belongs to God, not to the people. If, for example, the people allow sexual relations outside marriage, even if they are unanimous on this point, that unanimity has no value. The minority who do not agree with these deviations 'have the right to combat them by killing until the evil is uprooted' (p. 46). The only legitimate form of government is the caliphate. The caliph may consult a parliament, but in the end 'he alone decides in accordance with God's law' (p. 51). 'There is no public liberty in Islam' because man's hands are 'tied' in relation to 'everything he must and must not do' (p. 55).

When we learn that GIA militants in Algeria have killed monks praying in monasteries, or slit the throats of pregnant women, babies and old people, it seems to us that such savagery is inexplicable, that the wave of madness is of mysterious origin. But there is nothing mysterious about it; the literature used to brainwash such militants is enough to explain their behaviour. It convinces them that they have a divine mission to cleanse the earth of everything that 'smells foul', and that this will guarantee them a place in Paradise.

It is their business if Islamists oppose all progress and cling to ancient traditions, or if they wish to fan the thousand-year-old antagonism between Crescent and Cross instead of promoting the fruitful dialogue that is beginning to develop between the religions. It is their business – but only so long as they use exclusively peaceful means and remain at the level of ideological debate. The fact is, however, that they have a different strategy and employ different means.

Between 1989 and 1992, with the same watchwords and similar slogans, they conducted violent agitation in Tunisian colleges of higher education and attempted to draw secondary schoolchildren into a veritable uprising. This provoked a sharp response from the authorities, who were eager to prevent the kind of situation that Algeria had been experiencing.

Muslims and Islamists

In a recent work, Burhan Ghalioun analyses the Islamist phenomenon and (quite rightly) criticizes the mostly authoritarian political regimes in Muslim countries.[72] It needs to be said, however, that political phenomena are particularly complex: there is a dialectical relationship which means that different factors can serve as each other's cause and effect. Authoritarianism may lead to Islamism, but Islamism may also lead to authoritarianism and even provide it with a cast-iron alibi.

It is certainly the case that democracy is not viable, or even provisionally feasible, if a significant section of the population considers itself to be in possession of the absolute truth, and to have a right, or even a duty, to impose it by force: that is to say, if it subscribes to an anti-democratic ideology. It is also the case, unfortunately, that fundamentalism exists in varying degrees in virtually all the Muslim countries. So, an elementary question may well be asked: does Islam necessarily generate an anti-democratic culture? Certainly not. My aim here is to show that there is nothing inevitable about fundamentalism, that what is involved is not a matter of religion but a problem of culture and education. In fact, we must distinguish between Muslims and Islamists.

For Muslims, Islam is a peaceful religion of the people. It is first and foremost a religion, in the sense that its beliefs offer an answer to the nagging question of life and death, an effective way of soothing the anguish of existence, a hope of a life after death that is filled with justice and happiness. It simply means that God, the almighty power who created the world, imparted a message of love, equality, fraternity and peace to an ordinary mortal, Mohammed, a man with strengths and weaknesses like all other men. Mohammed experienced enormous difficulties, because he was denigrated, hunted and nearly killed by his own people. This led him to defend himself, but apart from that self-defence his message is essentially one of peace and harmony.

The message contains various obligations – to say prayers, to fast, to abstain from certain foods, and so on – which each Muslim will observe or not in his own way, for various personal reasons and according to the strength of his conviction. In all religions, there are practising believers and others who practise little or not at all. It is their own personal business, in which no one else has a right to interfere. The Koran (6:158) is clear about this: 'Each man shall reap the fruits of his own deeds: no soul shall bear another's burden. In the end to your Lord shall you return, and He will resolve your disputes for you.'[73] No individual, group or state may dictate the conduct that an individual is obliged to follow.

With regard to collective relations, Islam is like the other world religions as they are understood and applied today: it contains a morality or general orientation in life. The word *sharia*, in its primary sense, denotes *path*. It is the path along which Muslims travel in accordance with their *ijtihad*, their effort of reflection. Thus, in drawing up the legal rules governing life in society, Muslims will consider how best to adapt to the circumstances of their time. Democracy, universal suffrage and popular sovereignty are the most appropriate rules today for the designation and regulation of the powers that formulate such a body of law. These are the powers of the state, which, from the death of the Prophet down to the present day, has always been a purely human organization.

In the lands of Islam, there are and nearly always have been many different states. Each Muslim comes under the authority of a state that is sovereign within its territory and has a history of its own. Islam, then, is neither a legal system nor a state nor a political orientation nor an identity. It is a religion. Indeed, given its essentially universal vocation, it cannot be tied to one people, territory or state, and least of all to one political orientation.

The Islamist conception of Islam is the exact opposite. For Islamists, it is not God who must be worshipped but a certain 'history'.[74]

Fundamentalists have been indoctrinated by their theoreticians and leaders in such a way that their heads are full of a highly distorted and idealized history. In this view, God created humanity to obey Him, and chose the Prophet Mohammed, a perfect man, to pass on his orders to humanity. Mohammed was followed by a small band of devotees who were all good and noble-minded, and he was combated by a host of wicked men who were all haughty, deceitful, pernicious and grasping. With the help of God, the tiny forces of Good triumphed over the forces of Evil. The history of Islam is a Manichean epic.

After the Prophet's death, the struggle continued between 'the good and the bad'. The Prophet's companions and their successors – men who, if not perfect, were very nearly so – established a state and a system of law. The task today is to reconstitute that state and to apply that law without changing one dot or comma. In any event, since the law was established by holy men on the basis of the Koran (as they understood it) and the sayings of the Prophet (as these were written down a century later), no one has a right to touch it. The successors of the Prophet's companions were good disciples, and those who opposed them, from within or without, were all wicked men. This struggle of the forces of Good against the forces of Evil has never ceased.

Muslim law clearly differentiates between *Dar al-Islam* and *Dar al-Harb* – literally, 'the house of Islam' and 'the house of war', or, in other words, the lands obeying the jurisdiction of the Islamic state and others against which war should be waged whenever possible. For Islamists, this injunction of sharia law is still valid today. In March 1989, for instance, in issue no. 16 of *Al Munqid*, the organ of Algeria's Islamic Salvation Front (FIS), this bipolar vision was summarized in Point Ten of the FIS platform.[75] Today, then, the struggle is between pure, resolute Muslims, the only genuine ones, and everyone else – a rag-bag category including both the West and bad Muslims. The West is imperialism, Zionism, colonialism and materialism; it is exploitation of the weak in the Third World, moral degradation, consumer society, prostitution, drugs, corruption and so on … It has to be fought against. The struggle will not be so hard, because the West has been undermined by its own vices. If we don't manage to crush it today, this is because it has cunningly planted a fifth column among us, composed of sceptics, democrats, liberals, emancipated women and other vermin who have to be wiped out. Algerian intellectuals know well enough what that means.

Muslims with the strongest religious beliefs can engage in some degree of dialogue with the more moderate Islamists. But one is talking of a very marginal group. In Tunisia, in the late 1970s, a minority faction within the Islamist party tried to open a debate on the need to revise certain basic concepts of Islamism. When it was unsuccessful, it split from the party and in the 1980s published an original and highly interesting journal, *15-21*, a reference to the fifteenth century of the Hegira and the twenty-first century of the Christian era. In its attempt to pose the fundamental issues, it signalled a wish for dialogue with other religions and civilizations and underlined the need for Islamists to engage in a rethink, not to say a cultural revolution, before they turned to political action. But *15-21* came under attack from the Mouvement de la Tendance Islamiste (now known as the Ennahdha) and did not have enough support from non-Islamist Muslims to survive for long.

The unfortunate failure of the *15-21* experiment is, in the end, fairly understandable. The journal was unacceptable to fundamentalists because it undermined the foundations of their ideology, but its remaining odour of Islamism meant that it was unable to attract Muslims in general. Its problem was the problem of the whole Muslim world: lack of clarity about the relationship among Islam, law and the state.

2

Islam and Law

No duress in matters of religion.

The Koran

Sharia and *fiqh* – that is, classical Muslim law – is a voluminous body of legal rules concerning all problems of life in society. This juridical monument was developed by hundreds of authors, in thousands of works dealing with various branches of law. One finds there criminal law, rules defining personal status, property law and what we would today call civil law (dealing with contracts and obligations) or administrative litigation (*mazalim*).

Despite the great divide among Sunnis, Shiites and Kharigites scarcely thirty years after the Prophet's death, and despite the further division of each of these families into different rites (four within the Sunni family alone), Muslim law retained a certain unity because the various schools remained in agreement over the main choices, the essential issues. The extreme diversity of schools and authors, sometimes within a single school, did not prevent Muslim law from remaining a coherent system, which regulated urban Muslim society from the second century of the Hegira (approximately the eighth century CE) until a century ago in some cases and until more recently still in others – that is, until the early attempts of Muslim states to modernize through a codification of law. Although the law resulting from this codification contains sometimes important changes, in most Muslim countries it is still inspired by classical Muslim law, especially in matters concerning personal status. Comparative jurisprudence considers that, alongside

English common law and Roman-Germanic law, Muslim law and the more or less modern systems inspired by it constitute one of the four or five great juridical families in the world.

Several branches of this law have important similarities with other legal systems, including modern ones: its provisions regarding sales and rental contracts, for example, differ only in minor details from other bodies of law. There are also highly original elements, however, which may be grouped under three categories in accordance with the attitude that Islamists take towards them: those they agree to forget, those they would like to forget, and those they insist on restoring (for example, penal law) or maintaining (for example, personal status as defined in most Muslim countries).

First, the elements that Islamists agree to forget, without this appearing to cause a problem, are a number of defunct categories such as *venzel*, *kirdar*, *musakat* and *mogharsa*, which used to regulate land ownership throughout the period when Muslim law held sway but today count as nothing more than museum pieces.

The second category – rules of Muslim law that Islamists would prefer to forget – are all those relating to slavery. We are not just speaking of a single law permitting one man to own another man; there is a seemingly endless series of laws that specify, for example, the reasons for which a person may become a slave, the conditions for the valid sale of a slave, the hidden defects (hidden in the slave's body) that allow the sale to be invalidated, the right of the owner of a female slave to have sexual relations with her (so that she becomes a concubine while remaining a slave), the prohibition on a free woman having similar relations with her slave, the paternal line of descent of the children of a concubine, their inheritance rights, and so on. In fact, such rules are spread among all the various sections of Muslim law, but they could be grouped together in quite a bulky code of their own.

The institution of slavery is so integral to sharia law that, although fundamentalists studiously avoid mentioning it, it sometimes finds its way to the surface. Cheikh Lakhoua, for example, the head of the Islamist slate for the Tunisian legislative elections in 1989, clearly stated in an interview with a probing journalist that, in accordance with Muslim law, prisoners taken in war should be reduced to slavery.[1] That speaks volumes about the supposed moderation of Tunisian Islamists. Similarly, in 1988, when leaders of the Palestinian Islamist movement,

Hamas, adopted their charter, they asserted in Article 12 the 'individual obligation for every Muslim, man and woman, to struggle against the enemy. Women are authorized to go and fight without their husband's permission, and slaves are authorized to do so without their master's permission.' This shows the extent to which an Islamist imbued with classical culture is unaware of the enormity of such propositions, for what they are saying, indirectly but clearly, is that in normal circumstances a woman is subject to her husband and a slave to his master.

Now, slavery certainly existed in Islamic civilization, as in all the old civilizations, whereas today it has disappeared in Muslim as well as all other countries. The issue is therefore not especially problematic for Muslims. But it is extremely embarrassing for Islamists, since it poses a question of principle of the greatest importance.

There are only two possibilities: Muslim law may be considered either as a human, non-religious creation, or as a divine creation that is, by definition, just and immutable. In the first case, it is a product of history and has to evolve like all other legal systems in the world – which means giving up not only slavery but corporal punishment and discrimination against women. In the second case, where Muslim law is supposed to stand the test of time and to be valid for all countries, it is not clear why its provisions concerning slavery should be abandoned.

Moreover, even if one distinguishes between rules of Muslim law with a clear textual origin in the Koran and those with only an indirect religious inspiration, the provisions concerning slavery indisputably belong among the former and are therefore logically not subject to change.[2]

Today, Islamists and theologians do not generally call for the restoration of slavery and do not appear to believe that it is either possible or desirable. But why should they abandon slavery while still clinging to polygamy or corporal punishment in the name of their supposedly sacred character? No religious reason or other coherent explanation can justify such a distinction: this is the fundamental contradiction in the Islamist position. And so, they simply try to ignore that part of sharia law and do not tolerate any mention of it. It makes them feel uncomfortable, because they demand on religious grounds the restoration or maintenance of other parts of sharia law that are equally inappropriate to our times.

The third category of Muslim law – the one to which Islamists are firmly attached – mainly covers the areas of personal status, penal law and freedom of conscience. This is the real bone of contention between modernists and Islamists, since sharia law is conspicuous for its anti-feminism, its inhumane penal provisions, and its blows against freedom of conscience.

Discrimination against women

It is well known that sharia law discriminates against women, and it has become commonplace to denounce it on this score. We must take it up again here, however, because several aspects are considerably less familiar.

Unlike the Christian religion, Islam recognizes the legitimacy of sexual desire and pleasure; in themselves they are neither a sin nor a necessary evil justified only by the necessity of procreation. In a way, sharia allows a very large degree of sexual freedom, almost licence, the only real limit being that this freedom is reserved for men and totally denied to women. If a man is careful to respect certain forms, there is no limit to the number of women he can have.

First of all, he has a right to be married to four women at once – a right which, until the attempts in recent times to start new *ijtihads*, went unchallenged for thirteen centuries. The justification given for this has been the need to avoid sin: if a married man meets a woman or girl, widow or divorcee, and takes a fancy to her, then it is better to allow him to marry her, so that he will not be tempted into illicit relations. It does not matter if he is not sure that he loves her enough to marry her for life, or even for a long time, because he can repudiate her whenever he likes once the marriage is consummated and his desire assuaged. 'Sceptics' may well ask why a man should stop at two wives. And indeed the ulema reply by justifying a third or a fourth wife in exactly the same terms.

Next, during the first thirteen centuries of the Hegira, sharia law gave a man the right to buy as many slaves as his means permitted and to have sexual relations with all his female slaves. Thus, from the very beginning of the Umayyad empire, thirty years after the death of the Prophet, down to Atatürk's abolition of the caliphate in 1924, nearly all the caliphs (that is, leaders of the Islamist state who had the religious function to which Islamists are so attached) enjoyed their own 'exclusive' harem of women. This could run into the hundreds, or even thousands, and was an essential part of the imperial court. To keep the wolf out of the fold, these women were served by eunuchs – although, of course, the demand for fidelity is an expression of jealousy, itself a consequence of love, and cannot be applied to thousands of women at the same time. One is left baffled by all these inhumane practices, which recall the droit de seigneur in European feudalism.

In any event, the ulema never showed any concern for the emotional well-being or physiological needs of these countless concubines, who waited in their 'palace prison' in the constant fear, or constant hope, of being the favourite for one night.

It might be argued that although slavery and harems were regrettable, they are now a thing of the past, and that sharia law should be appreciated for its many other applications. But, concubines aside, the fact remains that the sharia gives men the right to an unlimited number of marriages, so long as they have no more than four wives at any one time. A polygamist may repudiate one of the four at any moment, thereby freeing a 'position' to be occupied by a new wife – who may then be later repudiated in the same merry-go-round. The man can even know with certainty that he will want to be with the new wife for only a limited period of time: one year, one month or one week (the duration of a holiday, for example); the marriage will still be valid. For Sunni Muslims, it will be simply a marriage followed by a divorce; theologians find no fault with those emirs in the Gulf states, for example, who practise this kind of legal prostitution for their pleasure trips to poor countries in the Indian Ocean. Shiites, for their part, are less inhibited about such matters. The Jafari rite explicitly recognizes a marriage of *mutaa* (pleasure), which is by definition a temporary marriage or, to be perfectly clear, a disguised and regulated form of prostitution.

This freedom for men to enter into as many marriages as they wish is made easier by the simplicity of marital repudiation, which has very few negative consequences for them. Women, by contrast, have to observe a minimum wait of three months before they can remarry. The gender inequality is as blatant for the dissolution of a marriage as it is for the rules under which it can be contracted in the first place.

A husband demands unfailing fidelity from his wife, any breach of this being punishable with death by stoning. But his own infidelity with one of the other co-spouses is considered legitimate. In short, the man has jealous feelings that must be scrupulously respected, a heart that must never be wounded, an honour that must on no account be damaged. The woman is supposed to have none of these things.

Islamists use a number of arguments to try to justify this blatant inequality. The first concerns the need to avoid confusion in the attribution of children: when a man marries several women the maternity and paternity of any progeny remains assured; but if a woman had relations with more than one man it would not be known who was the father of her children. This argument never held in the case of sterile or menopausal women, and today's methods of contraception and biological analysis make it redundant in other cases as well.

Next there is the demographic argument that is trotted out over and over again. There are more women than men on earth, it is said, and so the authorization of polygamy is actually a favour to the female sex. All that needs to be said about this is that no statistics have ever shown it to have a solid foundation.

An ostensibly humanitarian argument is that, in cases where a wife is ill or sterile, it is better to allow the husband to marry a second woman without abandoning the first. However, when it is pointed out that today's emancipated women, with means of their own, might claim the same right in relation to a sick or infertile husband, the fundamentalists say they have never heard anything so outrageous.

Finally, there is what we might call the sociological argument: that urban lifestyles, the housing shortage and similar factors are removing the ground on which polygamy used to flourish. This is true. Tetragamy is certainly becoming a thing of the past, and even bigamy is rare. But, even after the minor reforms introduced in certain Muslim countries, there will never be equality in the couple so long as the law upholds polygamy and allows a husband to take a second wife. The wife will continue to live beneath a sword of Damocles, as the legal discrimination inevitably unbalances the relationship and leads to a situation of dependence and inferiority, both in reality and at the level of each partner's conduct.

As to the dissolution of marriage, we have already seen that the classical practice of repudiation is available to the husband alone. It may take one of two forms: *beïn* (final) and *raji* (provisional). In the provisional form, the husband may remarry the repudiated wife without consulting her – the idea being that the time apart will have given him time to reflect and taught her to behave better in the future.

It is true that sharia law also provides for dissolution of the marriage bond on the wife's initiative, but the conditions and procedures for this are so strict that it mostly remains only a theoretical possibility. In theory, a judge can 'divorce' a married woman if her husband gravely fails in his legal obligations or if she pays him an indemnity (that is, in effect, buys back her freedom). But usually the judge – whose intervention is always necessary – comes from such a misogynistic culture that the process drags on and on until it becomes lost in the shifting sands of endless reports and procedures.

In practice, a woman who can no longer bear to live with her husband has no other option than to take refuge with her parents, brother or uncle, while waiting for her husband to lose patience and agree to repudiate her. Until that day of deliverance from her trials and suffering, the sharia gives her husband the formidable weapon of 'prison for a recalcitrant wife', whereby a judge orders her to be confined until she agrees to return to the marital home. It is true that this institution is so intolerable that it is tending to disappear in most Muslim countries. Nevertheless, it is a provision that has applied until very recent times – and those who call today for a return to sharia law need to be reminded of this. The small number of Tunisian women who have been indoctrinated by fundamentalists have no idea that such a prison, the Darjoued,[3] used to exist in Tunis and that it disappeared only with the emancipation of women under the Code of Personal Status adopted in 1956.

Many other provisions of sharia law indicate its discriminatory attitude to women: for example, the husband's right to strike his wife; the husband's legal guardianship over the children of a dissolved marriage (scrutiny of their education, general supervision, all the noble tasks) and the wife's responsibility for their everyday care (meals, clothing, special tasks in dealing with infants); the limitation of women's inheritance to half as much as that of men with the same degree of kinship; a ban preventing women from exercising any leadership function; the obligation to wear the veil – an exhaustive list would be too long to reproduce here. The point of our emphasis on polygamy and dissolution of marriage has mainly been to show that there are not just a few general principles of inequality in the sharia, but that the ulema went as far as possible in laying down detailed rules that sharpened its discriminatory character. The same is true of the rules directed against freedom of conscience.

The sharia against freedom of conscience

'No duress in matters of religion', the Koran tells us.[4] With a divine word as clear as that, one might have expected the ulema to construct a grand theory of the freedom of conscience. But the opposite is the case. They handed down to us a set of rules directed against the freedom of conscience – for Muslims, for the peoples of the Book and for everyone else.

Non-Muslims

Several verses of the Koran glorify Abraham, the Jewish religion and Christianity and command respect for Christians and Jews. For example, verse 69 of sura 5, 'The Table', explicitly states: 'Believers [Muslims], Jews, Sabaeans, or Christians – whoever believes in God and the Last Day and does what is right – shall have nothing to fear or to regret.'[5]

It was necessary to wait until the Second Vatican Council before Catholicism abandoned the principle of 'outside the Church, no salvation'. Muslims could have taken the lead fourteen centuries earlier, since the Holy Book tells us that all deists, and *a fortiori* all members of monotheistic religions, should be considered as having 'nothing to fear'. Yet we had to wait for the modern Tunisian thinker Mohamed Talbi to rehabilitate that verse,[6] to grasp its meaning, to conclude from it that respect should be shown to members of other religions, and to make it the correct and most suitable basis for the wished-for dialogue with other religions.

Unfortunately, that is not at all how the ulema interpreted the verse in question; they argued instead that it applied only to people who were Christians or Jews before the advent of Islam, or who remained such as long as the message of Islam had not yet reached them. This human, all too human gloss, so restrictive as to deform the verse's meaning, expressed a wish to dominate others, an egoism of nations that has been common to all civilizations, virtually without exception. *In several respects, then, sharia law was constructed by men against the principles of the Koran.*

To be sure, in their application of Muslim law, the ulema generally extended protection to priests and rabbis, churches and synagogues. Indeed, remarkably for the time, ecclesiastical and rabbinical courts were allowed to continue applying their own laws to fellow Christians or Jews; on the whole, therefore it was a favourable system of autonomy.[7] Throughout the Middle Ages, Jews, for instance, encountered much more tolerant and benevolent conditions in Muslim countries than anywhere else in the world. This is recognized in his *History of the Jews* by the well-known Israeli politician Abba Eban, whom no one could suspect of being friendly towards Islam or the Arabs. He shows how, in the Diaspora, Jews have known only two periods of prosperity when their personality has been able to flourish: in the United States today, and in Muslim Andalusia.[8] By contrast, after the Christian *reconquista* of Spain, Jews and Muslims had only three options: conversion to Christianity, emigration or death.

We should therefore take care not to make a value judgement on Muslim law outside of its historical context; it would be a grave mistake to evaluate the past through the lenses of the present. Fundamentalists do think and argue outside time, hoping to turn the clock back a thousand years or more to a legal system that has become completely anachronistic. And it is because they reason in this way that we have been led to criticize the sharia in the light of the principles of democracy and human rights. One consequence of the fundamentalist phenomenon is that Muslims do not manage to put the past in its place and to live their lives to the full in the present.

If the fundamentalists wanted to carry us back to the golden age of Islam, with its great translations of Greek and Indian scholars or philosophers and its peaceful yet exciting debates between Mutazilites and traditionalists, they would find much greater acceptance. But what they actually want is to make us relive 'that period of the past which adopted tradition instead of reflection, and repetition instead of creation'.[9]

Although we should be pleased at the Muslim advances in the recognition of others, this should not stop us regretting that the ulema, in defining the relations of Jews and Christians to the Islamic state, gave them the status if not of protected foreigners then at least of second-class subjects. They were minorities who enjoyed guarantees with regard to personal security, enjoyment of possessions and freedom of worship, but who in a number of respects also suffered social, political and legal discrimination.[10] The status that Islam accorded to minorities involved a complex mixture of tolerance (remarkable for the time) and discrimination (unacceptable today). As Lévi-Strauss put it: 'Islam, which invented toleration in the Near East, finds it difficult to forgive non-Moslems for not abjuring their own religions in favour of Mohammedism, when the latter enjoys the overwhelming superiority over all other faiths of respecting them all.'[11] Some of the discrimination established by the ulema still persists in a number of Muslim countries,[12] and it will certainly become worse whenever one of the existing semi-modern, semi-religious regimes gives way to a fundamentalist regime. Let us not forget the ordeals inflicted on the Bahais since the day Khomeini replaced the Shah of Iran.

Even in the rest of the Muslim world, the fate of religious minorities is scarcely to be envied. There can be no justification for the official harassment of Egyptian Copts wishing to build a new church, or the obstacles placed in the way of their taking up various posts. The Copts were already in Egypt before the Islamic conquest fourteen centuries ago, and the fact that they are now emigrating to Canada, Australia or elsewhere says a lot about the difficulties they face as a minority. We should reject the argument that Muslims, being the majority, have every right to rule. For the majority that counts in a democratic system of government is the one formed around certain political opinions and projects, not around religious beliefs or ethnic origins. Léon Blum and Pierre Mendès-France were two of the greatest presidents of the Council of Ministers in France. John F. Kennedy was a great American president. Those great nations had everything to gain by entrusting the highest office to the best candidate of the day, without taking account of his affiliation to a religious minority by origins or beliefs. It was both the collective interest and a personal right. We are still a long way from that in the Muslim world.

The first requirement should be to eliminate and even forbid any reference to religion in identity papers, so that there is at least the appearance of legal equality and non-discrimination between citizens. This has already been done in Tunisia and should become general. Next, neither the constitution nor the national legislation should make any distinction between citizens, who should all have equal rights and duties. The rest is a matter of education.

Muslim law brought with it the great achievement of religious tolerance. But today Jews and Christians no longer accept that they should be merely 'tolerated' in the land of their birth; they rightly demand to be fully fledged citizens free from any discrimination. As to non-Muslims who are neither Christian nor Jewish, the sharia accords them only limited rights that are recognized only in particular circumstances. But its most intolerable attack on freedom of conscience is directed against Muslims. For the most pernicious invention of the sharia, which is still today its most disastrous defect, is the idea that 'apostasy' is a crime punishable by the supreme penalty.

Apostasy a crime?

Astonishing though it may seem, the ulema had no foundation in the Koran for their invention of this attack on the freedom of conscience. In the case of other rules that conflict with human rights, a more or less arduous labour of interpretation – open to dispute and widely disputed today – enabled them to claim a basis in the religion that they claimed or thought themselves to be explaining. For the 'crime' of apostasy, however, no such procedure was possible. Indeed, not only does no verse of the Koran suggest even indirectly that there should be such a crime or penalty; the text of the Holy Book states the exact opposite. We have already mentioned the verse (2:256) which says: 'No duress in matters of religion.' We could also add verse 29 of the 18th sura ('The Cave'), in which God addresses his Prophet as follows: 'Say: "This is the truth from your Lord. Let him who will, believe in it, and him who will, deny it"'; or verse 99 of the 10th chapter ('Jonah'): 'Had your Lord pleased, all the people of the earth would have believed in Him, one and all. Would you then force people to have faith?'[13]

At least in this world, then, God does not punish, or command others to punish, those who do not believe in him. On the contrary, he commands that no duress should be brought to bear against them. Is this not the liberal answer to the question posed by Jean Daniel in his fine recent book *Dieu est-il fanatique?*[14]

God is not a fanatic, but yesterday's ulema were, and so too are today's ulema and fundamentalists. It is true that most clerics have been or still are fanatics. As Sami Abu Sahlieh reminds us, the classical Muslim jurists 'resembled their contemporary Jewish and Christian counterparts in prescribing the death penalty for anyone who abandoned their religion. In fact, for those jurists religious freedom operated in only one direction: freedom to enter, no freedom to leave.'[15]

Christians and Jews have abandoned this shameful rule. Because of the theologians and the fundamentalists, Islam has not abandoned it. It is a question of levels of development. Underdevelopment is not only economic or social but also cultural and intellectual. Fundamentalism, in our countries, is the most evident expression of our underdevelopment.

Already in classical Muslim law, the Hanafites allowed a small exception to soften the injustice of this rule. They laid down that it should strictly apply only to men, and were content to order imprisonment in the case of women (perhaps as some compensation for their legal inferiority) until such time as they returned to Islam. On this issue, as on many others, the Hanafites were often more liberal than others. Ibn Khaldun's explanation for this is that the Hanafi rite in Baghdad, the imperial capital at that time, developed in an urban milieu, whereas the much stricter Maleki rite originated in the Hejaz desert region and was then adopted by the mainly Bedouin society of the Maghreb.[16]

Lacking any basis in the Koran for their rule on apostasy, the ulema linked it to a *hadith* (saying) supposedly spoken by the Prophet: 'He who changes religion, kill him!' However, the hadith in question belongs to the dubious *ahad* category (reported by a single person),[17] and the doubt becomes stronger when we know that the companion who reported it, Ibn Abbas, was only thirteen years old at the time of the Prophet's death. The weight of this hadith is further weakened by the fact that there were a number of apostasies during the Prophet's lifetime, most notably that of the Kindi. When the Prophet learned of the latter, he blamed it on their four kings (Gamad, Mihwas, Misrah and Abdaa)[18] – a legitimate enough reaction on his part. But there was never any question of war or punishment against them. Only after the Prophet's death was a war waged against the Kindi as a whole in order to end their defection and to force them back to Islam.

Conscious of the weakness of their case, the ulema appealed to the authority of the so-called *fijmaa*, or consensus, of the people of Medina.[19] However, since history does not tell us that the Prophet's companions explicitly pronounced on the creation of such a rule, the Hanafites invented a special category of consensus, *fijmaa sukuti*, or consensus by silence. To explain this rather bizarre concept, we need to look briefly at the actual wars of the apostates, which were a major political event in the history of Islam.

After the Prophet's death, Abu Bakr was appointed caliph – that is, head of the Muslim community – but his authority was soon disputed in a number of ways. He presented himself as the Prophet's successor or the one who continued his work. He was therefore not a head of state in the sense of having sovereignty over a particular territory, but rather a religious leader or guide of believers; in this connection, the difference between territorial and personal authority is fundamental. What happened next is that a number of tribes outside Medina sought to escape Abu Bakr's authority by declaring that they had abandoned Islam. Was their real aim to recover the tribal freedom that went back centuries in Arabia? Were they expressing opposition to the person of Abu Bakr and, through him, to the tribes of Mecca and the hegemonic ambitions of the Quraysh in particular? Or was it a real apostasy on the part of tribes or individuals who had only recently converted to Islam, perhaps half-heartedly, without great conviction, out of mere opportunism? Most probably, there was a little of all these elements. But in any event the phenomenon was much more political than religious, although this did not stop Abu Bakr from unfurling the banner of religion to legit-imize his bitter struggle to assert his authority.

It was during this time that the death penalty for apostasy was intro-duced and immediately applied. The best proof that it was a religious cover for a political choice is that it was applied with the same rigour to recently converted tribes that said they had changed their mind as to tribes that clearly said they were Muslim but challenged Abu Bakr's authority and refused to pay his agents the *zaket* (alms levy) as a token of their allegiance.

Right from the beginning, then, the death penalty was used as a measure against political opponents, rather as most regimes in Muslim countries today prosecute people for their dissident beliefs by dressing them up as a plot against the security of the state. The death penalty for apostasy is not a religious rule; it is a political rule, a rule in the service of authoritarian politics.

Most of Abu Bakr's companions supported his war against the apostates. It was in their personal interest to do so, as well as in the interest of their tribe, their clan and the state they were in the course of building. Since none of the Prophet's companions explicitly opposed this political attitude, the ulema later said that there had been a tacit consensus.

The point here is not at all to condemn Abu Bakr: he was one of the main founders of the Islamic empire, and in the history of all countries and civilizations the ways of building an empire have been more or less the same. But those who seek to enforce his style of political conduct today, as if it corresponded to a rule of divine law, commit an error of judgement that it is high time to correct. In fact, a large number of Muslim researchers have already spoken out in favour of abolishing the rule concerning apostasy – and anyway it no longer exists on the statute books of most Muslim countries.[20]

The political uses of apostasy

Throughout the early centuries of Islam, religion was used as a cover for authoritarian policies involving the murder of opponents. The ulema always identified *ridda* (apostasy) with *al-baghi* (violent or ideological opposition to the Islamic regime in place). This is how they justified the crushing of popular revolts such as that of the Zanj, or black slaves, a superexploited subproletariat which rose up between 869 and 883 CE. It is also how they justified the execution of the great Sufi thinker Al Hallaj (in 922) or of Zanadika (free-thinkers) such as the celebrated writer of Persian origin Ibn Elmokaffa, who translated into Arabic a number of literary works from the Indian and Iranian civilizations and was put to death in 757, at the age of thirty-six. These are just a couple of famous examples, but the supporters of many other schools (Mutazilites, Karamita, Jahmia, and so on) were exiled, hounded, imprisoned or slaughtered.

Such practices later died down. Perhaps – and this was certainly one of the causes that precipitated the decline of the Muslim world – the ever more violent repression discouraged and eventually stifled any attempt at reflection or innovation. In any event, the criminalization of apostasy seems to have become obsolete in the last few centuries. Although the new Muslim states present in varying degrees a religious coloration, they have looked elsewhere to ground their legitimacy. For regimes that emerged out of the independence movement, whose constitutions provide for election of the country's rulers, universal suffrage is the theoretical foundation of power. Hence, in most Muslim countries today, the criminal code contains no mention of apostasy, and one might have thought that it was safely dead and buried. But, unfortunately, theologians and fundamentalists are in the course of bring it back to life.[21]

The history of the Muslim world over the past hundred years has seen many successful or abortive attempts to modernize society and the state. These projects have always encountered opposition from the ulema, who represent a major force for inertia. The weapon brandished by the-ologians is to charge with apostasy any intellectual advancing a new idea, and then to put pressure on the state to try him. Let us here simply recall the early-twentieth-century campaign by the Zitunians to put on trial Abdelaziz Thaalbi, the founder of the Tunisian national movement; or the proceedings against the great Egyptian thinker Taha Hussein in 1926, in response to pressure from Al Azhar; or, much more recently, the proceedings started against the Egyptian secular thinker and activist Farag Fuda.

Still, so long as it was necessary to act through the judicial bodies of the modern state, such accusations did not lead to very much. Abdelaziz Thaalbi was sentenced to two months' imprisonment, and the proceed-ings against Taha Hussein were eventually called off (although, to calm things down, he removed from the second edition of *Pre-Islamic Poetry* a few pages that had especially angered the people at Al Azhar).

What is making the problem considerably worse today is that, because of the rise of fundamentalism, a charge of apostasy levelled by the ulema often produces results, either at official level in the few Islamist states or through criminal action on the part of fundamentalist groups in other Muslim countries.

One example of the former was the death sentence on Mahmud Mohamed Taha in Sudan, under the Nimeiri regime, when Hassan al-Turabi, the Islamist leader and ideologue, was justice minister. Taha was the founder and main driving force behind the Republican Brother-hood, and several of his works had fallen foul of conservative thinkers because of interpretations of the Koranic basis of Islam that would have entailed a complete recasting of the sharia. Taha was seventy years old when he was executed, having spent his life fighting for a more liberal and more egalitarian Islam. Three of his followers were sentenced to death at the same time, but they were immediately released when they took up the judges' suggestion that they renounce their ideas.[22] Taha himself stuck to his convictions and was hanged on 18 January 1985, before a crowd that admired the broad smile he wore until the end. Al Azhar, which had demanded his head, and the League of the Muslim World, whose headquarters are in Mecca, congratulated President Nimeiri after the hanging.[23]

When an anti-fundamentalist thinker, a bold new interpreter of the Koran or simply a liberal writer does not come under the jurisdiction of a fundamentalist state, the ulema of Al Azhar denounce him, and members of fundamentalist groups proceed to execute him on a street corner. Thus Farag Fuda, the author of several works criticizing the sharia and fundamentalism and the founder in 1987 of the Egyptian Enlightenment Association, was assassinated on 8 June 1992.[24] The killer told investigators that Omar Abderrahman, a key figure in the fundamentalist organization Islamic Jihad, had given the blessing of the law to those who 'spilled the blood of the opponents of Islam'.[25] When Sheikh Mohamed Ghazali − a leading Al Azhar figure and long-time adviser to the Algerian government under Ben Jedid − was called to testify on behalf of Fuda's assassin, he told the court that the execution of apostates was a duty for every Muslim so long as it was not being fulfilled by the state.[26]

Naguib Mahfouz, Egypt's winner of the Nobel Prize for Literature, wrote in 1959 a novel that Al Azhar banned as contrary to Islam. Thirty-five years later, an Islamist took it into his head to 'fulfil his duty' by trying to assassinate the writer. Other Egyptian Islamists do their best to get the courts to take action against apostasy in line with sharia law. Nasr Hamed Abu Zeid is just one to have suffered from such a process: a series of his reflective works on Islam and commentaries on the Koran, following a historical and rationalist method, were of too logical and enlightened a character to escape the charge of apostasy from the fundamentalists.[27] According to sharia law, an apostate who is due to be executed no longer has a legal existence as a subject of rights and obligations. As he is already dead, as it were, from a civil point of view, the question of his inheritance is open and his marital union is dissolved. Fundamentalist militants therefore applied to the Cairo court for the marriage of the Abu Zeid couple to be legally dissolved, on the grounds that Abu Zeid's wife, as a Muslim, had no right to keep the marital bond with a husband who was no longer a Muslim. On 14 June 1995, for the first time in modern Egyptian history, the Cairo appeals court issued such a divorce ruling under pressure from the Islamists. The fact that the Court of Cassation then refused to overturn this decision says a lot about the degree to which the judiciary in Egypt is being infiltrated by fundamentalists. It is true that the infiltration is not complete − and, by a procedural trick highly debatable in legal terms, the Cairo court did block implementation of the divorce ruling. But, with his life in danger, Abu Zeid was forced to go and live abroad with his wife.

We need hardly stress the gravity of the legal implications of this affair, and the intolerable violation of human rights that it involved. Let us briefly mention four points.

First, the court's ruling accepted that it was permissible to intervene in matters of individual conscience, merely on application by a third party that had no authority or personal interest in the case. Law No. 3-96 has subsequently reserved the right of initiative to the public ministry, but this only reduces the gravity of the interference without actually ending it. Indeed, although the conditions under which the procedure may be employed are now more limited, the right to interfere has been formally enshrined in the law.

Second, similarly, the court's ruling accepted a right of intervention in the private lives of individuals. It should be the business of the couple alone to ascertain whether their marriage is to be valid or invalid; any intervention by a third party in this field is quite intolerable.

Third, it is particularly unfortunate − and symptomatic − that throughout the Abu Zeid divorce proceedings there were long discussions about procedure, about the admissibility of the action, and about whether Abu Zeid was a Muslim or an apostate, but there was never any consideration of whether apostasy itself was a crime. Nor did the issue come up for consideration in the trial of Farag Fuda's assassin. No one dared say that the whole pernicious concept should be dropped, that it had no basis in the Koran or the hadiths, and that it was contrary to the most elementary principles of human rights.

The fourth point concerns the Egyptian judiciary, which, it must be said, is one of the most independent in the Arab world. This would be cause for rejoicing if it had been trained to respect individual liberties, but that is not what is suggested by the Abu Zeid affair, when the judges sitting both in the Court of Appeal and the Court of Cassation handed down verdicts against the advice of the public ministry representing the government. This made their ruling particularly anti-democratic. But, above all else, it showed that, whereas respect for public freedoms, regular elections and an independent judiciary are the means of democratic government, the education of young people (that is, of tomorrow's citizens) is the first condition for those means not to lead to anti-democratic results.

The trends mentioned above are ample proof that Muslim law stands in need of deep and thorough revision. One particular requirement is that freedom of conscience should be respected. One cannot claim that this freedom is respected unless a person's religion is disregarded, and indeed not mentioned at all, in relation to their rights and duties *vis-à-vis* the community and other citizens. Nor can one claim to respect freedom of conscience if one accepts that a non-Muslim may become a Muslim but does not accept the reciprocity of the rule. Such reciprocity is the logical meaning of the Koranic injunction 'No duress in matters of religion'; it is in conformity both with its spirit and with its letter. Although, for historical reasons we may consider justified or at least understandable, that injunction has long been obscured, we are not obliged to remain prisoners of that unfortunate past. Our main problem today, the powerful brake on our emancipation and development, is that we are still collectively chained to our past. For Muslims there will be no development without freedom and no freedom without escaping from our historical prison.

We are still waiting for Muslims to reach a sufficient level of culture, intellectual freedom and self-assurance to accept that a Muslim can cease to be a Muslim, as Christians accept that a Christian can become a Muslim. Meanwhile, however, the most urgent struggle is for Muslims to have the freedom to understand and interpret Islam according to their own lights. For the threat of being branded an apostate is used today, as it has been for a long time, as a way of preventing any reflection that leads to something new.

This is why the Tunisian League for the Defence of Human Rights stated in Article 9 of its charter that 'every individual has a right to freedom of thought and conscience; this right entails the freedom to choose one's religion or beliefs and the freedom to interpret them (*ijtihad*)'.

As a result of its adoption of this article – and of another on the freedom of marriage – the League underwent the greatest crisis in the first ten years of its existence, when Islamists operating a policy of 'entrism' in non-governmental organizations tried to invade the League as if they did not realize that certain human rights were incompatible with various rules of sharia law. Discussions of a draft charter showed that their real hope, in the name of cultural specificity, was to empty the concept of human rights of its content so that it coincided with the rules of classical Muslim law. They also carried the debate into the public arena, pointing the finger at League activists as execrable unbelievers.

But these activists did not buckle under pressure, and the League kept its public audience while adopting its charter by a large majority.

Article 4 of the same charter explicitly condemns corporal punishment.

Corporal punishment

Muslim criminal law is often presented as an extremely severe, even barbaric system, and it is because of this law and the sometimes truly barbaric conduct of certain fundamentalists that Islam has such a bad press abroad. In reality, however, the most severe provisions of the law have no basis in Islam as such; they are the work of the ulema. And many other provisions, explicable in terms of historical circumstances, could and should be discarded today.

The hodud

The truth is that Islamic criminal law is very rudimentary. It defines two categories of offence: a small number for which certain penalties (*hodud*) are prescribed, and others (the *taazir*) where the punishment is left to the judge's discretion. In the latter case, although it may be wise to allow the judge considerable flexibility in fitting the punishment to the nature and circumstances of the offence, it is wrong not to limit this power by clearly defining each offence and setting a minimum and maximum punishment. The principle of the rule of law in crime and punishment, which is today asserted in nearly every legal system in the world, is a victory for humanity. Muslims should not be deprived of the guarantee that it provides against the arbitrary exercise of judicial power. Indeed, the category of *taazir* offences seems to have been abandoned in both theory and practice. Iran and Sudan have adopted penal codes that define offences and prescribe certain punishments, so that even these two fundamentalist regimes have implicitly accepted the need to revise certain provisions of the sharia.

The problem is still posed in relation to the *hodud*. The two gravest and most inhumane *hodud* have no real basis in the Muslim religion: namely, the death penalty for apostasy (which, as we have seen, has no basis at all in the Koran and is of a purely political-historical character), and the punishment of death by stoning for those found guilty of adultery. The ulema put forward two arguments, each as disputable as the other, to justify this horrific punishment.[28]

First, they claim that a verse of the Koran states: 'If a married man and a married woman commit adultery, stone them to death – it is God's vengeance.'[29] What makes this verse strange, and indeed unique, is that it is not actually to be found in the Koran. Instead, God is supposed to have suggested it to the Prophet so that it would be known and applied without being read. In fact, the Koranic verses were collected in the Holy Book by the Prophet's companions, during the fifteen years following his death, on the basis of their memories and of the documents in which the verses had been written down as and when they were revealed. If the verse in question was never inserted in a chapter of the Koran, this must have been because there was no written trace of it and because only one of the Prophet's companions had reported it; the proof of authenticity would thus have been wholly inadequate, especially as another verse contradicts it by prescribing a less severe punishment for extra-marital relations and makes no distinction in this respect between single and married persons.

The second argument of the ulema refers to the Prophet's *sunna* or practical conduct, and in particular to the fact that he once sentenced an adulterous man called Maez to death by stoning. However, it is best to know this episode in its details before using it as the basis for such a grave legal rule.

Islamic historians tells us that Maez, feeling great regret for what he had done, confessed it to the Prophet and asked him to hand down a punishment that would allow him to be purified. The Prophet did not give an answer, and so the next day Maez tried again. The Prophet's attitude remained the same. Then, on a third occasion, he finally gave way and ordered his companions to stone Maez in accordance with the local customs of the time. The Prophet subsequently heard that Maez had tried to run away as soon as the first stone hit him; he then warmly rebuked his companions for continuing the stoning regardless, on the ground that Maez's evidently sincere repentance was sufficient to obtain God's pardon. Clearly, then, the Prophet bowed to ancient customs but displayed an initial reticence and later openly disapproved of the action.

The two foundations invoked by the doctors of the law are each as shaky as the other. This means that they have simply taken over ancient customs and attached them to Islam, as they have done with most of their other rules and regulations.

We should therefore exclude, as lacking any religious foundation, the two gravest *hodud*: the death penalty for apostasy and the penalty of stoning for those found guilty of adultery. The only offences punishable by *hodud* that may be accorded a religious sanction are the five explicitly mentioned in the Koran: banditry; theft; slanderous accusations against a woman's honour; homicide, blows and wounds punishable under the *lex talionis*; and adultery. The last of these requires a further remark, in addition to the general ones applicable to all the *hodud*.

Adultery is mentioned in three different verses, where the sexual act liable to punishment is defined in three different but complementary ways. According to Sadok Mazigh's French translation of the Koran,[30] verse 15 of sura 4, 'Women', refers to 'women who offend against their virtue'; verse 16 of the same sura to 'immoral acts'; and verse 2 of sura 24, 'Light', to men and women 'guilty of adultery'. The ulema thought up a coherent system of punishments: one hundred strokes of the lash when both partners in a sexual act are unmarried (the reference being verse 2 of sura 24), and death by stoning in the much graver case when the sexual relationship is complicated by adultery. But we have just seen that there is no basis in the Koran for the latter penalty, and so the claim of coherence is demolished. As it is wrong to equate the two acts and to prescribe the same penalty for them, only real adultery should be established as an offence. For it is adultery that offends against virtue (4:15) and constitutes an immoral act (4:16). In this connection, Sadok Mazigh was entirely correct to translate the term *zina* in 24:2 as 'adultery'.

The fact is that Islam, like other religions, calls for discipline and self-control in sexual relations. But although it strongly urges people to have such relations only within marriage, and although it regards them outside marriage as sinful, the sin is sufficiently serious to constitute a criminal offence only if it also involves conjugal infidelity. In modern systems of law, a clear distinction is drawn between civil offences and criminal offences. The laws of Tunisia, for instance, do not punish all sexual relations outside marriage but only adulterous acts. The penalty is quite severe – five years in prison – but it applies equally to both the male and female partner, and a criminal prosecution can be initiated only if the aggrieved spouse requests that this be done. It is a kind of private misdemeanour.

Aside from this special observation concerning the definition of adultery, we can see that the five deeds listed as criminal offences are indeed reprehensible. Nevertheless, a few remarks arise in relation to the whole *hodud* system.

Comments

It is regrettable that, when the Koran offers a choice between two or more solutions, the ulema opt for the most severe. Thus, in the case of adultery, the verse prescribing one hundred lashes is supposed to render null and void the two other verses that prescribe lighter punishments.

The term *had* (plural: *hodud*) means 'limit'. In this context, therefore, it refers to a 'maximum limit',[31] so that one would expect the punishment to vary between five and one hundred lashes, for example, or the range of options to include a fine, banishment or corporal punishment. But the ulema preferred to convert the maximum punishment into the fixed norm. As used in the Koran, the term *hodud* signifies that the judge must not exceed a certain penalty, but he has every latitude to order something less severe. In fact, on most occasions when the Koran prescribes a penal sanction, it adds that the offence may be forgiven or that repentance should be taken into account.

In the case of two persons taken in adultery, verse 16 of sura 4 ends as follows: 'If they repent and mend their ways, let them be. God is forgiving and merciful.' And 5:38, which speaks of cutting off the hand of a thief, is followed by 5:39: 'But whoever repents after committing evil, and mends his ways, shall be pardoned by God. God is forgiving and merciful.' In 24:5, in relation to those guilty of slanderous accusations, we find the same exception for 'those among them that afterwards repent and mend their ways. God is forgiving and merciful.'[32]

It appears beyond doubt, then, that neither the spirit nor the letter of the Koran rules out punishments less severe, more humane and perhaps just as deterrent in the case of people guilty of the offences we have just mentioned. Modern lawmakers who replace corporal punishment with prison sentences are not contravening the Koran. On the contrary, they are opting for solutions more in keeping with its spirit.

In any event, corporal punishment is among the 'degrading' forms condemned by Article 5 of the Universal Declaration of Human Rights. Muslims have a right to know why the Koran, which preaches mercy and love of others, envisaged such severe penalties. The answer, which can dispel all confusion on the matter, is to be sought in the circumstances attending the revelation.

In the late sixth and early seventh centuries CE, the Arabia where the Prophet Mohammed grew up and received the revelation was inhabited by mainly nomadic tribes. In this desert region, there was neither a river nor adequate rainfall to support agriculture worthy of the name, and the main sources of livelihood were the caravan trade and a little livestock breeding. As most of the people were not tied to the land, they lacked the urban structures necessary for the birth of a state. There was no administrative organization in any meaningful sense of the term, and still less any statelike structures.

Each tribe had its bard who sang of its epics and glories, as well as a chieftain who decided on the movements of the tribe, arbitrated internal disputes and sealed alliances with other tribes. These alliances were formed and terminated in accordance with the prevailing circumstances. Assaults by members of one tribe against members of another tribe were the source of constant and often bloody conflict. If the chieftains in question were able to reach a quick agreement about compensation, peace could be preserved and the two tribes could continue to coexist relatively smoothly. If such an agreement proved impossible, however, the resulting conflict could last a long time and bring a vicious cycle of raids and revenge raids. Historians tell of the twists and turns of the Bassu war, which originated in the theft of a camel and pitted various tribes against one another for forty years. It is probably a legend, but it certainly also contains an element of truth. In a subsistence economy where the caravan trade played an essential role and the security of the nomads' camels and possessions was of prime importance, it was essential that punishment of theft and blood crimes should be severe. Mere compensation of the victim was not a sufficient solution; such crimes called for vengeance – that is, the death of the perpetrator. In the case of intertribal offences, where strong ties of solidarity operated within each tribe, execution of the criminal by close relatives of the victim called down in turn further acts of vengeance. And so the cycle of wars was unleashed.

A city, being placed under a municipal authority, or better still a state authority, comes to possess a court, a security force and a prison. The imprisonment of criminals serves both as a way of giving satisfaction to the victim or his relatives and fellow tribesmen, and as a means of preserving the dignity and physical integrity of the culprit, who will eventually complete his sentence and be released.

Where a municipal or state structure is lacking, however, there are no prisons or guards. It is then little short of a miracle if one manages to appease the desire for vengeance without also killing the perpetrator of the act of violence. The Koran's solution, justified by this historical context, is to be content with cutting off the hand of a thief, wounding the person who wounds another, or lashing the instigator and accomplice of marital infidelity. It is certainly appalling, even barbaric, to cut off the hand of a thief. But in the Arabia of the time of the Prophet, where there was no state and there were no prisons, this form of justice made it possible to avoid killing the thief and unleashing a tribal war that might cost dozens or more lives. Paradoxically, corporal punishment then represented the least bad solution.

The Koran did not prescribe the *hodud* alongside various forms of incarceration, as Iran, Sudan or certain Gulf states do today, and as our fundamentalists would like us to do in Tunisia. It prescribed the *hodud* only to make up for the lack of prisons, itself the consequence of the lack of a state. This is not to say that the Koran has no place for imprisonment as a form of punishment. The word *sijn* (prison, captivity) and its derivatives are used on several occasions – in sura 26, 'The Poets', and especially in sura 12, 'Joseph' – but only to describe certain episodes in the relations between Joseph or Moses and the Pharaohs, that is, in a country (Egypt) which had a state enjoying such attributes as places of detention and an apparatus of penal administration.

A particularly distressing current example will serve to show the extent to which forms of corporal punishment prescribed in the Koran may, under certain circumstances, constitute a lesser evil. For a number of years Somalia has been undergoing a terrible civil war.[33] The state has completely broken down, and the population is divided among rival factions. In 1996 there were seventeen different ethnic groups, led by chieftains among whom it was impossible to find ground for a lasting understanding. There was no industry, very little handicraft production, very little agriculture. Somalia's population is currently one of the poorest in the world. Amid this complete deprivation, with poor distribution of international aid, people live mainly on what is left of pastoral activity. The theft of a sheep has thus become an unspeakable act that has catastrophic implications for the victim. The lack of a state structure capable of enforcing punishment and compensating the victim means that, if victim and perpetrator belong to different groups or sub-groups, tribal warfare becomes a virtual certainty, with its terrible wake of blood and tears. In this specific context, leading figures in certain groups have taken the initiative of organizing what they call Islamic courts, which order corporal punishment for want of prisons and a permanent public power. This use of corporal punishment has triggered indignant and perfectly understandable protests on the part of international human rights organizations. But, for Somalis, such punishments have often been a means of damage limitation that averts the risks of a slide into civil war.

This demonstrates how closely law is bound up with the level of social development. But, above all else, it shows that, whereas the general philosophy of Islam – its broad orientation and fundamental principles – is absolutely valid and cannot change in time or place, the specific rules and applications adopted during or immediately after the Prophet's lifetime were geared to the prevailing circumstances and should change to reflect different circumstances. We must therefore distinguish between Islam, which is immutable and eternal, and sharia law, which should be amended or abolished. Islamists maintain that, on the contrary, nothing has changed since the age of the Prophet. And they do not like it when the incompatibility between sharia law and human rights is pointed out to them. They prefer to pass over such things in silence.

The sharia and human rights

Fundamentalists often appeal to human rights when one of their militants is the victim of abuse, and they are right to do so. But the affirmation of human rights is meant to ensure that anyone can lay claim to them and denounce acts that violate those rights. The problem is that fundamentalists want people to believe that they subscribe to human rights, while at the same time they subscribe to and demand the application of sharia law. It is true that Muslim states have made this task much easier for them.

In 1990, at its nineteenth session of foreign affairs ministers, the Organization of the Islamic Conference (OIC) adopted the Cairo Declaration on Human Rights in Islam. In each point of the preamble, as in each of its twenty-five articles, this declaration logically takes Islamic philosophy as its starting point and source of inspiration. Unfortunately, however, it maintains the confusion between Muslim religion and sharia law. Thus, several rights are recognized 'within the framework of the sharia' (Article 12) or as open to be exercised 'in a legitimate way' (Article 15) or only in ways that are 'not contrary to the principles of the sharia' (Article 16). Article 10 proclaims the freedom of conscience. But it is so designed that in practice it affirms only the freedom to be a Muslim. Article 22 asserts that 'everyone shall have the right to express his opinion freely', but again only 'in such manner as would not be contrary to the principles of the sharia'. Finally, Article 24 is of sparkling clarity: 'All the rights and freedoms stipulated in this Declaration are subject to the Islamic sharia.' And, in keeping with this provision, no mention is made anywhere of the basic right to physical integrity of the human person, to equality between men and women, or to equality between Muslims and non-Muslims.[34]

Most of the regional instruments concerning human rights (European and American texts, and so on) are meant to deepen or guarantee the rights mentioned in the Universal Declaration on Human Rights (10 December 1948) and upheld in subsequent international texts and agreements. Why is it that only the Islamic declaration lags behind these international instruments? The fundamentalist regimes (Iran, Sudan) and traditionalist regimes (most of the Gulf States) are fairly consistent in subscribing to the Islamic declaration, since they apply sharia law internally. Other states, which have modernized to a greater or lesser degree, have a thoroughly inconsistent attitude, especially as several of them have also signed up to the international instruments. Is this just demagogy on their part? Or fear of the fundamentalists? Or ideological confusion? The fundamental problem for these states is that they take a more or less modernist attitude without facing up to its consequences. This has done a lot to disorient their populations, and in particular their young people. The field of what is left unsaid continues to grow.

The fundamentalists foster the same kind of confusion. Once they are driven into a corner, however, they admit or adopt a position that effectively acknowledges the incompatibility between elements of sharia law and certain human rights, while also expressing their preference for the sharia and justifying themselves by reference to the opposition between universality and specificity. This calls for a number of observations.

Each people has cultural specificities and may legitimately wish to preserve them. These concern its literary and artistic production, as well as the mode in which national solidarity is organized.

The truth is that the extraordinary growth of audiovisual communications in the last few decades has tended to erode the differences between cultures. We may welcome this greater closeness between cultures because it favours peace, coexistence and mutual support among nations, but we may also regret it because absolute uniformity and the disappearance of diversity involve an impoverishment of humanity. For this reason, measures to safeguard culture, especially through the encouragement of national cultural production, may be justified – on condition that they do not involve constraints or prohibitions and strictly respect the freedom of individuals.

Individual freedom is surely the finest, and perhaps the most important, human conquest of the last few centuries. If there is one principle that must not be sacrificed on the altar of cultural specificity, this is it.

The enactment of international legislation on human rights, together with the establishment of various supervisory mechanisms, is clearly designed to limit the harmful effect of certain local or regional specificities around the world. International conventions on human rights are thus the means whereby the concert of nations shows the way forward to any nation that is lagging behind, so that it can develop its laws and social practices, and hence certain of its specificities, in the direction of greater freedom for individuals. Human rights, in the universal sense of the term, are an attempt to express the ideal of humanity today.

The right to difference is both a very fine and a very dangerous invention. It is very fine because it assumes that human beings are free to choose their way of life and their practical actions, with the single condition that these do not harm anyone else. But it is very dangerous if it allows a group to oppress certain of its members, whether a particular sub-group or simply one individual.

Freedom is thus the best criterion for knowing which should take precedence in any opposition between universality and specificity. The other human rights all stem more or less directly from the principle of the freedom of the individual. Inasmuch as no one should be freer than anyone else, freedom necessarily supposes the equality of all human beings: equal rights and, by extension, equal opportunities, hence economic and social rights. It is not in the nature of men, or of women, freely to accept the privileges of others; these are always the fruit of coercion. Freedom therefore rules out discrimination.

When seen in its true light, the idea of specificity that fundamentalists invoke to counter the universality of human rights appears as a way of legitimating constraint, oppression and further assaults on human freedom and equality among human beings.

Equality between men and women necessarily supposes monogamy – that is, equal respect for the feelings and sensitivities of each spouse, including the wish not to share his or her partner with anyone else. The specificity invoked by fundamentalists is supposed to mean in this context that Muslim women have less feeling and sensitivity than non-Muslim women, and therefore a weaker or non-existent desire for monogamy. Muslim women, however, with a few exceptions who are thrust into the limelight, do not claim this right to difference, which mainly involves rules that discriminate against them.

Fundamentalists and traditionalists usually retort that strict monogamy is against nature and that Christian conceptions of marriage have not stood the test of time – so that today the West accepts marital infidelity and downplays the gravity of its consequences. But the answer to this must be that the phenomenon is by no means as widespread as fundamentalists claim, and also that there is no lover without a mistress and no mistress without a lover. If the West treats sexual relations more casually than in the past, it does so in a manner that is equal for both sexes. On the other hand, when Muslims claim that it is preferable to have a second wife rather than a mistress, they are defending neither morality nor religion; they simply display their attachment to male privileges.

The trends mentioned above point to two crucial conclusions. First, a large number of rules in classical Muslim or sharia law are contrary to human rights as these are today understood by the international community; each such rule is an affront to the principles of individual liberty, human equality in general and gender equality in particular, and to respect for the physical integrity of human beings. Second, these elements of Muslim law are not really religious in character; they were first put forward by human beings and should today be reshaped by human beings. This raises the question of why fundamentalists and traditionalists are so determined to perpetuate these injustices. We should not forget that respect for the sharia, or the demand to return to the sharia, is the main objective and very *raison d'être* of fundamentalism.

The reasons for attachment to the sharia

Three complementary reasons may be suggested for this stubborn attachment to the sharia.

First, Islamists, being unable to conceive that a non-Muslim should be a full citizen, see him if not as an enemy then at least as an alien and in any case as an 'other'. In their view, Islam is thus an 'identity' before it is a religion. An Islamist may concede that he is not calling for reintroduction of the sharia tax or *jizya* payable by *dhimmi* (that is, Jews and Christians), and he may accept that Jews or Christians should be able to join the civil service and even become senior members of the Council of State. What he cannot tolerate is that they should ever occupy leadership positions, since to his mind a Muslim should never come under a non-Muslim. This is why, in most Muslim countries (even the most modern among them), the constitution stipulates that any candidate for the presidency of the republic must be a Muslim.

It is a question of education, of the understanding and interpretation of Islam. Whether at school or (if he did not go there) at the mosque, the Muslim has studied the history of Islam far more than the history of his own country. An uneducated Egyptian is ignorant of the history of the pharaohs; an uneducated Tunisian is ignorant of the history of Carthage. On the other hand, they all know of the Prophet's struggle to escape the hostility and perfidy of the Mecca infidels, of his and his companions' enforced exile in Medina, and of the praiseworthy efforts they had to make to ensure that Mecca was once again 'open' to them. By virtue of his education, the Muslim will have thrilled to the struggle and identified with those who took part in it, especially as it was always a just struggle and the infidels, even those in Medina, were never loyal allies. Islam is presented, and therefore received, more in terms of struggle and solidarity than as a form of spirituality.

It is therefore understandable that, although a particular non-Muslim may be an honest man with whom one can do business or even spend time as a close friend, he will be like a foreign friend – that is, a person to be cherished and helped, without ever forgetting that he has his own history and affiliation, his own identity. Even at school, the history of the pharaohs in Egypt, or of the Carthaginians of Phoenician or Roman origin in Tunisia, is taught as foreign history that happens to have unfolded on the national territory.

This culture, handed down from generation to generation, encourages the emergence of a 'religious' rather than a 'national' patriotism. The independence struggle created in the population a new sense of solidarity and national patriotism, and the school system could have built on that struggle to reinforce the new sentiment. Instead, for reasons that will be discussed later, it performed this task in a one-sided and imperfect fashion, so that today's Tunisian, while having a clear national consciousness, also continues to have a sense of Islamic affiliation. Islamicity is therefore for him a kind of second identity. And Islamists try to deepen it so that it becomes the primary identity, in the belief that it is in fact the only identity.

For fundamentalists and traditionalists, a non-Muslim can never be entirely a fellow citizen. The converse is also true: a Muslim of foreign nationality is never entirely a foreigner. And, for a Muslim who changes religion, the problem is not a problem of consciousness but of nationality. Insofar as one always thinks of oneself as living in a period of struggle, not to say a state of war, a Muslim who changes religion is a national who has gone over to the enemy. It is a matter of high treason. Hence the death penalty for apostasy.

A few paragraphs hostile to the Prophet in *The Satanic Verses* might have passed unnoticed if they had been written by a John or a Paul, but from the pen of Salman Rushdie, a former Muslim by conviction or family origin – it's all the same – they aroused the wrath of millions of Muslims. Khomeini took advantage of this to issue his fatwa condemning the 'traitor' to death (even if he was not officially described as such) and offering a reward for his execution. The behaviour of Khomeini and the motley firebrands in this affair has been scandalous from any point of view. They have amply demonstrated their contempt for – or, worse still, their straightforward ignorance of – a series of principles: freedom of conscience, freedom of opinion, freedom of expression, citizenship rights and the territorial jurisdiction of criminal law. Is this despotism or ignorance? Probably both.

Islamists are so attached to the sharia, and laws that discriminate against non-Muslims, for a second reason: the fact that they live in a bygone age. This is also what accounts for their anti-feminism.

Let us not forget that the principle of sexual equality first appeared very recently in human history. Even in Europe, it was only in the twentieth century that women gained the right to vote and full recognition of their personality and legal capacity. If, as we have seen above, equality is the corollary of liberty, we should not forget that, at the level of ideas, liberty itself is the fruit of Enlightenment philosophy, and that in actual history it resulted from the evolution of English parliamentarianism, the American War of Independence and the French Revolution – that is, from rather recent history – whereas the subjugation of women is as old as humanity. The *paterfamilias* of Roman law had the right of life and death over his whole family, and therefore over his wife. The legal systems of all the ancient civilizations discriminated against the female sex. And, in modern times, every nation has had difficulty 'swallowing' the great innovation of gender equality. Nor was it easy to win a majority for the new and truly revolutionary principle of democracy, even in the countries that invented it. There were ebbs and flows. After the Constituent Assembly and the Convention, France experienced the Restoration; after the achievement of universal suffrage came a return to a voting system based on a poll tax. It is therefore not at all surprising that new ideas are today meeting resistance in the Muslim world, especially among the least-developed layers of the population. Antifeminism is one of the chief manifestations of intellectual underdevelopment.

It might be objected that there are many fundamentalists among educated people or university graduates. There is a simple explanation for this, as the spread of education has fortunately promoted the evolution of children from the least-privileged sections of the population. How many children born in the back of beyond are today working as doctors or engineers! Nevertheless, it is much easier to learn a new technology than to absorb and internalize new social ideas. The traditional family does not pass on any *a priori* hostility to biology or mechanical engineering. From an early age, though, children have seen their father dominate their mother, or an uncle beat his wife, and learned that this is a normal part of life. Unless the principles of liberty, equality and democracy are inculcated through their parents' speech and behaviour, children require a long period of apprenticeship. The modernization of a society cannot be achieved in the space of one generation. The existence of fundamentalists in our society is proof of that.

The same logic lies behind the attachment to corporal punishment. The well-known phenomenon of flight from the countryside has not spared any developing country, and it has led to interaction between two ways of life, two mentalities. One may think that city life will rub off on the newcomers, but the change cannot be completed within a single generation. Meanwhile, a section of the urban population will live a transitional life in which rural reflexes coexist with newly learned urban patterns of behaviour that are understood and absorbed in widely varying degrees.

Abderrahman ibn Khaldun already drew a distinction between urban society and Bedouin society, each with its specific mentality and relations with the state and law. More recently, Durkheim contrasted *societies based on mechanical solidarity* (traditional societies whose members are alike in their lifestyle and social tasks, and where the law is highly repressive) and *societies based on organic solidarity* (more modern societies where the division of labour has led to a major differentiation of tasks). In the latter case, solidarity springs from complementarity and the law is less repressive.

Corporal punishment disappeared in Tunisia centuries ago, in both town and countryside. But the rural population has always had a rougher temperament, more brutal forms of behaviour and more severe forms of punishment. When a city child learns in school that Islam prescribes corporal punishment, he or she tends to be repelled and generally forgets the legal provision soon afterwards. The psychological predisposition of children from rural families is rather different: they will tend to accept the legal provision as just, and they will fail to see why it is not applied in practice.

The rise of fundamentalism can be explained by the conjunction of several factors, one of the most important being the way in which Islam is taught at school. In this context, we may distinguish several Islams: a popular Islam and a scholarly Islam, a religious Islam and a juridical Islam. Which is the most authentic? To answer this question, we need to go back to the origins of the identification of Islam with a legal system.

How Islam came to be identified with a legal system

We know that apart from *kyes* (argument by analogy) and *ijmaa* (ulema consensus), which are both indisputably human, Muslim law has two main sources: the truly sacred source of the Koran, the word of God revealed to Mohammed by the angel Gabriel; and the *sunna*, all the actions of the Prophet and his words (the *hadiths*).

The sunna

The hadiths are a controversial source of Muslim law. There is no argument about their obligatory force, but there is a problem concerning their authenticity. For it was only a century after the Prophet's death that work began on gathering them together; each hadith was associated with the person or persons who heard it from the Prophet's lips and of all those who passed it down from generation to generation. The later the transcription, obviously, the longer the chain and the less certain the actual content of the hadith. The drawback of oral testimony is that it is based on memory that is sometimes defective, often subjective and distorting. The main criterion used by the ulema to check the authenticity of a hadith is the honesty of the Prophet's companion who reported it and of those who handed it down. But, in formulating a hadith, even the most honest and devout reporter could be influenced, unconsciously and therefore honestly, by his own opinions, or even by events he had experienced or was still experiencing a century after the hadith was spoken.[35] Schisms began to occur in Islam barely thirty years after the Prophet's death, and suddenly each clan developed its own hadiths to serve its cause. The same hadith might be handed down along different chains in different versions, giving rise to the possibility of divergent interpretations. Law was always, if not at the service of politics then at least under its influence, and the establishment of hadiths was the most convenient way of laying the basis for a new law.[36] It is unlikely that the hundreds of thousands of reported hadiths were all actually spoken. And so, the ulema researchers devoted great labour to the task of distinguishing between reliable hadiths and those that were dubious, implausible or simply concocted. This was one of the main problems facing the great ulema who founded schools of their own, and one of the main issues in dispute between them.

Ibn Khaldun identified no fewer than eight categories of hadith, ranging from the most reliable to the most doubtful.[37] Ibn Hanbal, one of the most conformist authors, kept fifty thousand hadiths on his list, while Abu Hanifa, the founder of an equally classical but more liberal school, retained no more than seventeen.[38]

For many centuries now, all the Sunni ulema have considered reliable the hadiths reported in the *Sahihan* (the two genuine treatises) due to the *Sheikhan* (the two great masters), Bukhari and Muslim. In these works of reference we find, among the hadiths endorsed by these reputedly most reliable sources, a number of statements that cannot reasonably be attributed to the Prophet. Abdelmajid Charfi has listed a number of what he calls 'problem hadiths'.[39] One example is the hadith about the setting of the sun reported by the *Sheikhan*: 'Every evening the sun goes away to prostrate itself before the throne [of God]; it asks for permission … it does not receive permission and is told to return … such is the meaning of the verse which says: "And the sun too, which continues its course to a fixed point."'

If hadiths of this kind are thought reliable, what possible credence can we give to others, especially those that are contradictory? In contemporary compilations of laws, where even reliable and precise texts can often give rise to divergent theories and practical conclusions, what are we to make of texts that are fragmentary and uncertain? Thus, although the hadiths as a whole are useful as a tool for the understanding of religion as spirituality, metaphysics and the promise of an afterlife, or as an indication of the general guidelines for individual morality and behaviour in society, they cannot serve as a source of law. Jurists need reliable and precise texts in order to construct their theories and to deduce practical rules that are capable of being applied. The Koran is the only source that escapes all these criticisms of unreliability.

The Koran

Since the early twentieth century, in the framework of the movement to renew Muslim thought, a number of researchers have tried to rid themselves of the non-religious dross passed down by history, and to this end have adopted the basic idea that 'Islam is the Koran alone', as Mohamed Taufik Sidki put it.[40]

The Koran, which, being the word of God, is the sacred text *par excellence*, is an essentially religious message. It is true that, along with strictly religious elements (origins of the universe, fate of humanity, etcetera) and moral prescriptions (charity, help for the poor and sick, etcetera), it contains a number of rules that have some of the features of laws.

But how should we make the distinction between a moral rule and a legal rule? It is extremely difficult; in principle it depends on the degree of obligation. With this in mind, the number of lawlike rules in the Koran has been variously estimated at between 200 and 500 verses out of a total of 6,236.[41] Prima facie, some of these verses are sufficiently precise and detailed to constitute rules with a legal character. They concern only two areas: criminal law and inheritance law.

With regard to criminal law, we have already examined the definitions of crimes and the corresponding punishments, and we have concluded that the punishments in question were part of a stage of social evolution that has been left behind. As to inheritance matters, many verses define the quality of inheritor and specify the share accruing to each. The great innovation in these verses is the recognition of the woman as a potential inheritor, whether as mother, daughter, wife or sister. To be sure, her share remains limited to half of a man's share, but this still represented a considerable gain. At the same time, we can say that that all these verses have no more than indicative value; this is proved by the fact that the Koran accepts the validity of a will and even recommends it as a way of assigning the inheritance. All in all, we may consider that the Koran is telling the testator which degree of kinship to take into account and advising him to give a woman a share equal to at least half that of a man.

The capacity to make a will is affirmed in verse 180 of sura 2, 'The Cow': 'It is decreed that when death approaches, those of you that leave property shall bequeath it equitably to parents and kindred. This is a duty incumbent on the righteous.'[43] Even in cases where the deceased has not left a will, the Koranic law of succession is, reasonably enough, inapplicable unless a legislator intervenes to make it more specific and to solve problems of interpretation. For example, there is no system of automatic inheritance in a direct line – which means that, if an uncle is still alive, the prior death of their father deprives grandchildren of their grandfather's legacy. The Tunisian legislature has corrected this blatant injustice through the technique of the 'compulsory will', but in certain situations this does no more than limit the injustice.

Similarly, there are cases where the percentage shares of a legacy add up to a total of more than 100, and others where the son's share paradoxically ends up being smaller than the daughter's.[44] Such hypothetical situations, which are not merely classroom inventions, disturb the coherence of the system and show just how necessary it is for certain prescriptions to be interpreted. Interpretations that refer to the spirit of the Koran are here far superior to the kind of literal interpretation favoured by the ulema, which leads to absurd results.

Thus, in the only area for which there exist Koranic verses with a juridical import, a legislator is required to clarify them and to solve the difficulties of application. These verses anyway have only an optional character, since people always have the right to dispose of their possessions by drawing up a will. This optionality should already be enough for modern legislatures to recognize the legal validity of wills that share an estate among offspring without discrimination on the basis of gender – until the day comes when equality of inheritance is made compulsory with all the force of the law.

The role of the ulema

In seeking to play a legislative role, and thus to create a system involving legal compulsion, the ulema took literally the Koranic verses that prescribe a certain apportionment of a legacy and maintained that the verse concerning the freedom to bequeath property in favour of close relatives was overridden by the verse according to which the male inheritor should receive twice the share of the female inheritor. God, it would seem, granted the legator the freedom to write a will and then rescinded that very freedom – which is a patent absurdity. Examples of a verse that cancels another verse are certainly not unknown in the Koran. In each case, however, there is a convincing explanation for this phenomenon, usually bound up with particular historical circumstances. For example, certain obligations and prohibitions were introduced by stages, such as the one urging people to abstain from the consumption of alcohol, which began with a simple ban on praying in a state of inebriation. But we find no explanation of the kind in relation to the two verses on inheritance, and we should conclude that one rescinds the other only if the two are indeed absolutely incompatible. Such is not the case, however. In every system of laws, anywhere in the world, inheritance by means of a will is recognized alongside inheritance *ab intestat*. So, why should it not be accepted that the two forms coexist in the Koran? Arguments to the contrary simply do not hold water. The ulema sensed the problem and took refuge in a hadith which states: 'God has given to each heir his proper share. Therefore, no will in favour of the heir.' Is this not rather odd? The Prophet's word is supposed to rescind a Koranic verse, a secondary source to override the primary source – as if a particular law were to override the Constitution.

In any event, this is the shaky legal basis on which the ulema established the rule disallowing a will that names close relatives as heirs. All the Muslim countries still drag along this rule in their legal systems. Thus, a Muslim father who believes in the principle of gender equality would today be unable, by writing a will, to bequeath equal shares of his property to a son and a daughter. The ban on wills in favour of appointed heirs is a major obstacle to equality between men and women.

When the ulema laid down this prohibition, they were probably guided by the best of intentions towards women. We should not forget that, in allowing even a half-share to female heirs, the Muslim law of fourteen centuries ago was considerably ahead of most other civilizations, which, at that time, gave no scope at all for women to inherit property. The men of Arabia certainly did not accept with good grace the new progressive law. Indeed, if the ulema had instead accepted the validity of wills in favour of named heirs, most men would have taken the opportunity to bequeath all or nearly all their property to their male offspring. The law disallowing wills therefore operated to the benefit of daughters; it provided them with a legal guarantee.

But the ulema could not for long resist male pressure and had to find a safety valve that would placate the most anti-feminist heads of families. The device of the *waqf*, developed by theologians to make property inalienable, was theoretically supposed to guarantee that the legator's estate would not be squandered by his heirs. However, once the *waqf* system made it possible freely to appoint the beneficiaries of a bequest, it no longer served its ostensible purpose and was mainly used to exclude women from inheritance.[45]

This example, chosen among many others of the same kind, amply demonstrates that the general guidelines and principles in the Koran require rules of application if they are to be effective. The passage from the abstract to the concrete can just as well be the means of deepening a principle as of betraying it. In laying down rules of application, the ulema took considerable account of the economic, social, cultural and political circumstances of their age. The legal system they elaborated is a human creation, one that was useful in its time and sometimes worthy of admiration but which has been overtaken in today's much-changed circumstances.

If we can draw this conclusion in relation to the law of inheritance, concerning which the Koran contains the largest number of detailed verses with a legal import, the demonstration is even simpler and the conclusion even clearer for other areas of the law.

As far as contracts and obligations are concerned, a number of passages in the Koran enjoin that once someone has given their word they should respect it. For example, sura 17, verse 36 states: 'Keep your promises; you are accountable for all that you promise.' This idea is the common denominator of all the legal systems in the world, both past and present. In Roman law the principle was *pacta sunt servanda*; in canonical law, it was known as respect of the given word. In French law, Article 1134 of the Civil Code stipulates that 'agreements … serve as law for those who make them', and Article 242 of the Tunisian code on obligations and contracts states: 'Validly created contractual obligations serve as law for those who have made them.'

Nevertheless, in the hundreds of articles drawing consequences from this general principle, each of these systems has peculiar characteristics that make the body of law distinctive of its time and country. Following the example of all other jurists, the ulema built a system of laws relating to contracts and obligations, which might have been called Arab law, Omayyad law or Abbasid law. For historical reasons that will be considered below, it was called Muslim law or sharia law.

The same considerations apply to the whole area of personal status: that is, family relations, the settlement of marital issues, divorce, lines of descent, and so on. For example, in speaking of divorce, the Koran says in sura 2, verse 231, 'When you have renounced your wives and they have reached the end of their waiting period, either retain them in honour or let them go with kindness.'

For the ulema, who interpreted it literally, the verse is addressed to men and at this level has a juridical character. It gives men, and only men, the right to take the initiative in severing the conjugal bond. The power lies with the husband; there is no question of intervention by a third party, especially a judge. We are therefore talking not of divorce but of repudiation, which does not need to be properly motivated or to comply with certain forms. Under Muslim law, all a husband has to do to break the tie is to utter the simple oath 'I repudiate you', perhaps even in the heat of a household dispute. It is true that the verse refers to honesty and generosity. But that is a question of morality, and it involves no more than recommendations. Generosity is, by definition, voluntary. The judge has no business interfering. Such is the sharia system as it was established by theologians and as it is still applied in most Muslim countries, whether traditional (like Saudi Arabia) or fundamentalist (like

Iran) or modernizing (as in the case of the Egyptian state, which has not dared to legislate on family matters).

For the Tunisian legislature, by contrast, the fact that the Koranic verse is addressed to men proves that it was dependent on the circumstances of the time. The forms of expression used in the male-dominated Arabia of fourteen centuries ago cannot be used as the basis for a contemporary law that is supposed to have the immutable force of a religious edict. God addressed the men who dominated society at that time, to issue recommendations on divorce that may be summed up in the requirements of honesty and generosity. That is the heart of the verse; it is not merely advice on which the husband is left free to do as he wishes. Means have to be developed which will ensure that the recommendations are actually respected.

To guarantee 'honest' and 'generous' treatment, the modern Tunisian legislature considers that the matter cannot be left to the husband's discretion, good will or arbitrary decision, and that it is therefore necessary for the courts to intervene. According to the Code of Personal Status, divorce must always be a judicial affair, to be decided by mutual agreement that is verified by a judge. If it results from a marital offence on the part of one or other spouse, he or she will be liable to pay damages to the injured party. If the divorce follows a request from one of the spouses without any accusation of misconduct, it is the applicant who has to pay damages to the other party. This upholds the Koranic principle that divorce is a right which may be requested and obtained even on a whim. The innovations introduced in Tunisia therefore come down to three points: both spouses may take the initiative for divorce and are responsible for the consequences, being treated on a basis of complete equality; compensation shall be paid to the non-guilty party; and the courts ensure that the divorce takes place in accordance with the law.

As we have seen, the ulema made certain verses inoperative (on the grounds that they were mere recommendations) and gave other verses the force of law. For the Tunisian legislature, on the other hand, a Koranic verse is not an article in a legal code; it is not part of a body of law. It is God addressing men in a language they understand, and expressing a general recommendation to them. It is then up to the legislature in each country to adopt the laws that best correspond to that recommendation in a given epoch. In the world in which we are living today, it is the task of the state to make itself the expression of universal suffrage. The legislature should therefore not be tied in any way by sharia law, a purely human creation that has been largely overtaken by history.

Let us take as another example the particularly sensitive issue of illegitimate children. Under Muslim law, a man's sexual relations are legitimate if they are with one of four wives or with a concubine; any act performed outside that framework is *zina*, a crime subject to harsh punishment. The child of *zina* is therefore the fruit of sin; he has neither legal ties to his father, nor any right to maintenance in his father's lifetime or to a share of the inheritance after his death. It is a harsh solution for the child, and an unjust one for the mother who has to suffer alone the consequences of an act committed by two people. In the eyes of the theologians, however, this injustice is inevitable.

The solution is not specifically laid down either in a Koranic verse or in a hadith. It derives from a process of legal reasoning on the part of the ulema, which starts from the ban on *zina* and leads to the conclusion that the illegitimate child has no rights. Let us look more closely at this reasoning.

– Is any extra-marital sexual relation an instance of *zina*? Yes, the theologians answer, and they include in the same category not only prostitution and adultery, but also free unions and concubinage, as well as cases where an engaged couple do not have the patience to await the marriage date fixed by their parents. Clearly, what we are considering here is a gradation from the most immoral to the most innocuous actions.

– Even if we accept that all these cases should be grouped under the same category of immorality, is it right that the child should bear the consequences of his parents' sin? The Koran states in sura 6, verse 164, 'Each man shall reap the fruits of his own deeds: no soul shall bear another's burden.' Is it right that the child should carry the burden of his parents' sin? Or that the mother alone should carry the burden of a sin that she did not commit alone but with another person?

– If an an illegitimate child cannot be recognized because of his immoral origins, if he must therefore be excluded from his father's family and denied any share in the inheritance, is it not at least possible to recognize his right to damages or maintenance, that is, the possibility of compelling the father to contribute to his upkeep until he reaches maturity? In the 1950s, in France, Germany and other European countries, the legislature established a right to paternal maintenance for the child of an adulterous liaison, without officially accepting that he or she was part of the father's lineage. Since then the legal reforms have gone further still. But even the right to maintenance goes some way to reducing the injustice of which the child born out of wedlock is a victim.

We have seen that, in starting from the religious injunction against *zina* and continuing with a series of dubious syllogisms, the theologians acted as if illegitimate children were conceived by their mother alone. But, for a healthy mind free of fanaticism, all children deserve care and attention, and their rights deserve to be protected. Even if one insists that their rights should depend on the character of the relations between their parents, it seems obvious enough that the relations between an engaged couple before marriage are incomparably more honourable and deserving of sympathy than those a rich man has with a female slave bought an hour earlier at the market and abused by her 'owner' because she has no choice. The likelihood that the child is the fruit of a loving act is much greater in the case of a cohabiting or engaged couple, even if they subsequently break off the engagement, than in the case of a harem owner and his slave. Yet sharia law condemns the former circumstance and accepts the latter. Such law is not and cannot be the work of God. It is a purely human creation.

A human creation

Muslim law is based on three fundamental inequalities: the superiority of men over women, of Muslims over non-Muslims, and of free persons over slaves. It recognizes the maximum advantages in the case of a free and rich Muslim male, and the fewest rights in the case of a non-Muslim female slave. The main thing she has going for her is the recommendation that her master should treat her well – a moral recommendation of no great practical consequence. Muslim law is therefore fundamentally discriminatory. It might be said that this is a harsh judgement. Indeed it is – an unfair judgement even. But what makes it necessary, unfortunately, is the existence of a fundamentalist movement that demands a return to the sharia and therefore compels us to measure the past by the standards of the present. An objective evaluation would require us to place Muslim law in its historical context and to compare it with the legal systems of other old civilizations. It then takes on a rather different aspect.

In Greco-Roman antiquity, the foreigner was a *hostis* – a root word that gave us *hostile* and *hostility* long before *host*, *hotel* and *hospitality*. Fustel de Coulanges showed centuries ago that the ancient city was based on religion,[46] and that since foreigners did not take part in the same cult they could not benefit from the same laws. There was thus a confusion between affiliation to a particular religion and membership in a particular community. In ancient Greece, a foreigner lacking the protection of the city's laws could neither marry nor acquire property nor even ask the courts to compensate him for damages incurred.

The fathers of philosophy, Plato and Aristotle, approved of the law of Lycurgus that barred foreigners from settling in Sparta.[47] The situation of foreigners markedly improved only after a long evolution of Greek civilization. From the Code of Hammurabi and throughout antiquity down to the era of Roman law, war prisoners were systematically reduced to slavery.[48] Mosaic law established polygamy and excluded women from inheritance. And in medieval Europe, the system of inheritance was based on primogeniture and male privilege.

Compared with earlier or contemporaneous bodies of law, Muslim law represented a general advance in human history with regard to the rights of non-Muslims, slaves and women, a considerable step towards liberty and equality and hence towards the foundations of human rights as we conceive of them today. The sharia is a set of laws which appear unjust by the standards of today. But the ulema who drew them up were chained to the circumstances of their time. I have criticized them above, as I have also criticized Muslim law. But in essence they were mostly people of good will. They realized that some of the laws they put forward were too harsh and tried to tone them down, but without shaking the foundations of Muslim law. If they had not done so, the whole edifice would have been in danger of collapse. Their method was to make a law less harsh, not by changing it (which its religious basis precluded), but by adding more and more exceptions where it did not apply. Here are just a few examples of this extremely common technique.

– Death by stoning for adulterers, and even the hundred lashes for others guilty of sexual relations outside marriage, are overly harsh, inhumane, barbarous forms of punishment. The ulema certainly felt this and therefore prescribed rules of proof that were extremely difficult, almost impossible, to fulfil: for example, not only were four eye-witnesses required, but each one had to have seen 'the pen in the inkwell', to use the colourful euphemism. In other words, the system was designed in such a way that the crime was always defined as a crime but the penalty was never applied.

– The hand of a thief should be cut off. But there are endless possibilities if the judge wishes to substitute a milder penalty. Hence the development of the *shubha* concept – a term signifying doubt about whether an action should be described as a crime of this sort, or more generally about whether the action occurred at all. For example, since theft involves the wrongful taking of something that belongs to another, it is necessary to be certain that the thing does not in fact belong to the person who took it. If the object in question is directly or indirectly owned by the state, it is the property of the whole community and therefore of everyone, including the person accused of theft. Of course, it belongs to him only in a minute proportion, but that is sufficient to constitute a case of *shubha*.

– A child conceived outside wedlock has no father. But there are endless means of finding one for him. Thus, when a woman gives birth two, three or even four years after her divorce or the death of her husband, it will be said that the child was conceived before the divorce or the death but then fell asleep in its mother's belly and awoke to start growing again only a few months before the birth. In the nineteenth century, when Europeans first came to learn of Muslim law, they often poked fun at it because of this theory and held it up as proof that the ulema did not have even the rudiments of scientific knowledge. The truth is quite different. Arab science and medicine were among the most advanced in the world during the Middle Ages. The ulema were not deceiving themselves, but invented the theory of the sleeping embryo as a way of guarding the child's interests that did not imply recognition of sexual relations outside marriage. The underlying idea remained the same: 'Hide from me that breast which I'm afraid I can't see.'

The ulema tried to adapt the law to the realities of their society, if necessary by ignoring clear Koranic injunctions or by deciding the opposite of what a particular verse decreed. Sura 2, verse 282, for example, states: 'Believers, when you contract a debt for a fixed period, put it in writing. Let a scribe write it down for you with fairness.'[49] This stress on the need for written proof of fixed civil obligations is an important feature of the modern world: for example, in bodies of law such as the Tunisian Code of Obligations and Contracts (Article 473) or the French Civil Code (Article 1341). However, the rule would have been too far ahead of its time for the largely illiterate Muslim society of the Middle Ages. The ulema could have decided that the obligation to put an agreement in writing held only between parties to a contract who knew how to read and write, or only when it was possible to use the services of a scribe. But in fact they preferred to go further. Despite the use of the imperative in the Koranic verse ('Put it in writing. Let a scribe write it down'), the ulema said that the rule was not an imperative but a simple recommendation.

Similarly, the ulema tried to satisfy economic requirements by using various *hyals* (legal ruses or tricks) to circumvent the ban on interest-bearing loans. The peasantry often need seasonal loans, and the owner of a grain field needs money for harvest expenditure before he can dispose of his produce. The owner of an olive grove has to advance the fairly high costs of gathering and transporting the crop, as well as the costs of pressing it at the mill, before he can sell the oil that is the end product. Farmers often find that by the eve of the harvest they have spent all their savings from the previous year. To borrow a sum of money then becomes a necessity. But, under Muslim law, the lending of money at interest is regarded as usury and forbidden. It is not always feasible to borrow the required sum without interest from a brother or friend, and anyway no economic system can function only on the basis of the kindness of others. Everyone has to get something out of it. And so, the ulema thought up the *salam* contract, or 'selling for delivery with the price paid in advance'. The farmer sells his crop. He has to deliver it only after the harvest, but is immediately paid the price that gives him the liquidity he so badly needs. In fact, this involves a form of disguised interest, dressed up as a sales contract. Little tricks of this kind are common in Muslim law.

Islamic banks, which have multiplied in the age of petrodollars, operate on the same basis with contracts known as *taajir, musharaka, mudharaba* or *murahaba*;[50] these are in fact disguised interest-bearing loans, with the peculiarity that the interest is not clearly established in advance. The so-called association between the Islamic bank and its customers allows all manner of unpleasant surprises for the latter.

Sometimes the conduct of these bankers is sheer daylight robbery, as the scandal of Egypt's Islamic banks in the 1980s amply demonstrates.

In modern economic systems, bank loans are subject to monitoring by the central bank, which ensures that interest rates are reasonable and that usury is avoided. The creation of the Bank of Tunisia in 1984 immediately made it possible to establish a code of ethics for financial operations and to lower interest rates from the levels previously charged by usurers. Interest on secured loans fell from 25 per cent to 10 per cent, the discount rate on commercial paper from 12 per cent to 7 per cent, and mortgage interest rates from 20 per cent to 8 per cent.[51] A banking system that is straight and to the point in its provision of interest-bearing loans can be effectively monitored by the state and at the same time constitute a means of economic growth.

Certain legal regulations that are considered secondary nevertheless play a primary role in the development of nations. In Europe, it was the law of primogeniture and male privilege in regard to inheritance that made possible the emergence of feudalism, whereas the system of inheritance in the Muslim world, though morally and socially superior, led each generation to divide up legacies and therefore failed to promote the accumulation of wealth necessary for development. Similarly, the constitution of the banking system in Europe promoted the formation of capital and the emergence of a bourgeoisie that ushered the region into the industrial age. Such an evolution was not possible in the Muslim world because of the ban on interest-bearing loans.

The origins of this ban lie in the Koran's condemnation of *riba* and the way in which theologians interpreted this concept. We distinguish today between legally permissible loans at a reasonable rate of interest, regulated and controlled by the central bank, and illegal forms of usury in which the rates are excessive, immoral and harmful to the economy. The theologians did not have in mind this distinction – it did not even exist at the time – and therefore interpreted *riba* not only as usury but as any lending at interest, however minimal. Yet the definition of this concept suggested in the Koran makes us think more of usury than of mere lending at a reasonable rate of interest. Verse 129 of sura 3, 'The Imrans', says: 'Believers, do not live on usury, doubling your wealth many times over.'[52] This is a clear allusion to the practice in Arabia before Islam, when a borrower had to repay twice the sum or quantity borrowed – at a rate, that is, of 100 per cent – and when, if he failed to repay on time and was given an extension, he had to find twice the doubled sum or become the slave of his creditor.[53] This is what the Koran forbids.

By interpreting the concept of *riba* too broadly, so that the prohibition covers any interest-bearing loan, the ulema created a social and economic problem. Subsequently, in order to solve this problem, they came up with little ruses such as *salam* selling, a contract that used to be widely practised in the Tunisian countryside. In the early twentieth century, the legislature then respectfully followed tradition and incorporated the Islamic rule into Articles 712 to 717 of the code on obligations and contracts. But the cure turned out to be much more damaging than the original malady. The neediest peasants, fearing that their crop would begin to rot, had to sell it under a *salam* contract at any price, often for no more than half its true worth.

Thus, two systems existed alongside each other in Tunisia. A contract regarded as religiously legitimate, the *salam*, virtually forced the peasants to sell their crop for 50 per cent of its value, while bank loans, regarded as religiously illegitimate, covered them for the one or two months of the harvest at an annual rate of interest of 12 per cent, so that they eventually had to repay the principal plus 1 or 2 per cent.

Immediately after independence the Tunisian legislature, reputedly not respectful towards religion, did not hesitate, on 28 January 1958, to include among its many reforms the repeal of the whole section of the code on obligations and contracts relating to 'selling for delivery with the price paid in advance' (*salam*). With all due respect to our ulema and their contemporary heirs the fundamentalists, this was a salutary measure. For, throughout the late-nineteenth century and the first half of the twentieth, when the two systems existed side by side, no Zituna scholar ever dreamed of issuing a fatwa or teaching his students that it was necessary to make the *salam* legal and bank loans illegal.

Yet some of the ulema were great scholars, and others were as honest and devout as saints. They must have felt – clearly or obscurely, according to their degree of knowledge and intelligence – that the *salam* was much less favourable than bank loans for people in need, that the theft of an object belonging to a public school or hospital was in no way less reprehensible than theft from a private bank or business, and that an embryo never goes to sleep for four years inside its mother. They must surely have understood that the lawlike force of certain rules in the

Koran depended on the circumstances in Arabia fourteen centuries ago, and that this was true *a fortiori* of the theories and interpretations put forward by the Prophet's successors and the founders of schools. The fact that they developed various dodges or escape clauses (*hyal*) obviously proves that the rules in question were no longer applicable.

They therefore became aware that certain rules were inappropriate in the changed circumstances of their time – which is to say that they were no longer compulsory. If a rule is inappropriate and non-compulsory, this implies for any rational mind that it should be revoked. But the ulema never dared to take that step, thereby storing up a major problem for the future. Islam and Muslims today lug around various rules that they – or, anyway, the best minds among the ulema – know to be inappropriate and religiously non-compulsory, yet no one dares to say that they have been or should be revoked. And, since the rules have not been revoked, they are still taught in schools and universities or at the weekly sermon on Fridays; they still fuel religious discourse. This clash between appearance and reality, between what people say and what they think, fuels the schizoid way of thinking that is such a distinctive fetter on the Muslim world.

Among those listening to this discourse, there will always be some simple minds who take it literally and wish to see it applied – hence the disturbances and the popular demands for a return to an anachronistic body of law. How are we to explain this intellectual timidity or conservatism of our ulema? A number of factors seem to be in play.

During the first thirteen centuries of the Hegira, up to the emergence of modern states, Muslim countries were unlike all others in the world in that the state never exercised legislative power. Whether in the great Omayyad and Abbasid empires or in the dismembered states of both East and West (Aghlabite, Almohad, Hafsite, etcetera), the state never gave itself the capacity to enact legislation. The sovereign always enjoyed, usually in the most personal and authoritarian manner, extensive prerogatives in military, diplomatic or financial matters and in the whole field of 'justice and repression', but he never had the power to make laws. For historical reasons that will be examined below, it was the ulema who had that monopoly. They stood out because of their religious knowledge and the lessons they gave in the mosque. Of course, it was the sovereign who appointed the judges, but he was under a moral obligation to make his selection from men publicly known for their erudition. These legislators, who were not official representatives of the sovereign and were not elected by either the whole people or a particular corporation, therefore had no political or popular legitimacy. Their only legitimacy came from the fact that they were supposed to speak the religious truth. For this reason, the ulema always pegged rules of their invention to a religious precept; their power was legitimate because they were merely interpreting the divine will. This gave them great authority, but it also limited their room for manoeuvre. Once they presented their rules as divine rules, they could not amend or correct or, still less, revoke them. The great advantage of the *hyals* was that they got round the law without revoking it or even making any alterations. For the sharia cannot move: it is here for all time.

A lay legislator, whether a dictator or a democratically elected assembly, may say one day that interest-bearing loans are prohibited and then, through a new law, change its mind and permit such loans on conditions that it is free to define. Such a change of mind does not in any way damage the lay legislator's credibility, as it never claimed to be infallible. But a theologian who claims that God has prohibited any interest-bearing loan cannot suddenly turn round and say the opposite. Nor can he accept that his venerable predecessors made a mistake, because his own authority and scholarly pretensions rest upon his reputation as an heir carrying on where they left off. Nor, above all, can he say that changed circumstances call for a change in the rules, since that would mean that the sharia itself can change, that it is not fixed, and therefore that it is not the work of God; the whole edifice would crumble. Thus, when circumstances made it necessary, the ulema came up with the idea of the *salam* contract. The poor debtor now had to repay the actual amount of the loan plus an increment of 50 per cent, instead of a mere 2 per cent. This was unfortunate, but still a lesser evil. For it kept what was really essential: the formal prohibition on lending at interest. The rule did not change.[54]

This basic feature of sharia law was compounded by the historical decline and ossification of the Islamic society and state. We know that the major schools of theological, philosophical and legal thought came into being and reached their peak during the first three centuries of the Hegira. The great period of intellectual creation corresponded – evidently not by chance – to the apogee of Muslim civilization and imperial power.[55] Immediately afterwards began the 'dark centuries'.

The onset of decay at the intellectual level was marked by two major events: the crushing of the Mutazilites and the end of the *ijtihad*.

The crushing of the Mutazilites

The term 'Mutazilites' is used for the ulema whose school of thought became important in the mid-eighth century (CE) and who ascribed a key role to reason in their research – as opposed to the Muhaddithin who constantly invoked the hadiths in their creation of new laws. For the latter, 'good is what God commands and evil is what God forbids'. For a Mutazilite, by contrast, it is not enough to demonstrate that a hadith is authentic; it is also necessary to study its content to check whether it is acceptable to reason. Good and evil are thus grounded upon reason; the legal sphere itself is rational. This led the Mutazilites to explain the Koran itself by constantly referring to reason. 'The Mutazilites made reason the very criterion of religious law.'[56] In this way, they were able to develop extremely bold legal constructs. For example, faced with the abuses that already marked the practice of marital repudiation, at least some of them ventured to argue that it should be allowed to go ahead only with a judge's agreement.[57] The method of the Mutazilites was thus, to some extent, the method of the philosophers, of which Averroës could write: 'We categorically state that, whenever there is a contradiction between the result of a proof (or of rational speculation) and the apparent meaning of a revealed text, the latter must be subject to interpretation.'[58] And he added that interpretation meant searching for the figurative sense beyond the literal sense, in the light of rational knowledge.

The method of reflection and theoretical construction, as adopted by the philosophers and Mutazilites and grounded upon reason, has similarities with a secular approach. It was already a sign of decay that the Mutazilites were hunted down as infidels as early as 846 (CE), during the caliphate of Al-Mutawakkil, and that their writings were so thoroughly destroyed that one used to have to guess at their ideas from works directed against them by their enemies. It is only in the last century or less, since the rediscovery of ancient manuscripts, that we have had direct access to their writings. With the crushing of the Mutazilites, the spirit of imitation carried the day over the spirit of reflection.

The end of ijtihad

The second event that marked the onset of the intellectual decay of Muslim civilization was the fall of Baghdad during the Tatar invasion of 1258, which caused the death of numerous ulema and the loss of many of their manuscripts. With this general weakening of Muslim society, the ulema lost all hope in the future. Thinking that it would be impossible to improve on their predecessors, fearing that Islam would lose itself in interpretations ever more remote from its essence, they decided by a kind of consensus that – to use a hallowed expression – it was necessary to 'close the door of *ijtihad*' (reflective effort). From then on, new researchers did no more than take up the work of the ancients and add a clarification here or a timid comment there;[59] by and large they limited themselves to almost slavish exposition of the ideas of their predecessors.[60] Even among the ancient authors, it was only the most classical who would be accepted as authorities. The situation continued to grow worse, since after a time one of the commentators on an ancient work would acquire such authority that no one in later generations would dare to contradict him or do more than add a few points to justify or clarify what he had said. It was rather like the phenomenon of the glossators and post-glossators after the golden age of Roman law – a resemblance not only in essence but also in form, insofar as certain works of both Muslim and Roman law mixed together an original text by a great author (*matn*) and the texts of a glossator (*sharah*) or post-glossator (*hashia*). Nor is this striking affinity a matter of chance. It proves that, in similar circumstances, even quite diverse societies often react in the same manner. Perhaps this involves a kind of cycle that all the ancient civilizations went through. After the golden age came the twilight of old age, when the imagination shrank, the creative faculties diminished, and thought grew stiff and rigid.

From that time down to the present day the same attitude has prevailed among the ulema – that is, among the magistrates of the sharia courts, the muftis and the professors at theological universities (such as Al Azhar in Egypt or the Zituna in Tunisia), who might be called the representatives of official Islam. A few rare exceptions may be singled out. For example, the Egyptian Mohamed Abdu took some courageous and innovative positions, but although a number of modernist authors embraced his ideas he remained an isolated figure among theologians. The overwhelming majority have done no more than repeat the theses of the ancients.

In the early nineteenth century, when the Egyptian government, as one of its many efforts to promote social development and an opening to the modern world, sought to introduce the teaching of mathematics and the exact sciences, it felt obliged to consult the sheikh of Al Azhar to 'cover itself' before embarking upon the path of innovation. The sheikh thought he was displaying a highly modern spirit by lending his approval to the project, but he added that it would be necessary to show what purpose it served.[61] That is the kind of innovation of which official Islam is capable.

The sharia is for the Muslim world what Roman law was for continental Europe. Created by great minds, they have each been admirable legal monuments and have each rendered the best services in their time. Today they have been overtaken by circumstances. Europeans have been able to discard, without too much trauma, a large number of the Roman conceptions that are no longer suited to our times. This is more difficult in our case because of the religious coloration given to Muslim law. For a century or more this has been the fundamental problem for Muslim societies, and many thinkers have tried various ways of solving it. The first to be proposed was what is sometimes called in Arabic *talfik*, which might be translated as 'the makeshift approach'.

Talfik

For each rule in Muslim law that is considered inhumane or contrary to human rights and modern principles of liberty and equality, the *talfik* approach tries to go back in time and find the original defect. If the rule is attached to a particular hadith, an investigation is conducted to determine whether the hadith is dubious or authentic. If it is attached to a Koranic verse, attempts are made to reinterpret that verse. Such research is not dishonest, since the point is neither to make the verse mean the opposite of what it says, nor to sow doubt concerning a hadith that is very likely to be genuine. But nor is it entirely objective research without preconceptions. For the researcher has already set a goal and is trying to find historical or semantic arguments that will enable it to be achieved. He is not seeking to understand religion for its own sake, but rather to find in it the justification for a new rule that he considers to be more just and worthy of application. Though not spurious or subjective, the research may be described as guided research. For this reason it may appear artificial or slightly suspect, and will not always have a lot of credibility.

The arguments used for the abolition of polygamy are a good example of both the legitimacy and the limits of this method.

Polygamy is a kind of fetter on the spread of progressive ideas in Muslim societies. Being contrary to the principle of sexual equality, it has been abandoned by modern civilizations and remains a peculiarity of the Muslim world,[62] doing us no honour and giving others a revolting image of Islam. Naturally enough, therefore, attacks were made on this practice right at the beginning of the Muslim renaissance, just after the successful abolition of slavery. Mohamed Abdu, one of the first Egyptian reformers, followed by the great Tunisian reformer Tahar Haddad, set out to reinterpret the Koranic verses dealing with polygamy. The first prescription is set out in verse 3 of sura 4, 'Women': 'You may marry other women who seem good to you: two, three or four of them. But if you fear that you cannot maintain equality among them, marry one only.'[63] Taken literally, the verse contains a permission, an obligation and a piece of advice: permission to marry up to four women; the condition or at least obligation, implicit yet clear and indisputable, that wives should be treated with equality (the Arabic *adl* means justice and therefore, by extension, also equality); and advice to be content with only one wife, for all who are not sure they can be fair and equitable or who are incapable of ensuring equal treatment. In the same sura, another verse (4:129) says on the same subject: 'Try as you may, you cannot treat all your wives impartially.'

If we compare the two verses of the Koran, we can conclude that it is acceptable for men to marry up to four women, so long as all are treated equally, but that men are incapable of satisfying this condition. In other words, the tolerance of polygamy is only apparent; the bottom line is a prohibition. The reasoning is consistent and the deduction logical. In order to avoid a head-on clash with age-old habits, the Koran gives the impression of not forbidding polygamy but actually hedges it around with a condition that makes it virtually impossible. Sooner or later, a Muslim is expected to understand the secret of divine thought and to grasp the incompatibility between conditional tolerance and an impossible condition that amounts to cancellation of the tolerance.

To justify the abolition of polygamy in Tunisia, under the Code of Personal Status decreed on 13 August 1956, Bourguiba took up and popularized these ideas that had already been developed timidly by Abdu and rather more vigorously by Haddad. Bourguiba was able to do this because, at the time, there were no fundamentalists and the ulema had been weakened by their past subservience to the colonial rulers. The decision to end polygamy certainly required great political courage as well as extraordinary lucidity. What made this possible was the homogeneity of the new ruling group, its deeply modernist convictions and, above all, Bourguiba's popularity following the successful struggle for independence that he had led. A victorious leader has huge scope to introduce bold reforms; the talent of a politician is to seize the right historical moment to make the difficult choices.

What interests us here is the choice of method. Whereas, in Turkey, Kemal Atatürk abolished polygamy in the name of a secular politics directed against Islam or existing alongside it, the same course was pursued in Tunisia in the name of a renewal and reinterpretation of Islam. The difference between the two approaches is to be explained by the different historical circumstances. Following on from the reformers of the second half of the nineteenth century and the Young Turks of the early twentieth century, who had struggled for freedom against the religious regime of the caliphate, Atatürk led a war of liberation against foreign occupiers and against the power of the caliphate that had compromised with them. His victory thus ended in abolition of the caliphate and its logical sequel: the establishment of a secular regime. In Tunisia, however, as in all other Arab countries, the national liberation movement was directed only against the colonial power, and its leaders did not hesitate to mobilize activists by drawing on the religious sentiments of the population. Independence was a national victory against the foreigner, not a revolution for liberty against a religious power. The ensuing reforms were therefore presented not as a turning away from religious laws but as the result of a reinterpretation of religion.

The guiding principle was that one should not impose on society a body of law contrary to its religious beliefs, but that the law could be reformed if sufficient impulses were found in the religion for it to be understood in a different way. There was some resistance; yet on the whole Tunisians accepted the new legal code, because it was not contrary to Islam but the fruit of a better understanding of Islam. The encounter between intellectuals and politicians, if both are reform-minded, can produce real miracles.

No other Muslim country took the same path. It is true that the failure of thinkers and men of action to join forces was one of the main reasons, but it was not the only one. The method based on reinterpretation has its own limits. The Tunisian interpretation was logical, consistent and certainly viable, but it was not the only one possible. The science of interpreting legal texts is such that it only seldom yields an entirely certain result. And, in the absence of case law, one can rarely be sure of the meaning of a rule contained in a particular text. Often the text is open to two or more equally tenable interpretations, and often the choice between them is political or ideological – or dictated by the circumstances of the time.

To return to our two verses, one might very well notice the contradiction yet solve it in a different way. It might be argued that the Koran cannot give with one hand what it takes away with the other, that such a procedure ill becomes a sacred text. It could then be concluded that the tolerance of polygamy has a legal, therefore obligatory, force, whereas the need to treat wives with equality is no more than a recommendation. This was the position taken by the ulema, and it is still that of the fundamentalist or traditionalist regimes. It might also be suggested that the tolerance of polygamy should be reduced but not entirely ended – for example, that tetragamy should be scaled down to mere bigamy, perhaps with the further proviso that the first wife must be ill or that the husband must be financially capable of satisfying the needs of two wives. Or it might be stipulated that the judge should give formal permission in advance, having convinced himself that the conditions prescribed by the law have been met. Some timidly reformist Muslim states have opted for one or another of these solutions.

The textual ambiguity is such that none of these interpretations is obviously wrong. Each legislature adopts the solution that its particular circumstances dictate or permit. Reinterpretation of the sources, if based only on semantics or grammatical analysis, may appear an artificial method or seem to be a matter of politics or even demagogy. Thus, one author complained: '*Ijtihad* – an Islamic concept – is perhaps a method currently used to move social practice and law away from its Islamic source.'[64] But another author, who calls for modern values to be welcomed in Tunisia, emphasizes the freedom of the legislature and prefers to avoid 'absurd mental gymnastics'.[65]

The *talfik* or 'makeshift' approach was first used by the precursors of the Islamic renaissance, Jameleddine al-Afghani and Mohamed Abdu, although neither arrived at clear practical conclusions.[66] Their chief merit was to make people aware of the need for reforms that would reconcile Islam with modernity.

The *talfik* method has not yielded convincing results when attempts have been made to break free from particular constraints and to group together the best rules from a number of different rites. It was with reference to this mixing of rites that the term 'makeshift' was first used by those who characterized the whole approach as opportunist.

Some analyses that stretch the texts too far are criticized on the basis of other texts. The line of reasoning that takes the verses on polygamy and draws conclusions in favour of monogamy is able to proceed only by disregarding the end of verse 129, sura 4, which, after noting that it is impossible for men to treat several wives with perfect equality, states: 'Do not set yourself altogether against any of them, leaving her, as it were, in suspense.' The way out of the impasse is therefore indicated by the Koran itself. It does not enjoin monogamy but issues a recommendation, or perhaps an order, that men should be more impartial.

Mohamed Iqbal, a Pakistani thinker and politician, has tried to construct a theory of sexual equality on the basis of sura 2, verse 228: 'Women shall with justice have rights similar to those exercised against them.' But others have accused him of ignoring the end of the same verse: 'Men have a status above women.'[67]

In fact, a method that partly consists of playing on words is today frequently used by traditionalists or fundamentalists who wish at all costs, and in the most artificial ways, to find everything in the Koran. If it is claimed that astrophysicists invented the theory of the big bang, they will retort that the Koran already foresaw it – in a passage where it speaks of thunder! This kind of argument makes it possible to speak of Islamic astronomy, Islamic medicine, Islamic science or Islamic philosophy; Abu Zeid, for instance, complains that we merely wait for new Western discoveries in order to claim that they were anticipated by the Koran. In the view of Abdelmajid Charfi, such behaviour is designed to compensate Muslims for their lack of involvement in the contemporary production of science; hermeneutic interpretation is offered as a more convincing path that makes it possible to escape the criticisms and drawbacks associated with that failure.

Hermeneutics

This is the most appropriate method from a religious point of view, the idea being that we should not linger over the analysis of words but seek out the spirit of the Koran and try to place each question within a divine global purpose. Such research assumes that the time factor is built into the picture. A rule may have been useful at a given moment, but as the circumstances have changed over time it has become inappropriate and should itself be open to change. Even the Koran adopted a kind of stageist policy, as we can see from the abrogation of certain verses by other verses. Over the twenty-two years of the revelation, a number of rules were prescribed and then replaced with more appropriate ones. Circumstances changed in that space of time, making it necessary to change certain rules. If that happened over such a short period, all the more should it take place over a longer period of time: the fourteen centuries separating us from the death of the Prophet. The wheel of history did not cease turning with the end of the revelation. This does not mean that the whole of sharia law should be repealed, or that we are left without any points of reference in deciding on new laws. Rather, we should be guided by the goals of religion as they may be ascertained from the Koran and the life of the Prophet. The simple point is that the evolution that began a long time ago should be continued.

Apart from the immutable principles governing man's relations with God, the Koranic message contains precepts concerning people's relations with one another that were evidently too revolutionary in the tribal and, in some respects, primitive society of the Arabian peninsula in the seventh century. It was a society incapable of understanding those precepts, still less of accepting them. Unless a degree of flexibility had been shown, the Arab society of the Hejaz would have rejected Islam, and the Prophet would have failed in his mission. Today, fourteen centuries later, we must therefore identify the core principles of Islam and assert them over and above the detailed applications that may in some cases contradict them.

Tahar Haddad, who has developed this theory at considerable length, gives several examples in its support.[68] His most convincing argument, against which all attempts to hold back innovation in Muslim law break down, concerns the practice of slavery.

We know that slavery was practised in the Roman Empire and

throughout the ancient and early-medieval world. The works of historians such as Charles Verlindin have shown that it continued throughout the Middle Ages in many parts of Europe, especially in Spain, Portugal and Italy.[69] Pre-Islamic Arabia was no exception in this respect. The practice persisted there under the Omayyads and Abbasids, when there were Muslim slaves and the servile condition became hereditary. In principle this is rather surprising, if we consider that Islam is a religion that preaches the equality of human beings. One need only think of the Muslims ranged side by side in the same position in the mosque, or wearing the same dress for the pilgrimage, or observing the same fast during Ramadan. After death, too, equality is apparent in the simplicity of the cemeteries and the identical character of the graves. Islam is a religion of love among Muslims, as we can judge from the *zaket* (the duty to give alms, which is one of the five pillars of Islam) or from the many obligations of mutual aid. The Koran explicitly states in sura 2, verse 177: 'The righteous man is he who believes in God and the Last Day, in the angels and the Book and the prophets; who, though he loves it dearly, gives away his wealth to kinfolk, to orphans, to the destitute, to the traveller in need and to beggars, and for the redemption of captives; who attends to his prayers and renders the alms levy.' One would therefore have thought it out of the question that one man should own another.

And yet, Islam did not abolish slavery (any more than Christianity did). It strongly encouraged the freeing of slaves,[70] and both sura 2, verse 92 and sura 57, verse 3 make this obligatory for anyone seeking pardon for a number of sins. It also recommended that slaves should be well treated. But it did not go so far as to urge the abolition of slavery.

Should we conclude that, since a number of Koranic verses speak of slavery as a social fact without condemning it, the institution should be maintained in order to comply with the letter of the Koran? Or should it be abolished on the grounds that, whereas the spirit of the Koran is eternal, its letter is bound up with a certain place and time? Clearly, the recommendation to treat slaves well and the many encouragements to free them are an evolutionary step towards the abolition of slavery. Similarly, in comparison with the period before Islam when polygamy was unrestricted, the tetragamous limit was a step along the evolutionary path towards monogamy. In comparison with the *jahilia*, under which women could not inherit, the recognition of their right to half a man's share was a step along the evolutionary path towards equality of inheritance.

The Tunisian Mohamed Talbi, a devout man who has conducted profound research and advanced various bold proposals, has taken up and developed the ideas of Tahar Haddad.[71] In his approach, which we might call the 'vectoral' method, the historical evolution from the *jahilia* through the age of the Prophet and down to our own times is not a straight line whose direction is unknown to us. It is a line with a clearly defined direction, like a vector. God created human beings, mapped out a path for them, endowed them with reason and gave them the task of continuing to move in the same direction. In support of his theory, Haddad offers a highly interesting personal reading of the word 'trust' in sura 33, verse 72 of the Koran, which says: 'We offered Our trust [that is, God's spirit] to the heavens, to the earth, and to the mountains, but they refused the burden and were afraid to receive it. Man undertook to bear it, but he has proved a sinner and a fool.'[72] This trust borne by human beings is what distinguishes them from other creatures: it is their intelligence, their capacity for judgement and discrimination, their reason, which is not only the faculty of distinguishing good and evil but also that of penetrating to the essence of things and understanding the meaning of life and the human mission on earth. It is thus a question not of blind submission but of rational reflection, to discover the direction of the vector and to take new steps in that direction. Does the Koran not describe man as God's 'deputy' on earth (2:30), who has benefited from the breath of God's spirit (38:72), from the faculty of reflection (16:78, 6:104, 75:14), from wisdom (2:269) and from the capacity to learn the sciences and to understand the universe (2:31–3, 2:151, 10:101, 20:114, 29:20, 39:9, 55:1–4, 61:53, 96:1–5, 108:11, among others)? Such, according to this school, is the way of the future, the way of Islam as it should rightly be understood.

The eternal and the specific

The third approach is that of Mahmud Mohamed Taha, who, as we have already seen, was executed in Sudan for apostasy after a trial organized by the fundamentalist leader Hassan al-Turabi. For a long time Taha's numerous works were little known outside Sudan,[73] but one of his disciples, Abdallah Ahmed Naïm, a lawyer who defended him at his trial before taking refuge abroad, has published a work of his own summarizing Taha's thought.[74]

We know that the Muslim revelation stretched over approximately twenty-two years. It began in the twelve-year period when the Prophet preached the new religion in Mecca, which has given us the Meccan chapters or *suras* of the Koran; and it continued for a further ten years, after the Hegira, when the Prophet escaped the Quraysh persecution by moving with his followers to Medina and found refuge and support there (the period of the Medinese *suras*). Taha remarks that the general tone of the Meccan *suras* is one of preaching for a religion of peace, fraternity, love, freedom (including religious freedom) and equality, especially between men and women. They include such fine passages as sura 16, verse 125: 'Call men to the path of your Lord with wisdom and kindly exhortation. Reason with them in the most courteous manner. Your Lord best knows those who stray from His path and those who are rightly guided.' The Medinese *suras*, on the other hand, contain some verses with a legal appearance and others that accompany the Prophet and the group of Muslims around him in their attempts at defence and their conflicts with the idolaters.

Taha concludes from this that the essence of the Islamic message is contained in the Meccan *suras*, which impart a message of religion and morality to the whole of humanity, irrespective of time and place. It is the eternal message. The Medinese *suras*, associated with the struggle of the Prophet and his companions and the twists and turns of life in Medina, contain passages incompatible with the spirit and sometimes the letter of the Meccan message. In these chapters we find elements of discrimination between men and women or Muslims and non-Muslims, as well as a few verses that have a certain martial tone (especially in Chapter 9, 'Repentance').

In these *suras*, it is as if God considers the Meccan message too advanced for the Medinese and gives them a second message more in keeping with their circumstances, their way of life and their mentality. It is therefore a specific, more realistic message, which tends to help them advance while waiting for them to reach the level of the Meccan message.[75] Taha infers that the Medinese *suras* played a role and fulfilled their purpose, but that only the Meccan message concerns Muslims and the whole of humanity in the twentieth century.

Taha also uses more technical arguments of a textual nature. We have already mentioned the problem that some verses are rescinded by others. The ulema, for their part, always solved the contradiction between two verses by arguing that the later verse rescinded the earlier, just as in legal theory a later law abrogates earlier laws. Taha takes issue with this interpretation. In his view, since the two messages in the Koran do not have the same authority, the Medinese message could only ever suspend the effects of the Meccan. This is the technical argument used by legal experts, who maintain that a special law does not abrogate a general law but only makes it inapplicable in particular circumstances. Taha here refers to the Koranic verse (2:106) that addresses this very issue: 'If We abrogate a verse or cause it to be forgotten, We will replace it by a better one or one similar' – from which he concludes that there is a difference between abrogation and deletion from the memory ('causing to be forgotten'), especially as the two propositions are linked by an 'or' instead of an 'and'. They are two alternative possibilities. We might add that the Arabic verb *nacia* used in this verse can mean either to forget or to postpone, as the classical author Tabari pointed out long ago in his commentary on the Koran. Thus, the verses that concern us here were not abrogated; their application was only postponed until better times. Today is the right time.

For all these reasons, Taha concludes that if there is a contradiction between two verses or sets of verses the Meccan ones should take precedence over the Medinese. This is the opposite of what all the ulema have decided up to now.

Freeing the law

Taha was perfectly correct in stating that the key verses on equality or religious freedom that were revealed at Mecca, and which have since become basic principles with universal validity, cannot be abrogated by Medinese verses bound to a particular time and place. Nevertheless, Taha's arguments go a little too far. It is not easy to say, or even to imply, that all the Medinese verses (roughly one-third of the Koran) have been abrogated, just as it is not easy to accept the existence today of a second message that is a kind of new religion.

Furthermore, the theory of hermeneutics and the idea of a distinction between the eternal and the specific verses share the drawback that they risk solving one problem while creating another in its stead. It is true that Taha tends to be more explicative and Talbi more normative. But both writers argue for one religious body of law to be replaced with another religious body of law. This is an important drawback of their writing.

Religious laws are often taken to be immutable laws. But the whole idea of immutability is contrary to the nature of things. Even in the case of the *ibadats* – that is, everything concerning man's relations with God (prayer, fasting, etcetera) – few rules exist that could be valid for all times and all places, as the sharia would like them to be. At the beginning of the twentieth century, when ambassadors and Muslim travellers were appearing in Nordic countries, the ulema were faced with the problem of determining the hours of the Ramadan fast. To abstain from food and drink between sunrise and sunset is bearable for people living in equatorial, tropical and temperate regions, but what provision should be made for the inhabitants of polar regions where the days are sometimes endless? According to the fatwa issued at the time, diplomats were permitted to fast during the daylight hours of their country of origin. But this was only a stopgap solution, for it overlooked the fact that some Swedes or Norwegians might be attracted by Islam and have to face the problem in all its original force.

More recently, ulema assemblies in Hyderabad and Cairo have decided that the hours of sunrise and sunset at the 45th parallel should be applicable as far as the pole in each hemisphere – in other words, that the hours of fasting in Helsinki or Oslo should be determined by the hours of daylight in Bordeaux.[76] This seems a reasonable solution. Yet the Koran says (2:187): 'Eat and drink until you can tell a white thread from a black one in the light of the coming dawn. Then resume the fast until nightfall.' The ulema therefore had to avoid taking the Koran literally and to adopt a solution logically consistent with its spirit. Is this not striking and irrefutable proof that the Koran spoke a language that the inhabitants of Arabia understood fourteen hundred years ago, and that, outside that time and place, its letter is often inappropriate and sometimes entirely inapplicable?[77]

We see, then, that even typically religious rules need to be adapted to circumstances. The same is true *a fortiori* of the *mwamalat*, the field of law properly so called, which deals with relations among human beings. Economic, social and cultural circumstances are subject to rapid change, and laws must constantly keep pace with their rhythm. For this adjustment to be regularly performed without arousing passions on each occasion, it is necessary to erase the impression that the law is religious.

Religion is a problem of conviction, a matter of the heart. The conscience of each human being should be absolutely free. To believe or not to believe, to choose one's belief, is a strictly private area in which no one else has a right to interfere. Any constraint in these matters is against nature. In the case of fasting, for example, what does it mean in religious terms to abstain from food and drink merely out of fear of how the state or one's neighbours will react? The act of abstaining would not be God-directed and would therefore be devoid of meaning. Religion involves certain obligations and prohibitions, but these require voluntary submission and a daily renewed act of will free from duress on the part of the state or even society.

The law, on the other hand, involves duress by definition. It organizes social relations and delimits each individual's sphere of freedom in such a way that this does not encroach upon those of other individuals. The field of liberty should be as large as possible. The only limit, at once reasonable, acceptable and necessary, is the obligation to respect the liberty of others.

The ulema, the fundamentalists and the traditionalists have a classical response to this line of argument: since we are Muslims, we should obey God's dictates and apply Muslim law. (They also think, but do not say, that Muslims who disagree with it are apostates and should be killed.) But it is easy enough to come back and insist on God's command in the Koran (2:256): 'No duress in matters of religion.' Addressing his Prophet, God tells him (10:108): 'Say: "You people! The truth has come to you from your Lord. He that follows the right path follows it for his own good, and he that strays does so at his own peril. I am not your keeper."'

The Koran that contains such phrases must not be confused with a code which, by definition, makes certain laws obligatory and cannot but make them obligatory. It is true that the Koran contains recommendations, but these are bound up with particular circumstances. The first caliphs clearly understood that this was so, and that the recommendations would have to change with the times.

Omar, reputedly the most just and irreproachable of the four 'wise caliphs', set the example by taking huge liberties with the Koranic recommendations: Whereas the Koranic punishment for theft was amputation of the hand, Omar suspended its enforcement during a year of drought.[78] Whereas the Koran provides for war booty to be divided among the victorious combatants (59:6–10), Omar decided not to apply this rule during the conquest of Iraq and avoided distributing the land among the conquering forces, so that they would not sink roots there but continue the fight elsewhere.[79] Whereas the Koran provides for a share of war booty to be given to 'those whose hearts are sympathetic to the Faith' (9:60), Omar considered that this rule could serve to encourage those sympathetic to Islam when Muslims were in difficulty and needed their support, but that there was no longer any reason to apply it once the times had changed and Muslims had become stronger.[80] Whereas the Koran permitted Muslims to marry Jewish or Christian women, so that such unions became common during the great conquests, Omar responded to the protests of Muslim women by banning mixed marriages.[81]

Of course, what concerns us here is not the practical content of these solutions but the fact that Omar, a great authority in the eyes of all Muslims, whether fundamentalist or not, never took the Koran to be a legal code. For him, the so-called legal verses are no more than recommendations bound up with particular circumstances and liable to change with them.

It is high time to put an end to sterile debate about the meaning of this or that supposedly legal verse of the Koran. Instead, a clear distinction must be established once and for all between law and religion.

Furthermore, all Muslim peoples yearn for democracy, and it must be established in places where it does not exist. That is an urgent necessity. However, democracy is not viable where a majority of the population do not believe in pluralism. The France of 1848, the Germany of 1932 and the Algeria of 1991 each proved this in its way. Even among nations that have enjoyed freedom for one or two centuries, where the pluralist tradition is by now strongly rooted, a genuinely democratic debate needs to be calm and not heated. For elections to be held normally and in an atmosphere of calm, the principal contenders must all be democratic forces which respect the peace. The alternation of parties in government can take place without disturbances only if the outgoing majority keeps a reasonable hope of peacefully regaining power and a certainty that it will actually take the reins of government if it again wins a majority. On the other hand, if the outgoing majority knows that it risks losing power for ever and will be held down by the new regime, there is a strong possibility that it will resist the transfer. The elections will then be rigged, and the use of violence against the opposition will provoke violence in return. In the end there will be no alternation.

Such outcomes are all the more likely in Muslim countries, where democracy, if it exists at all, is still in its early, faltering stages, and where it therefore needs to be encouraged and protected. The intrusion of fundamentalists into this debate is liable to distort the rules of the democratic game; it is an element of serious disturbance, a powerful brake, a veritable catastrophe. For the debate immediately becomes passionate and overdramatized – as well as perfectly sterile. To believe or not to believe in angels, devils and *jinns*, to judge whether the story of Abraham, Hagar, Isaac and Ishmael is legend or historical fact, to decide on a thousand and one other questions of belief: this is up to the conscience of each individual. To avoid poisoning political life, and to make it easier to establish democracy in our countries, political debate must be separated from religious debate. It is incomparably more sensible to leave religion above and outside the sphere of politics. This is not to say, however, that Islamists should be prevented from expressing themselves or from organizing in a peaceful manner; liberty and democracy are indivisible. Attempts should therefore be made to integrate the Islamists into political life while continuing to denounce any confusion between religion and politics.

These conclusions are diametrically opposed to the fundamentalist view that the main task is to restore the 'Islamic state'. We should now turn to a consideration of what that expression means.

3

Islam and the State

Your duty is only to give warning: you are not their keeper.

The Koran (88:21)

On 23 March 1924 Kemal Atatürk abolished the caliphate in Istanbul. This pivotal event in the modern history of Islam is seen by some as a liberation, and by others as a veritable catastrophe whose consequences are still with us today.

The caliphate was a major obstacle to the modernization of Islamic thought, to the emancipation of Muslims and to the development of Muslim society. The Tanzimat reforms of the mid-nineteenth century had begun to create the seeds of a modern Turkish state, but the caliph had only grudgingly consented to them under the pressure of an elite that, at the time, was the largest and most advanced in the Muslim world. Subsequently he went back on the concessions at the first opportunity, clinging to age-old prerogatives of a personal absolutist regime. The institution of the caliphate was also discredited by its collaboration with the foreign powers. The great prestige acquired by Atatürk, who raised a people's army in Anatolia and successfully liberated the country and guaranteed its independence, made it possible for him to abolish the already moribund caliphate. Liberal Muslims enthusiastically welcomed this as a source of hope for the future. Exceptionally, there were even some bold and intelligent ulema, such as the Algerian Ben Bedis, who felt pleased that it had happened.[1]

For most ulema, however, especially those at Al Azhar and Zituna universities, the abolition of the caliphate was the collapse of the institution on which the Islamic state had rested for thirteen centuries. The event created a veritable trauma among the theologians, who have always considered the state and religion as two elements inseparably bound up with each other. Ignoring the concept of liberty, they have always taught that it is necessary to impose Islam on the rest of the world – on Muslims by threatening them with the death penalty for apostasy; on non-Muslims by waging *jihad* (holy war) whenever possible. In their eyes, duress has always been legitimate in matters of religion, and the state has been the means of exercising such duress. The disappearance of the Islamic state, traditionally represented by the caliphate, therefore caused serious disarray. The compass spun wildly round. The reference points were lost.

It was not by chance that the Muslim Brotherhood was founded in Egypt in 1928, almost immediately after the events in Istanbul. Its starting point was that the abolition of the caliphate had resulted from attempts to modernize society along Western lines; this was the high period of colonialism, when it was easy enough to attribute the whole ghastly evolution to a Western plot against Islam. The movement then developed a set of ideas in opposition to any modernization drive and demanded a return to the sharia and the Islamic state.

In later years, the Muslim Brotherhood underwent a number of splits which gave rise to the most diverse tendencies. But demands for both a return to the sharia and the rebuilding of an Islamic state remained common to all the Islamist groups and parties, even if some openly stated their aims while others were at pains to camouflage them.

Two facts will show the extent to which the goal of restoring the caliphate was essential to Islamist ideology and represented a key objective for all fundamentalist militants.

Under the monarchy, the Iranian mullahs always combated the republic and republicans in the name of Islamic dogma and opposition to any imported European institution.[2] When they took power, they felt obliged to establish a republic with elections and a parliament. But a committee of religious experts – the supervisory council – keeps a close watch on parliament to ensure that its laws are consistent with religious tradition (Articles 91 and 94 of the Constitution). Besides, both constitutionally and in reality, all institutions in Iran are under the control of the *faqih*, the 'guide of the revolution', a supreme religious leader appointed for life by the religious authorities, without any form of popular consultation. His status and powers, which are indisputable and undisputed, make one think of a caliphate with special Shiite features.

In 1994 the Algerian Armed Islamist Group (GIA), which is well known for its radical positions and the barbaric violence of its operations, announced the restoration of the caliphate and the appointment of a caliph.[3] In fact, the GIA was merely trying to implement one of the points in the FIS programme of March 1989.[4]

To listen to the Islamists, one would think that the existence of an Islamic state – preferably in the form of a caliphate, and in any event with theologians at the helm – was a pillar of Islam, a religious necessity. But the truth is different. The caliphate was a purely human creation in history, envisaged neither in the Koran nor in the Prophet's *sunna*. Added by men, it does not form part of the religion.

The Koran and the caliphate

We find two mentions of a caliphate in the Koran. In sura 2, verse 30, God tells the angels that He intends to 'place on earth one that shall rule as my deputy'; this is Adam in particular or man in general. But, if it is the latter, we should stress that there is no talk of a state or a ruler. In sura 38, verse 26, David is appointed caliph in the sense of a ruler. The Koran also uses the term *shura*, which means consultation or deliberation. Thus Muslims 'conduct their affairs by mutual consent' (42:36), and the Prophet is told: 'Take counsel with them in the conduct of affairs' (3:159). Finally, the word *dawla*, which can mean 'state', is used in sura 59, verse 7, but in quite a different sense.

A few points should be made in relation to these verses.

Let us first examine the concept of *shura*. Those who wish at all costs to find everything in the Koran, even attaching the most recent scientific theories to particular verses, or those who think we have nothing to borrow from others, especially in the West, claim that democracy exists in our own heritage and that all we need do is deepen the Koranic *shura*. For fundamentalists, the ideal government is that of the emir who consults his lieutenants – or technical experts – before taking his decisions alone, in the manner of the 'wise caliphs' of old. Such consultation is supposed to serve the function of democracy. But it is a false approach, more akin to what we have previously called *talfik*. That a leader should consult his companions and subordinates is simple common sense or, at most, a precondition of intelligent conduct in government. It is by no means sufficient to allow us to characterize a government as democratic. To take an extreme example, we may recall that Stalin – who personally directed several battles during the Second World War – used to gather his generals and consult them on tactics before taking any important decision. Even in emergencies, he found the time to consult top army commanders.[5] And yet he was one of the bloodiest dictators that humanity has ever known.

The Koran named Adam and David as caliphs, but not the Prophet Mohammed, and still less his successors. It does on several occasions use various Arabic words with the same root as 'caliph', but these refer to the whole of humanity as the beneficiary of all the goods created on earth.[6]

Finally, and most important, the Koran never speaks of an Islamic state or of the state *tout court*. The state is therefore not a religious institution; no religious function is attributed to it. It is a question that does not come up for discussion. It logically follows that the state and politics are not part of religion.

If the form of rule were of any interest to religion, if the state had any kind of religious mission, the Koran would not have failed to speak of it – for there are even verses that deal with secondary matters. The Koran contains no reference and no allusion to the mode of appointing rulers, or to the possible ways of supervising or removing them. Later, the Prophet's companions and their successors tore one another apart in fratricidal wars because there was no rule that could settle their political rivalry and adjudicate their claims to legitimacy. The only logical, coherent and rational conclusion from the silence of the Koran on these vital issues is that the state and politics concern life in the world below and are of no interest to religion. God actually stresses in the Koran (6:38): 'We have left out nothing in the Book.' If such a crucial matter, one with such dramatic consequences as the character of the political regime, is passed over in silence in a book from which 'nothing' has been left out, then this must be because it is not part of the subject matter.

The five pillars of Islam are: *shahada* (belief in God and his Prophet), prayer, fasting, almsgiving (*zaket*) and the pilgrimage. Other obligations of lesser importance also receive a mention in the Koran. Thus, to add a sixth pillar is to claim that the contours of the Islamic religion were not set once and for all by the end of the revelation, at the death of the Prophet. It is also to fly in the face of the Koran, where God states (5:3): 'This day I have perfected your religion for you.'

Fundamentalists ought to re-read our sacred text and comply with what it says.

Sunna and caliphate

We must look at the Prophet's mission as defined in the Koran, before we go on to examine the methods he used to accomplish it.

The Koranic definition of the Prophet's mission

Unlike Adam and David, Mohammed was never named in the Koran as a caliph, still less as a king, ruler or emir. On the contrary, one verse distinguishes between the obedience due to him as Prophet and that which is due to an emir or a civilian or military ruler (4:59): 'Believers, obey God and obey the Apostle and those in authority among you.'[7] Obedience to God and the Prophet is, as we have seen, a religious obligation to be fulfilled voluntarily; obedience to rulers, who for their part employ various forms of constraint, is advised in order to avoid anarchy. But the idea that Prophet and rulers should coexist is clearly visible here.

Verse 65 of the same sura orders Muslims to seek the Prophet's arbitration of matters in dispute among them and to accept his judgements with good grace. Arbitration was a common practice in Arabia, where there were no state and no courts. What was more normal than that Muslims should accept the Prophet's arbitration during his lifetime? But this is a far cry from the command functions of a king, an emperor or the state in general.

Outside of these two verses, which theologians and Islamists try to manoeuvre into their theories of an Islamic state, the Koran is clear that the Prophet's mission is to preach, not to command or constrain. Let us briefly mention a few of the numerous verses that confirm this point.

The Prophet's mission is to pass on God's message. The Koran expresses this in restrictive terms: 'You are only a messenger'.[8] On the ways of passing on the message, the Koran says: 'Call men to the path of your Lord with wisdom and kindly exhortation' (16:125). The Prophet's role is to bear happy tidings,[9] but these also contain a message of warning: 'Your mission is only to give clear warning' (16:82).[10] The

Prophet's role is also defined negatively. He has not been sent to be the 'keeper' of others (4:80); his mission does not involve 'using coercion with them' (50:45). 'Had your Lord pleased, all the people of the earth would have believed in Him, one and all. Would you then force people to have faith?' (10:99). No, surely not; everyone is responsible for the attitude that he or she freely chooses. The Koran adds: 'Say: "You people! The truth has come to you from your Lord. He that follows the right path follows it for his own good, and he that strays does so at his own peril. I am not your keeper"' (10:108).[11] Finally, there are the two verses that summarize the Koranic teaching on the Prophet's role by recalling what he should do and what he should avoid: 'Your duty is only to give warning: you are not their keeper' (88:21–22).

These verses should not need interpretation: their obvious meaning is that the Prophet had a duty to preach, not a power of command, and that this excluded any quasi-state function. In his book *Islam and the Foundations of Power*, to which we have already made reference, the great Egyptian thinker Ali Abderrazak based himself on these verses to argue that Islam needed no caliphate and that the latter was a purely historical creation.[12] This drew the fire of the conservative ulema and cut across the plans of King Fouad, who was dreaming at the time of declaring himself caliph. Under ulema pressure, the Egyptian government removed Abderrazak from his post and ordered his books to be burned.[13]

Interpretations that distorted the meaning of these verses were used to combat Abderrazak's theory – interpretations reminiscent of those put forward by the ulema in the early centuries of the Hegira. Those ulema of old, subject to the political authorities in place, never dared to challenge the legitimacy and supposedly sacred character of the Islamic state, and they were forced to use the most specious arguments to avoid deriving a theory of freedom from the verses cited above.

So it is that conservative commentators writing today have been able to claim that the words 'You are not their keeper' mean that the Prophet was not responsible if he failed to convince non-believers,[14] whereas in fact this interpretation obviously does not correspond to the text on which they are commenting. A rather more serious, though unfounded, explanation is the one put forward by ancient commentators: that this verse was abrogated either by other Koranic verses[15] or by a hadith in which the Prophet supposedly said that God had commanded him to combat non-believers.[16] We may easily discard the idea of abrogation by a hadith, since, as we have already seen, a lower rule is meant to explain or apply a higher rule and can never contradict it. The idea of abrogation by other Koranic verses deserves a little more discussion.

It is true that many verses deal with *jihad*, whether to define the forms in which it should be waged, or to encourage Muslims to participate in it, or to criticize those who refuse.[17] The clearest in this respect is the one that prescribes a duty to engage in *jihad*: 'Prophet, make war on the unbelievers and the hypocrites and deal rigorously with them' (9:73). There does seem to be a contradiction here between the two sets of verses. Commentators have taken advantage of this to claim that the verses dealing with *jihad* abrogate those dealing with freedom of belief. We have already mentioned Taha's view that the latter are part of the Meccan core that defines the eternal message of Islam, whereas the former are bound up with a particular time and place in Medina and have since become obsolete.

Nevertheless, without going so far as to accept Taha's theory, it is perfectly legitimate to challenge the case for abrogation. In order to maintain that one set of verses abrogated another of the same grade but did not actually say that it was abrogating them, we would first need to be satisfied that the two were absolutely incompatible with each other. The idea of abrogation is especially grave, above all when it is a question of the word of God. But that is not what is involved here.

In fact the Koran says: 'God does not forbid you to be kind and equitable to those who have neither made war on your religion nor driven you from your homes. God loves the equitable. But He forbids you to make friends with those who have fought against you on account of your religion and driven you from your homes on account of your religion or abetted others to drive you out' (60:8-9). Or again: 'Fight for the sake of God those that fight against you, but do not attack them first. God does not love aggressors' (2:190).

These verses are perhaps able to reconcile the two sets by assigning to each a distinctive field of application. In normal times, the Prophet and all Muslims should exercise no constraint for religious reasons, but when they are being attacked and driven from their homes they should defend themselves. War can be described as holy only if it is defensive; that is the only legitimate *jihad*. All aggression, all wars of conquest are forbidden – in the past as in the present.

It is true that the ulema interpreted the theory of *jihad* more broadly. But in reality the theory was virtually never applied from the Middle Ages down to the period of colonization. In the mid-twentieth century, to mobilize as many as possible for the struggle against the colonial powers, leaders of the national liberation movements used the concept of *jihad* in addition to their political arguments. But the decades following decolonization saw a calming of relations between Muslim and other countries, and a period of friendly cooperation succeeded the old relations of domination. The whole world periodically expressed the esteem in which it held Islam and Muslims. The President of the Italian Republic ceremonially opened a mosque in Rome; the French interior minister opened one in Lyons. The Pope sent his best wishes to Muslims each year on the occasion of the month of Ramadan, as did the President of the United States on the Eid holiday[18] – until the day when relations again became poisoned as a result of the actions of a violent wing of the Islamists. The murderous attacks of September 2001, plus those in Nairobi, Bali, Casablanca and elsewhere, have resulted in a situation where many Western governments and commentators no longer make a distinction between Muslims and Islamists. Islam as such is associated with fanaticism and violence.

Today, relations between Muslims and others suffer from a vicious circle. On the one hand, absolutely nothing can justify the fact that Palestinians and Chechens are still deprived of their right to self-determination and the establishment of an independent state; it must be hoped that a just solution to these problems will be found as soon as possible, and that the Afghan and Iraqi peoples will quickly regain full sovereignty over their national territory. On the other hand, nothing can justify the killing of civilians anywhere in the world, whatever their religion or nationality; it is desirable that a representative and credible assembly of ulema should one day proclaim that the idea of holy war, and especially of offensive *jihad*, has been abandoned for ever, and that any attack on an innocent person is to be condemned, whatever the circumstances.

Certainly the Prophet would never have approved of the acts of violence committed in recent years in the name of Islam. And this whole interpretation is all the more persuasive if we consider that the Prophet accomplished his mission in accordance with divine prescriptions.

Achievement of the Prophet's mission

From the beginning of the revelation, the Prophet started to preach the new religion. We have already seen that this upset the polytheists of Mecca, who banded together against him and oppressed his followers, especially the more vulnerable ones who did not have the protection of noble birth or tribal solidarity. The Prophet and his companions patiently bore this persecution, until their growing numbers made the Quraysh feel threatened in their social position and economic interests; the decision was then made to make an attempt on the Prophet's life. He chose to go into exile in Medina, where his many supporters could protect him and his people.

This event, known as the Hegira, was a turning point in the history of Islam. Relations between the Prophet and his opponents were now governed by a logic of war, which lasted until his death ten years later. The persecution suffered by Muslims in Mecca, and the fact that they had been 'driven from their homes' (as the Koran puts it), were the origin of the defensive violence used by Muslims themselves. It is true that particular acts of war may be described in isolation as offensive, but these too were part of the wider logic dictated by the attitude of the Quraysh.

In Medina the Prophet continued to spread the word, especially by sending letters which suggested to nearby tribal leaders that they adopt the new religion. The rapidly growing numbers of Muslims made an impression on several of these tribal leaders, who decided to join the rising group. When a region informed the Prophet of its wish to embrace Islam *en masse*, he sent a representative to explain to it the rules of the new religion. At the same time, he played the role of arbiter in disputes.

Throughout this period, the Prophet did not find in Medina or elsewhere either a state with which he might have coexisted or a monarch whom he might have combated and replaced. The particularity of Islam is that it was born in a semi-desert, in the midst of a tribal society that lacked any statelike structure. There were only the tribal leaders, who, even after a mass conversion, kept their titles and prerogatives. It was therefore normal, given the Prophet's moral authority and his prestige as God's messenger, that Muslims should consider him their leader. But he himself, in a hadith that no one challenges, said: 'You know better than I the affairs of the world below.' In other words, apart from the requirements of self-defence with which he had to concern himself, he behaved only as a religious leader. Neither in Mecca nor in Medina did he find or establish a state structure. No currency was minted in the name of a new state. There was no civil service, no permanent courts, no army, prisons or guards. All those structures, which are characteristic of a state even in the ancient understanding of the word, were conspicuous by their absence.

In fact, apart from his mission to pass on the divine message, the main purpose of the Prophet's activity in Arabia was to end the permanent inter-tribal warfare and to form a community organized 'on moral more than strictly political foundations'.[19] He also succeeded in breaking the resistance of the Quraysh and their allies, who had sole control over the Kabah in Mecca (long the most important shrine for all Arabs). The liberation of Mecca by the Prophet took place without bloodshed, as there were already a large number of converts in the city. There can be no doubt that these historical events later made it easier for Abu Bakr and Omar to establish a state. But only an excess of ideological enthusiasm could allow anyone to jump to the conclusion that Mohammed himself founded a state and acted as its head.

A conclusive point in support of this analysis is that any head of state with the slightest sense of responsibility would have tried to ensure that a successor continued his work and maintained the continuity of the state he had founded. In the course of what historians call the 'farewell pilgrimage', the style and tenor of the Prophet's sermon prove that he felt his death approaching; it can even be argued that God foretold his death in a verse of the Koran: 'This day I have perfected your religion for you and completed My favour to you' (5:3). And yet the Prophet did not choose a successor or give the slightest indication about the method that should be used to elect one.

Paradoxically, orientalists, fundamentalists and the ulema all commit the mistake of claiming that the Prophet was the founder of a state, although they do so for very different reasons. All start from the assertion that Mohammed was a great man, one of the giants of history. Orientalists, not being Muslim, see him as a politician who thought up an ideology to build a state that soon became an empire; he was, in this view, essentially a statesman. The ulema, wishing to legitimize the caliphate, consider that the four 'wise caliphs' merely continued the work of the Prophet, who thus becomes the founder of a state. As for the fundamentalists, their goal of reconstituting the Islamic state leads them to embrace the theory of the ulema.

A correct, objective reading of the religion and history will enable us to disentangle the elements that the ulema jumbled together, and to see that the turning point came with the death of the Prophet. That was the event that marked the end of the revelation, ushering in the caliphate and the purely human construction of an Islamic state and empire.

The caliphate

The ulema, now followed by the fundamentalists, have a habit of extreme embellishment or idealization, which allows them to attach a sacred aura to the history of the caliphate in general and the four 'wise caliphs' in particular. However, the atmosphere at the election of the first caliph was not one of reverence, piety or devotion to the cause of religion and the public interest. At a place called Sakifat Bani Saida, a small number of Medinese notables gathered to select a new leader in haste, even before the Prophet had been laid to rest. They were on the point of choosing Saad ibn Ubada, the head of one of the main tribes in Medina, when a few Muslims from Mecca heard of this and quickly joined the proceedings. The lively discussion that ensued did not centre on either the Koran or the *sunna*. The only argument of the Meccans was that the new leader should be chosen from the Prophet's own tribe, the Quraysh. Through a kind of *coup de force*, Omar and four other Meccans proclaimed Abu Bakr the new leader (he later chose the title 'caliph' or 'Prophet's successor'); it came to blows and Saad was defeated.[20] But Saad never recognized Abu Bakr or his successor, Omar, and he was assassinated in obscure circumstances.[21] Ali – who, as the Prophet's cousin and brother-in-law, had ambitions of his own – recognized Abu Bakr only six months later, after the death of the prophet's wife Fatma.[22]

The Abu Bakr caliphate was a period of constant warfare. Most of the tribes rose up against him, but since they were divided and had no common programme or leader, Abu Bakr was able to pick them off one by one and break their resistance. The accusation made to justify these wars was that of apostasy. But we have shown above that, even when this was true, apostasy was not sufficient grounds for punishment, still less for the declaration of war, especially as, in addition to religious apostasy properly so called, there were what historians describe as 'economic apostasy' (whereby tribes calling themselves Muslim refused to pay the *zaket* to the caliph's agents) and, most important of all, purely political apostasy. The various tribes of Arabia had admiringly welcomed the Prophet's liberation of the holy places in Mecca (holy both for Islam and before Islam) from the yoke of the Quraysh. But since Abu Bakr, himself a Quraysh, had been proclaimed the Prophet's successor, they rightly feared that the Quraysh might again capture power and 'impose their monopoly on the other tribes'.[23] The wars waged by Abu Bakr were thus political acts, not religious acts.[24] They were certainly important, because when Omar succeeded Abu Bakr he found an Arabia entirely pacified and unified. He then threw his troops into the conquest of the countries of the Sham (Syria and Palestine), Iraq and Egypt. Abu Bakr had laid the foundations of the state, and Omar went on to lay the foundations of empire.

The ulema always tried to attach a sacred aura to the conquests of the caliphs, which they considered by definition just and beneficial on the grounds that they tended to Islamize the local population. In fact, the main result of these wars was to Arabize the countries that today speak Arabic; they could have been Islamized without the need for bloodshed. In Central and Western Africa and South-East Asia – the regions where the largest number of Muslims live today – Islam spread in a peaceful manner, without those wars and invasions whose justification by the ulema helped to disseminate the false concept of offensive *jihad*. Wars occurred in some of those countries, of course, as wars do everywhere in the world, but Islam did not take root there through a strategy of conquest based on *jihad* and violence.

Muslims need a critical re-reading of their history in order to recover their religion in its original purity, free of the deposits left by the vicissitudes of history. The first two caliphs were great political strategists; their deeds could not have been successful without the ruses, calculations and alliances inherent in all political action. Reasons of state explain a number of their decisions. For example, when Abu Bakr learned that Khalid ibn al-Walid (whom he had placed in charge of his troops during the war of the apostates) was committing crimes unworthy of a Muslim leader,[25] he left him in his position in order to continue benefiting from his great military skills. The first two caliphs were great politicians who served the cause they had given themselves with both intelligence and single-minded commitment. But they were not saints. Unfortunately the third caliph, Othman, was even less of a saint.

It may be possible to criticize the actions of the first two caliphs, but only in the name of principles that appear evident to us today but which, in their own time, had no purchase on relations between peoples. As to their personal conduct, they were above all suspicion. Things were very different, however, in the case of the third caliph. His twelve-year reign, the longest of the three, was marked by nepotism and mismanagement of the public purse. He placed friends, close relatives and tribal dignitaries at the head of great provinces, on such a scale that the Omayyad era may be said to have begun with him.[26] 'He borrowed from the Bayt al mel [the public treasury] huge sums that he did not always pay back. He may have used them to engage in business dealings or lent or given them to others.'[27] He amassed a large fortune consisting of property, camels, horses and huge sums of money in dinars and dirhams. It is true that he was already rich before he was elevated to the caliphate. 'But the past riches appear paltry in comparison with those of the present.'[28]

A number of leading figures, including old companions of the Prophet such as the celebrated Abu Dhar al-Ghifari, vigorously protested against this outrageous conduct on the part of the head of state. Othman responded by issuing orders for corporal punishment against some and banishment against others;[29] he also surrounded himself with guards for fear of the consequences. In short, it was with Othman that the rot set in: the chain of misconduct, protests, repression and revolt.

The first revolt in the history of Islam was the one that led to the assassination of Othman and his replacement by Ali. Muawiyah declared war on Ali to avenge Othman and to punish his assassins. But in fact that was only a pretext: the proof is that he had known in advance that Othman was in danger and had done nothing to protect him. It had suited his purpose to allow the situation to degenerate.

The intrigues, calculations and political manoeuvres began well before the assassination of the third caliph. Aisha, 'the mother of Believers' and one of the Prophet's most famous wives, who reported a large number of hadiths, sharply criticized Othman and let it be understood that he might be killed.[30] But, as soon as the revolt turned to Ali's advantage, she organized against him an alliance with the two pretenders to the caliphate, Zubeir and Talha, who had previously sworn allegiance to Ali. She personally directed the 'camel battle' against Ali's troops. Then, when Ali was himself assassinated after a tumultuous five-year reign, the chapter of the 'wise caliphs' ended in blood and disorder. With the Omayyads began the so-called false caliphate: that is, the system of dynastic rule which persisted with frequent changes of ruler and capital down to the year 1924.

From time to time a caliph would appear who was remarkable for his intelligence and knowledge (for example, the Abbasid ruler al-Mamun) or his personal integrity (for example, the Omayyad Omar ben Abdelaziz, who is often held up for praise, even if it is not mentioned that his rule lasted only two years). But, with very rare exceptions, the conduct of the caliphs was never exemplary. Mostly, life in the palace was dominated by intrigues of all kinds, drinking bouts, pretty boys, harems run by eunuchs, and so forth.[31]

Power was always exercised in an absolute manner, and the frequent revolts were repressed with the greatest vigour. Thus, in the reign of Yazid ibn Muawiyah, collective punishment was meted out to the inhabitants of Medina, the city of the Prophet, where the soldiery was given three days to kill, destroy, steal and rape.[32] In the reign of Abdelmalek ibn Marwan, another punitive expedition against the inhabitants of Mecca involved an attack on the Kabah, the sacred Islamic sanctuary.

The policy of repression was intended not only to crush collective revolts and challenges but also to stifle individuals who dissented, or were suspected of dissenting, from the official line of the day, especially if they held a certain social or religious position. Three of the four founders of the main Sunni rites suffered the consequences of this policy. Malek (who died in 795 CE) was beaten because he was suspected of thinking that the *beya* (the oath of allegiance to a new caliph) had legal value only if was not made under duress. When Abu Hanifa (d. 767 CE) became a religious figure of renown, the caliph wanted to make him a *qadi* in order to integrate him into the political apparatus. He then interpreted Hanifa's rejection of the offer as a refusal to cooperate and ordered him to be severely beaten. Ibn Hanbal (d. 855 CE) was tortured because he refused to accept the theory of the created Koran (the theory associated with the Mutazilites).[33]

Thinkers, then, were kept under close surveillance. Arabs translated, taught and enriched the works of Greek philosophy – with the exception of Aristotle's *Politics*. Circumstances barred them from conducting research in that field.[34] This is why the Muslim law they developed was only a private law; the whole area of public law was too much of a minefield. No one dared to venture into it, except with ideas that strengthened the absolute power of the ruler. Both the Hanbalites and the Malekites clearly asserted a duty to obey the caliph, even if he was a tyrant or a corrupt individual.[35] The best-known (because quite developed) work of Muslim public law is the one we owe to Mawardi, but even that is not really a book of law.[36] It does not speak of mechanisms for the limitation of the caliph's prerogatives, but mainly consists of recommendations about the qualities (integrity, justness, virtue, etcetera) to be expected of a ruler. Does this not prove that the Islamic literature lacks a public law worthy of the name, or a theory of the state other than that dealing with the responsibility of the caliphate to apply sharia law and of the population to obey it? Mohamed Talbi summarizes as follows the work of the ulema on this subject: 'We may say, a little abruptly, that men of letters in Muslim civilization patiently and methodically applied themselves to the task of theologically whittling down all freedoms and promoting intolerance.'[37] The incompatibility between the sharia and freedom cannot be disputed. But it is not an incompatibility with Islam as a religion, since that does not contain a theory of the state. Islamists who use the slogan 'The Koran is our constitution' ought to be aware that there is no mention of an Islamic state in the Koran or the *sunna*. Nor has there been a real Islamic state at any time in history. All that happened was that religion was used in the service of political ends.

The title 'caliph of God's messenger' was chosen by Abu Bakr in the sense of a temporal successor: that is, 'he who comes after'. This sense developed to take in the more functional content of 'he who takes the place', 'he who plays the role' or 'he who continues the work' of the Prophet. Then the title itself evolved to become 'God's caliph', 'God's light' and 'God's shadow'.[38] These various self-given titles helped to paint the caliphs to their people as God's representatives on earth; anyone who dared oppose them thereby became an enemy of God whom it was justifiable to repress. Rule in God's name – or in the name of the sharia, which came to much the same thing – was based on a real or artificial confusion between politics and religion that inevitably brought dictatorship in its wake.

The confusion was real in the case of the first two caliphs, men of integrity who were both religious and political leaders and whose conduct was in tune with their discourse. They would consult their companions but took the decisions alone. They created no institution and did not permit the establishment of any countervailing power. Theirs was supposed to be the rule of virtue.[39] It was a system that, though lasting only twelve years, served a useful purpose thanks to the wisdom and exceptional stature of Abu Bakr and Omar. But it was not viable in the longer term.

We know today, after the lessons of Saint-Just and Robespierre among others, what 'the rule of virtue' can lead to – even in the presence of a national assembly. It is easy to imagine what it meant in the absence of any other centre of power.

The caliphate of Othman was the real turning point, as it gathered the Koranic *suras* into a single book, endorsed a single version and ordered the destruction of all others. Until then the *qurrahs* (those who recite the Koran) had had a kind of monopoly on knowledge and dissemination of the sacred text. Each had his own reading, which he propagated in the circle of those he taught and discussed with. These ancestors of the ulema, who were deeply upset by Othman's imposition of a single version, played an important role in the mobilization that led to his assassination.[40]

Later, with the benefit of experience, Muawiyah did everything he could to humour them. He established a clear division of tasks and powers in which each had his own sphere of responsibility: political and military authority for the caliph, religious teaching and lawmaking for the theologians. Although the caliph was theoretically also the religious leader ('Commander of the Believers'), he generally did not interfere in theological matters and contented himself with the role of protector of Islam. In return, the ulema were not grudging in their support for the caliph and were always at his service. The imam's sermon at the mosque before Friday prayers always ended with a reaffirmation of allegiance to the prince and an entreaty for God to come to his aid.

The outcome was disastrous for public liberties, which were never respected under the caliphate. Islamic society has always been stuck between a regime that represses people without restraint in the name of religion and ulema subservient to the regime who, owing their privileges to it, do not dare speak out against it. Islamic society has never been able to produce either the intellectuals to develop a theory of liberty or activists capable of struggling for democracy.

It clearly follows from what has just been said that there can be no liberty or democracy without a separation between the spheres of religion and politics, and that the Islamic state, envisaged neither by the Koran nor the *sunna*, is a man-made institution that has used religion for political ends,[41] to justify military conquests, exploitation of the people and the pleasure-seeking of caliphs. Summarizing and commenting on the thought of Ali Abderrazak, Abdu Filali Ansari writes that the theory of the caliphate 'did violence to the community, religion and reason'.[42]

This critique of the caliphate cannot be taxed with hostility or denigration with regard to Islam as a religion and culture. During its golden age, Islamic civilization was particularly dazzling: the Islamic contribution to science and universal knowledge has not been insignificant, and the importance of the philosophical works of Farabi, Kindi and especially Averroës no longer has to be demonstrated. The same is true of the invention of algebra or Khawarizmi's research in mathematics. In medieval Europe, medicine was taught from textbooks in Arabic or translated from the Arabic of Avicenna, Ibn Zohr or ar-Razi.

Beginning with the rule of the caliph al-Mamun (813–33), who gave considerable encouragement to scientific research, Arab astronomers developed instruments such as the astrolabe and conducted extraordinary measurements of the sidereal year and the movement of the planets, all the more extraordinary if we consider that they used rudimentary devices such as the water clock. Their measurements and their theories later served a number of European scientists, especially Copernicus, whose heliocentric theory revolutionized our conception of the world.

We should also bear in mind that the violence and the wars of conquest in the name of Islam resemble the aberrations experienced by many other religions. A brief comparison with the other monotheisms will easily demonstrate this point.

Judaism, Christianity and Islam

For each of the three monotheistic religions, faith is essentially a question of conviction belonging to the strictly private sphere. Yet, for various historical reasons, each one went through episodes of violence and holy war.

The kings of Israel, who had both a religious and a political character, traditionally waged cruel wars in the name of Yahweh. Deuteronomy precisely specifies who was required to go to war and who was exempted, and it clearly distinguishes between the rules governing defensive wars and those governing offensive wars (for which the exemptions were a little more numerous). To give some idea of the appalling nature of these wars, let us quote the Bible: 'When Israel had finished killing the inhabitants of Ai, in the countryside and in the desert where they had pursued them, and when every last one had fallen to the sword, the whole of Israel returned to Ai and put the population to the sword. The total number of those who fell that day was twelve thousand, all people from Ai.'[43] Or again: 'They put everything in the town to the sharp edge of the sword, both men and women, young and old, bull, sheep and ass.'[44] These are just two passages, which are unfortunately by no means exceptional.

On the Christian side, the Crusades were a straightforward case of aggression against the Muslim world. Europeans tend to forget this when they say that they will wage a 'crusade' against a particular evil such as drugs or unemployment. Perhaps without realizing it, they use an expression that recalls a dark period in the history of relations between East and West, a campaign of aggression that lasted two centuries and brought in its wake untold death, suffering and depredation. Alain Finkielkraut has recently reminded us that in 1550, on the orders of Charles V, a royal commission of theologians and legal experts met in the chapel of San Gregorio convent in Valladolid to answer the question: 'Is it lawful for His Majesty to wage war on the Indians [of America] before preaching them the faith?' The commission was unable to complete its work. But it was argued there that such a war was justified for several reasons, including 'the needs of the faith, since their subjugation will make it easier and quicker to conduct the preaching that will be made to them'.[45] That is the point of view that won acceptance.

Justinian established the death penalty for Christians guilty of apostasy. As this decree and associated excesses were widely applied, whole communities such as the pagans disappeared[46] – and we know that the Inquisition costs tens of thousands of their lives.

These points remind us that intolerance and the use of violence have been a common feature of religions with universal pretensions. Rousseau wrote: 'In paganism, where each state had its own cult and its own gods, there were no wars of religion.' Perhaps the universal pretension already contains the seeds of a tendency to expansion, and hence to domination and compulsion. But, since religions also contain the principle of freedom, true believers have to make a considerable effort in relation to themselves; they have to do violence to themselves in order to refrain from all violence. They believe in absolute truth and should also believe absolutely in each person's freedom to share or not to share this truth, and to understand it by his or her own lights.

Much of Western public opinion today has a poor view of Islam and Muslims because of the barbaric acts committed by fundamentalists that are so often in the headlines. Violence is no more part of the essence of Islam than it is of the other monotheistic religions. The only point is that, whereas the great majority of members of other religions have left behind that stage of history, Muslims are still living through the pain of a transitional period.

Let us not forget that in 1789 the Roman Catholic Church was outraged by the Declaration of the Rights of Man and the Citizen and by the abolition of divine right, or that the Pope reacted in the strongest way to the French law of 1905 on the principle of secularism. Until then, religious freedom had been considered a pernicious invention of atheists to turn people's minds from the 'true faith'. But subsequently, under the pressure of events, the Church really went to work on itself and experienced a considerable evolution.

The decree of the Second Vatican Council on religious freedom, dated 7 December 1965, constituted a major turning point and was 'painstakingly formulated and hotly debated'.[47] Tolerance is no longer a compromise but an affirmation of the primacy of freedom. As Cardinal Roger Etchegeray, president of the Pontifical Councils, put it: 'The decree on religious freedom is based on the rights of the human person, not on the rights of the true religion', for 'it is more comfortable to be a slave than to be a master. In the end, one only ever has the freedom that one is capable of assuming. Only people already free within themselves can be made free.'[48] On the question of human rights, the Church's thinking passed from rejection to engagement – which marked 'a real break with a tradition running through the whole history of the revealed religions'.[49] Since then, the synod of bishops has declared (in 1974): 'The promotion of human rights is a requirement of the Gospel, and it everywhere occupies a central place in the ministry of the Church.'[50] In the new approach, then, faith first requires freedom. Only then can one freely adhere to the faith.

This kind of approach is not inconsistent with the Koranic texts. But it cannot be embraced in the absence of structures officially representing the Muslim religion, along the lines of the Church or the councils. Instead, the whole issue is currently left to the judgement of believers. Enlightened modern thinkers have clearly asserted the compatibility of Islam with human rights, but this is not a majority view because the Muslim peoples live in countries that are still developing. In the end, the existence, number and violence of our fundamentalists are both the consequence and the chief manifestation of underdevelopment, which is intellectual before being material.

The fundamentalists call for democracy, which in itself is a perfectly legitimate demand. But they leave out the crucial point that no one has ever governed democratically in the name of religion. The European experience provides ample evidence of this: democratization has always gone hand in hand with some kind of distinction between the political and religious spheres. Brushing this aside as a bad example, fundamentalists insist over and over again in their speeches and writings – so that it has become accepted by Muslim public opinion as an undeniable truth – that Islam, unlike Christianity, does not restrict itself to spiritual matters but is a 'total' religion, in the sense that it governs all aspects of the life of believers.[51] Secularism, they argue, may suit Christianity and other religions, but it cannot suit Islam. This false argument, contrary to both theological and historical truth, is so widespread that it calls for a response.

For a very long time, the Roman Catholic Church laid down minutely detailed rules for the creation and functioning of the family. It continues to do this, in fact, but the triumph of the secular principle means that such rules no longer have the force of legal obligations. The present code of canon law dates from 27 November 1983, its 1,752 articles involving a degree of simplification in comparison with the 2,414 articles contained in the code of 1917. It governs the conditions and the form of marriage, the status of children, the rights of parents, and so on.[52]

During the Middle Ages, all the details of life were subject to a series of obligations and prohibitions which strike us today as quite amazing. Alain Peyrefitte writes: 'Today it is hard to grasp the inhibitory power that the Church retained until the dawn of modern times. For example, on several occasions it anathematized or at least rebuked people not only over linen, handkerchiefs or fine cuts of meat but also over wine, secular music or even laughter.'[53] Later (to humanize a little the last of these prohibitions), Saint Bonaventure, Saint Albert the Great and Saint Thomas Aquinas distinguished immoderate from 'moderate' laughter, the latter being tolerated outside places of worship and times of penance.

The history of interest-bearing loans is indicative of identical problematics and similar evolutions in Islam and Christianity, the only difference being the different timing of change that again rubs in how far we have lagged behind. All the ancient civilizations were hostile to the idea of lending at interest, and it is condemned both in the Bible and in Aristotle's *Politics*. Saint Ambrose permits it only in relation to 'those whom it would not be a crime to kill' (the enemies of the Church), on the grounds that where there is a right of war there is also a right of usury.[54] Pope Alexander III waged relentless war on interest-bearing loans, and the Lateran Council of 1179 reaffirmed the prohibition. To get round it, people came up with the idea of 'selling forward at an increased price', which resembles the *salam* technique we encountered above in Muslim law. In 1185 the Pope condemned this too. And in 1227, Gregory IX condemned bottomry contracts (a precursor of marine insurance), in a move curiously reminiscent of the problem that insurance poses for our ulema.

The Reformation gave the green light for interest-bearing loans, but the Counter-Reformation took a tougher line. The Council of Trent declared: 'Usury was always a most grave and odious crime, even among the pagans ... What is it to lend with usury? What is it to kill a man? ...There is no difference.'[55] Various thinkers tried to find a solution by inventing a distinction between reasonable interest and usury. But Soudret answered them: 'The arguments are pointless; it is necessary to obey or to cease being a Christian.'[56]

It was Calvin who secularized credit by arguing that it was a matter for the civil government, not the Church. From the seventeenth century, interest-bearing loans then began to develop, together with commercial and financial activity, among the Dutch – the 'new Phoenicians' of Europe[57] – and later in Switzerland and England. More generally, with the development of Protestantism, a wind of liberalism and decentralization blew across northern Europe and put an end to 'intellectual inhibition'. Peyrefitte follows Max Weber in concluding: 'Piety, if externally controlled through the prohibitions and commands of a hierarchy, is likely to be an unfavourable environment for the spirit of initiative and innovation. If internalized, however, piety is favourable to it.'[58]

The major difference between Christianity and Islam, which had decisive repercussions in the field of politics, was the existence of the Pope and of Churches that were autonomous *vis-à-vis* states, whereas the clergy of Islam (the ulema) have been intertwined with the state administration. This difference has its roots not in the content of the religions but in history.

Mohammed preached in Arabia, exactly as Jesus had brought the good tidings to Palestine. Both preached a monotheistic doctrine. Without disowning the essential legacy of Abraham and Moses, each of them announced a new religion that challenged the widespread ideas of the time and threatened the interests of the regional notables. Inevitably, they ran up against intense opposition. Their discourse was of peace and they demanded no more than the freedom to preach. But, since their ideas were well received and attracted more and more followers, the opposition to them turned violent. Then came what some call miracle, divine will or predestination and others call an accident of history. Jesus was arrested and crucified. Mohammed, having had similar experiences, escaped death and took refuge among his supporters in Medina, who welcomed him and enabled him to continue his preaching and, once his following became very large, to reconquer Mecca by peaceful means. At the moment of the Hegira, the essence of the divine message – the dogmas, the five pillars of Islam, Islamic morality – had already been revealed.

Ultimately, the key difference between the two religions lies in the conduct of their respective followers after the crucifixion of Jesus and the death of Mohammed. The companions of Jesus adopted a strategy of seeking survival. To avoid persecution and extermination, they offered assurances to those in power that they would not compete with them politically, in accordance with the principle of rendering unto Caesar that which is Caesar's and unto God that which is God's. Each had its distinct field of operation. This was not a slogan or a tactic: it was a fundamental doctrine. Saint Paul explained this as clearly as one could wish: 'My Gospel has nothing to do with temporal affairs. It is a thing apart which concerns only the soul, and it is not my responsibility to unravel or dispatch temporal matters; there are people who have those as their vocation: emperors, princes and authorities. And the source from which they must derive their wisdom is not the Gospel.'[59] At this price, the supporters of Christianity were tolerated by those who held political power. They grew in numbers and were able to organize. In this way the Church established itself in parallel to the state, without any direct ties.

By the end of the third century, however, the Christians had grown so numerous that the conversion of the Roman emperor was a necessity; this is what happened with Constantine the Great, in the year 312 CE. He was not a man of great moral rectitude: he had a court with eunuchs; and, following various palace intrigues, he arranged the death of his eldest son (by his first wife, Minervina) and then that of his second wife, Fausta. Historians have discussed his conversion and concluded that it was probably sincere.[60] But, in any event, he went on to use his new religion to the advantage of his politics. It became the ideology of the 'Christian empire' and he took the title of 'Emperor by the grace of God'. He asserted his will over the Church. It was he who summoned, presided over and conducted the first ecumenical council, at Nicea in 325, a council of the highest importance since it settled the great dogmatic issue of trinitarian theology by declaring that the Son was consubstantial with the Father. The council also solved the problem of Aryanism, and the Emperor subsequently took authoritarian measures against the only two bishops who remained in solidarity with Arius. From that time on, the view was that political stability was intimately bound up with a consensus on religious matters. Several Roman emperors after Constantine imitated him by calling a council of their own: Theodosius II at Ephesus in 431, Justinian at Constantinople in 553, and so on. In short, the structure of the Church remained autonomous because it already had three centuries of existence behind it, but a great interdependence developed between clergy and state – both in the Roman Empire and in the European kingdoms that followed it. The coexistence of political and religious hierarchies was not always an easy business. Investiture disputes and excommunications were dramatic moments in the history of conflict between the two authorities. In the end, however, there was a large degree of cooperation and collusion between them, each using the other while agreeing to serve it.

From the time of the Enlightenment, the struggle for liberty was directed against the monarchy as an authoritarian form of state based on divine right. Democracy could genuinely and lastingly take root in Europe only through the affirmation and application of the state's neutrality in matters of religion. The Church resisted as much as it could but accepted it in the end. Christian thinkers then discovered in their legacy the old principle of rendering unto Caesar that which is Caesar's and unto God that which is God's – a long-forgotten principle but one that should be welcomed today.

Muslim theologians cannot find such a principle in our legacy because circumstances did not favour its emergence. After the Prophet's death, his companions behaved in a very different way from those of Jesus. First of all, the place was different: not Palestine, a province of the Roman Empire with long-established administrative and judicial structures, but an Arabian desert inhabited only by more or less nomadic tribes. Next, the religious Guide was not crucified; on the contrary, he triumphed over his enemies and regained control of Mecca, his birthplace and the religious capital. With the wind in their sails, his companions were therefore tempted to form what had not existed until then: a state. The new religion would serve them as a support and an ideology in their conquests. Islam, instead of spreading peacefully, achieved expansion through force, mainly in Iran and what is today the Arab world. The nascent state needed and took control of the religion. For Muawiyah and the various caliphs who succeeded him, there was no question of helping the *qurrahs* to organize as spokesmen for the new religion and later as its clergy. On the contrary, the caliphs reassured and integrated them, with the aim of both dominating and using them.

The wars of Abu Bakr against the apostates, which had the result of unifying Arabia, had no precedent in the age of the Prophet and, as we have seen, cut across the Koranic principle of freedom of conscience. They were primarily a political operation. In the wars to conquer new lands that began with Omar, religious considerations were not absent, but the chief motive was to seek booty for the soldiers and expansion for their leaders.

The Muslim world is divided into Sunnis, Shiites and Kharigites. At the time when these divisions first appeared, no doctrinal differences separated them; a few nuances appeared later but even those were insignificant. The basis for the conflict was simply the opposition between Ali and Muawiyah, that is, a power struggle. Once Ali had been defeated, his supporters organized into a clergy independent of the state, out of which the ayatollahs and other mullahs of present-day Shiism took shape. As to the Sunni clerics, the victory of Muawiyah meant that they were lodged within the state and would never acquire autonomy. But, in return for using and controlling them, the state would respect the sharia law that they had created.

Thus, no distinction was established between Caesar and God. It was political considerations plus the accidents of history that imposed the confusion between state and religion.

Although, in the Prophet's time, the word *umma* could denote solidarity of the oppressed against their oppressors, the idolatrous Quraysh, and although, at a certain moment in history, it became charged with the sense of a struggle for liberty, the concept has today become an anachronism. The Muslim religion, which formally recognizes neither a clergy nor a Church, should have been and ought to become the religion that encourages the ending of individual alienation and the full affirmation of individual liberty and sovereignty in the choice of beliefs, ideas and behaviour. But instead, because of its history, it has been the religion in which the individual dissolves into the community, loses all autonomy and endures the most oppressive enslavement to society and the state. The legitimation of force by the ulema has prevented the emergence of a theory of democracy and human rights. The Muslim peoples have only ever dreamed of a 'just despot', the type of authority which, in the words of Slim Laghmani, 'inhabits our dreams and nurtures our hopes'.[61]

Whereas most nation-states have freed themselves from their history by submitting it to criticism, we have sacralized our history by ignoring a part of reality. As Ali Mezghani put it, 'in Arab-Islamic civilization, there is a gulf separating the imagination from reality'.[62] The result is that we forbid ourselves to have the slightest critical spirit in relation to history. It is time that we fundamentally changed our attitude, by emancipating the state from Islam and Islam from the state.

Before this can be done, there remains a problem to which Sunni Muslims have not yet found a solution: the handling of religious affairs.

The handling of religious affairs

For several decades, most activists campaigning for democracy and human rights in Muslim countries have laid claim to the principle of secularism, whereas the theologians and fundamentalists have displayed fierce opposition to it. This opposition has taken every possible demagogic form, so that for public opinion secularism no longer means simply the separation of state and religion. It has now become imbued with the meaning of atheism; the secular state is supposed to be necessarily hostile to religion. Most important of all, however, is the fact that French-style secularism is ill suited to Islam. The transfer of Western secularism to Shia Muslim countries will be possible only when circumstances are favourable – thanks to the existence of a religious hierarchy. Such a hierarchy does not exist among Sunni Muslims: they have no pope or church or clergy. If secularism means the separation of state and church, it would not be possible for Sunnis to practise it,[63] because for them it would be a separation between the state and nothing. A more suitable form must therefore be found for the separation of religion and politics.

The specificity of Sunni Islam is that the construction and maintenance of mosques and religious schools have always been funded mainly by the state.[64] Moreover, the state has always appointed the imams who lead prayers in the mosque, the lecturers at the theological universities, and the muftis who advise believers on religious questions. The whole of this sector has always been regarded as a public service. The nature of Islam is such that, in Muslim countries, the state cannot escape its religious obligations. Democracy entails not only the separation of Islam and the state but also, within the state, a separation between its religious and its political functions. That would be a reasonable compromise in keeping with the circumstances, so long as the two kinds of abuses observable today come to an end.

The first of these stems from the fact that fundamentalists, basing themselves on a tradition going back to the early days of Islam (when the mosque was both a place of prayer and a place of instruction and political debate), find it natural to conduct their oppositional political activity inside mosques. They are perfectly consistent in doing so, since they advocate that the confusion of religion, politics and the state should be maintained. This confusion also serves their interests, of course, insofar as they find in places of prayer a potential clientele for their slogans – a fact that the political authorities evidently find disturbing.

The second abuse stems from the fact that, even in modern states, the political authorities often use religion for political ends or interfere in purely religious affairs. In Algeria, for instance, under the Boumedienne presidency, the imams of mosques received every Thursday the text of the sermon they had to deliver the following day before Friday prayers, without changing a word. A similar, though less systematic, policy was attempted in Tunisia under Bourguiba, but it was not successful. What is certain is that it constituted an intolerable interference by the political authorities in religious affairs. In most Muslim countries, it is an age-old tradition that imams end their Friday sermon with prayers in favour of the king or president – a requirement that may trouble the conscience of believers. Such interference becomes even more unacceptable when the public power sets itself up as the interpreter of religion on *ibadat* issues (relations between the believer and God), such as prayers or fasting.

In the early 1980s, the Tunisian League for the Defence of Human Rights had to deal with a problem that indicates the kind of blockage that may result from the confusion of politics and religion in a climate of mistrust between rulers and ruled. In a village in the Sahel, practising believers complained to the League that the man who had been appointed as imam to their mosque was not, in their view, known for good conduct and was unworthy of leading their prayers. They therefore organized what we might call a 'prayer strike' – which was perfectly legitimate, since an imam has to enjoy the confidence of the faithful. After the complaint was lodged with the authorities, it turned out that they had interpreted the 'strike' not as an expression of distrust towards the new iman, but as an act of solidarity with his predecessor, who had been stripped of his functions for using them to conduct anti-government political activity inside the mosque. The attitude of the government was also legitimate, insofar as it wanted to ensure that the mosque remained a place where people could pray together in an atmosphere of calm, not a place riven by political conflict.

In Christian countries, following the legacy of Montesquieu, the secular principle of the separation of powers entails no more than that the executive, legislature and judiciary remain distinct, and that religious authority is represented by the Church. In Muslim countries, where there is no church and no clergy, the Western model of secularism is impracticable. The way of solving the problem would be to create a religious authority along the lines of the judiciary, independent of the other authorities and with no right to interfere in their functions. It would be essentially a moral authority, whose decision-making powers would be confined to the running of mosques. These would be places of prayer and meditation, undisturbed by any ideological dispute or agitation; their political neutrality would have to be clearly asserted and scrupulously respected. Imams would no longer have to pray for the rulers or defend their policies, but they would also have to refrain from any criticism of government action or of the attitudes of the various political currents. With the distinction between law and religion clearly established and universally accepted, muftis and imams would have to keep their words and gestures within the framework of the law, never outside and against it.

This fourth, religious authority would itself have to be democratically organized: there would be elections of imams in each mosque, and the imams in each region would elect both their own mufti and, together with imams from other regions, a Higher Islamic Council and a grand mufti at national level. The actual forms of election would have to be specified when the time came, but the basic principle would be that the imam of each mosque has to be chosen by the believers who usually pray there.

A caricature of our idea might accuse it of tending to establish a disguised church within Islam. But there is no basis for such a charge, since the essence of Islam involves a direct relationship between God and believer, and the institution we propose could not constitute a screen where no such screen can exist.

But the existence of the ulema for fourteen centuries proves that believers need guides to advise them on theological and moral questions. Most of the time, the ulema have been conservatives allied to the regime in power. But there is a strong chance that elected imams in non-political mosques would be more human, more credible and perhaps more audacious. An authority of this kind might one day declare that all the anachronisms of sharia law should be abolished, and such a declaration might be widely accepted by believers.

Finally, an authority of this kind could validly represent Islam in the dialogue with other religions – a dialogue that should be encouraged and intensified in order to improve mutual knowledge among nations and to bring them closer together.

This is a new idea, and there is a risk that, like everything new, it will raise a number of eyebrows. It will probably be met with many reservations and criticisms and, initially perhaps, a degree of rejection. Rulers will be afraid of what might happen if they no longer control the mosques and the whole religious sector. But they are wrong to think they really control it in the present situation; the truth is that they control the consequences, not the causes. They arrest terrorists, but they allow the functionaries of official Islam to spread their traditional false theories which are essentially incompatible with the basis of the modern state and which, by their nature and content, cannot fail to train fundamentalists, some of whom will inevitably give themselves up to violence. You cure a disease by attacking its causes, not its symptoms.

Between traditional official Islam and the fundamentalists, there are differences in behaviour but not at the level of analysis, theory and foundations. Hence links and bridges are necessarily created between the two. When governments finally recognize this evident fact, they will be more receptive to the idea of a fourth authority: that is, a religious authority that accepts the separation between religion and law, and a state that relaxes its hold on individual conscience and no longer uses religion or men of religion for political ends.

When that day comes, governments will rightly seek guarantees that the now-independent religious sector does not turn against the modern state and civil society. Constitutional reforms and appropriate legislation will be required to establish the mechanisms and institutions that ensure the non-political character of mosques and other religious bodies, and ultimately the viability of the system as a whole, through the real separation of the political and religious spheres. A high-level constitutional court will supervise the political neutrality of the religious authority and have the power to dissolve it if it departs from this principle.

The system outlined above is not yet workable because the fundamentalists would not play the game. They would take advantage of it to stir up trouble in the places of worship, to politicize the religious elections, to gain a monopoly over the fourth authority and turn it into a war machine from which to besiege the state. The existence of the fundamentalist current means that our proposal is a plan for the (perhaps distant) future, not a solution for the present. A minority of Islamists, who claim to be sincerely moderate, are calling for 'the organic autonomy of religious institutions'.[65] This certainly appears to be a just demand, but it becomes acceptable and achievable only if the great majority recognize the distinction between the political and religious fields. Such a system therefore presupposes major change in the ways people think of and relate to religion. This is not the same as saying that radical Islamists should become moderate Islamists, for the problem is that Islamism as such vitiates the basis of the distinction between the political and the religious. Observers today call moderate an Islamist who speaks a reasonable language before Westerners and does not openly choose violent action. But even if the peaceful style and the rejection of violence are sincere, the attachment of the movement to the sharia and to the sacralization of history means that the moderation remains provisional. Since the main components of the radicalism have not disappeared, the moderation suggests that what is really involved is a strategy of waiting for the right hour to come.

A good illustration of this point is the Dawa wa Tabligh, an organization created in 1927 and today present throughout the world, which officially preaches the 're-Islamization' of society 'from below' – that is, without aiming to seize power. It provides a classic example of a peaceful and moderate approach. Nevertheless, 'most of the leaders of the armed wing of Algerian Islamism came out of it, following the example of Kamreddine Kherbane, the patron saint of Algerian Afghans'.[66] An ostensibly moderate organization thus produced the most violent cadres for radical action, because *their theoretical basis was the same*.

Only when Islamists accept the legitimacy of *modern, non-sharia systems of law* will Islamism cease to be a politically subversive movement and become simply a reference to a fine and respectable religion; only then will the fourth authority that we have proposed become perfectly feasible. When this happens, Islamists will have accepted that since the Prophet's death all the events involving Islam have been historical and not religious. A large number of enlightened Muslim thinkers have been developing such ideas for the past century and a half, but their work has been little publicized and therefore remains little known.

The Muslim world has not carried out its cultural and educational revolution. In the absence of a Church-like religious authority, this mission falls to governments.

In all the Muslim countries, schools teach the Islamic religion to children. The structure and the extent of this teaching may vary from country to country, but the content is the same. In Turkey, where the state is secular, religious teaching is conducted by the private sector; elsewhere it is the responsibility of state schools. In Saudi Arabia, half of primary education is devoted to religion; elsewhere it has a more reasonable place in the timetable. But the many differences, which may seem important, do not change anything essential. From Turkey at one end to Saudi Arabia at the other, for all their constitutional, political and social differences, the whole spectrum of Muslim countries sees sharia law and Islamic history taught in the most classical manner, just as they were a thousand years ago. Everywhere those who attend such classes are told that it is necessary to cut off the hand of a thief, to stone those guilty of adultery, to kill apostates, to close banks and to wage war on infidels, and everywhere too they are told that the caliphate was the legitimate regime *par excellence* – even if, in the political, social, economic and legal spheres, the exact opposite is done. Believers are therefore torn between two contradictory ways of thinking: the one they learn and the one they practise. If this is combined with reasons for discontent, the drift into fundamentalism will inevitably begin to tempt a section of public opinion.

Here it is instructive to consider briefly the Turkish experience of the past fifteen years. In this country that has preached and practised secularism since 1924, the Islamist party Rafah scored a number of electoral breakthroughs, won a majority in 1990 in several large cities including the capital, and headed the government for a number of months. To explain this success, we should mention that in Turkey 20 per cent of children and young people pass through a private Islamic system of schooling (Koranic schools at primary level, *imama et khatabat* schools at secondary level, and theology faculties in higher education) – a system run by Islamists, or anyway people with a traditional formation, who teach the sharia in its classical form. At the same time, 20 per cent of the electorate voted for the Rafah. The identity of these two figures is evidently not accidental. The education received in youth largely determines choices in adult life.

Erbaken, the leader of the Rafah party, managed to become prime minister with the support of a parliamentary coalition and took a number of measures inspired by Islamism. The army opposed these, and as Erbaken had only one fifth of the electoral vote he was forced to resign. When the party was dissolved, in 1998, its members took the opportunity of the constitution of a new party to change their political line and to choose new leaders.

The ensuing Justice and Development Party (AKP), regrouping the old Islamists under the leadership of Recep Tayep Erdogan, has explicitly accepted the secular principle, no longer refers to sharia law and no longer describes itself as Islamist. In Ankara, on 12 October 2003, Erdogan stated to the first ('refoundation') congress of the AKP: 'We are a democratic conservative party. Our formation does not rest on either a religious or an ethnic basis.' He then quoted Kemal Atatürk and added: 'We intend to act in such a way that Turkey becomes part of the civilized world'; he promised a Turkey 'free of ideological approaches'. Journalists noted the presence of unveiled women and the fact that male and female delegates were not physically separated, whereas, at all congresses of Islamist parties, women had all been veiled and separated from the men.

At the same congress, the parliamentary deputy Eyup Fatsa, one of the party's founders, declared: 'We are sincerely engaged in establishing a genuine democracy in Turkey. Religion should remain a matter of personal choice and in no case an obligation. … Turkey has Muslims, Jews, Alevi [Shiites] and atheists. All are Turks, and the state must be neutral and secular.' Another delegate, Murat Mercan, added: 'Yes, we have changed, because we have understood that Turks do not want religion to be instrumentalized by politicians. The Koran does not solve the problems of society. It simply professes values: do not commit adultery, do not steal, and so on.' This is precisely the discourse of a secular Muslim. The observer Ahmed Sever concluded: 'The historical mission of this party is to show the world that Islam can live with secularism, modernity and democracy.'[67]

Observers agree that those who support the application of sharia law are a small minority in the AKP. Thus Turkish Islamists have concluded from their many failures that classical Islamism, with its call for the reconstitution of an Islamic state and a return to the sharia, is no longer viable in today's world. In this way the party has opened up to a large number of members who no longer invoke Islam as their point of political reference. The party managed to win a parliamentary majority at the elections of 3 November 2002 and to form a new government on its own. If the experiment is successful, it will be a huge step forward for the Muslim world and prove that it is perfectly possible to reconcile Islam with liberty and secularism.

Nevertheless, the coexistence of an officially proclaimed (and actually applied) secularism with a government of Islamist inspiration is a seeming paradox that deserves some explanation. Let us first recall that the AKP is far from having a majority of the popular vote; its 34 per cent gave it a parliamentary majority only by virtue of a most peculiar electoral law. Next, the electoral breakthrough came in the wake of the gravest financial crisis in Turkey's history, amid a wave of discontent caused by mishandling of the economy by a corrupt political class. These two conjunctural factors compounded the structural factor we have already mentioned: the existence of a large traditional sector in education which ensures that one-fifth of children are brought up to be Islamists. This private sector specializing in religious education is a consequence of the fundamental secular principle that forbids the teaching of religion in state schools. In the end, this self-denial of the state with regard to involvement in religious affairs has been a kind of trap, which prevents the state from acting as a driving force for liberty and social progress.

In the Muslim world, a secular state is not enough to separate politics from religion; action in the educational and cultural fields is also necessary. Where the educational system creates or encourages fundamentalism, it is through the educational system that fundamentalism can and must be combated.

Our proposed system involving a politically independent fourth authority is not viable so long as this disharmony remains between political life, with its economic and social content, and a value system conveyed by the traditional organs of culture and education. On the other hand, if education is reformed so that it spreads modern ideas in keeping both with the essence of Islam and with the evolution of social and political structures in most Muslim countries, then the fundamentalist temptation will disappear once a majority of believers have been educated in the new system. Or, at the very least, the influence of fundamentalism will be greatly reduced.

For the moment, then, the first priority for the Muslim world is a radical overhaul of the educational system.

4

Education and Modernity

Not all politics is dirty; not all action is vain.

Pierre Mendès-France

On 4 November 1995 Itzhak Rabin, prime minister of Israel, a lucid and courageous man who had decided to make peace with the Palestinians, was assassinated in a cowardly way by Yigal Amir, who was soon discovered to be a student at the Bar Ilan religious university in Tel Aviv. Was there a link between his abominable crime and the religious education he had received? The answer became a clear 'yes' when it was learned that all the Israelis who had distinguished themselves in recent years for their crimes against Palestinians had acted out of religious motives:[1] Baruch Goldstein, the killer of Hebron, who gunned down twenty-nine Palestinians at the Abraham mosque on 25 February 1994, and Noam Friedman, a soldier who wounded six Palestinians at a vegetable market in Hebron, are but two examples. Rabbi Yehuda Amichai, head of the moderate Zionist organization Meimad, concluded: 'We are guilty of the education we gave a whole generation, which has been making use of the dangerous and harmful religious tradition of *halacha*.'[2] The title of *rav*, awarded by Israeli Talmudic schools, is the crowning achievement in an ultra-specialized education that does not include in its syllabus even liberal Jewish thinkers such as Maimonides.[3]

It would seem to be a universal law that, if they are given a free hand, men of religion prefer to monopolize education, to keep it within the religious sphere, and above all to teach the most orthodox theories. That is certainly how things were for a long time in Christian civilization. In the year 529, Justinian closed the schools of so-called pagan philosophy;[4] there was no longer any intellectual life except in the bishops' palaces and the abbeys. The Church took charge of all the structures of education, which was made to conform to official orthodoxy and to serve the purposes mainly of religious instruction and liturgical chanting. In 1210 the Council of Paris condemned the teaching of Aristotelianism – a position reaffirmed by popes Gregory IX and Urban IV. The same applied to Thomism, the first truly profound and original Christian philosophy. Despite his apparent hostility to Averroës, Aquinas found inspiration in his work and sought to reconcile rationalism with Christian thought.[5] The Faculté de Décret in Paris – a precursor of the law faculty, created in 1213 – was supposed to teach nothing other than ecclesiastical law; Roman law, in particular, was a forbidden area.[6]

In 1524 the king created the Collège de France as a counterweight to the religious establishments. The rivalry between Church and royal power would prove beneficial, since it led academic authorities to accept a degree of openness and encouraged teachers to enlarge their field of knowledge and research. A green light was given for the teaching of Thomism and Roman law.

During this time, in the lands of Islam, the ulema abandoned all the profane sciences – the mathematics of Khawarizmi and the medicine of Ibn al-Jazzar were forgotten – and made do with religious knowledge that was 'supposedly unchanging and, like a clone, could reproduce itself *ad infinitum* in a time outside history'.[7] Those who held the reins of power let them get on with it for century after century.

In the Christian world, the existence of a political authority clearly distinct from the religious authority had a beneficial effect on cultural and scientific, and later economic, development, whereas in the Muslim world the bundling together of the two authorities favoured immobility.

In the early nineteenth century, the shock of Bonaparte's expedition to Egypt as well as Tunisia's uninterrupted contact with the northern shores of the Mediterranean encouraged the emergence of the first reformers: Kabadou, Bayram, Bouhajeb and Ibn Abi Dhiaf in Tunisia; Mohamed Ali and Tahtawi in Egypt, who both worked for an opening to the world (especially through the creation of educational institutions) but were unable to shake Al Azhar or the Zituna. Later, Thaalbi, Abderrazak and Haddad went further along the road of reform but were beaten down by those same traditional institutions. Then the religious institutions began to lose their influence, so that in the 1950s and 1960s the ulema came to seem relics, unable to compete with intellectuals and experts trained in Europe or the new national schools.[8] But the evolution was rarely linear, and since the 1970s we have witnessed a revival of fundamentalism.

The origin of this evil is to be found in the educational system. Modern governments, having given up hope of reforming traditional education, established a modern public sector alongside it. But this modern sector was always supposed to provide religious training. And, for the religious syllabus as well as for the teaching of Arabic, educationalists turned to the numerous former pupils of religious institutions, who brought with them their programmes, their methods and their mentality. *The worm was in the fruit from the start.*

In Tunisia, in the last years of the French protectorate, barely 15 per cent of children aged six were attending school. Immediately after independence, the new government adopted a policy of mass education but, for lack of personnel with a modern training, had to recruit many teachers with a traditional background. Morocco followed the same course, whereas Algeria relied on the assistance of Egyptian volunteers. But, in all these countries, teachers with a totally outdated training found themselves in a few decades training the whole of the youth. They created in their pupils a split mentality that resulted from the gulf between the system of values and references taught at school and the social and political reality. In extreme cases, this led to the production of schizophrenics and terrorists.

Thus, the birth of the fundamentalist movement resulted from a divorce between society and its educational institutions. The crisis will continue so long as a cure has not been found for this dangerous dysfunctionality, but it will go down in history as no more than a passing episode if the disease can be rapidly diagnosed and properly treated.

A brief look at the record of Tunisia over the past century or more will show the close link between the content of education at any given moment and the ideology dominating the minds of young people and adults a few years later.

The evolution of education in Tunisia

The first reforms

After some three centuries of social-economic stagnation and cultural slumber, Tunisia began to become aware of its backwardness and to initiate a process of renewal. The key date in this respect was 1840, the year of the founding of the École militaire polytechnique at Bardo, which began to teach foreign languages (as an opening to the world) and the exact sciences (as an initiation into the new technologies of the time). For the next forty-one years – the French invasion and protectorate date from 1881 – a series of reforms marked the beginning of a quiet revolution: the abolition of slavery in 1842–46; the adoption of the Fundamental Pact (a kind of declaration of human rights) in 1857; and the first constitution and legal code in 1861. These texts may appear inadequate to us today, but they were remarkable for their time.

The legal code, in particular, is of astonishing modernity. Article 203 lists the punishments that may be inflicted on lawbreakers: the death penalty, forced labour, imprisonment, banishment and fines. And Article 204 adds: 'It is forbidden to pass sentences other than those in the preceding article which might cause physical suffering.' Apostasy is not mentioned and is therefore not liable to punishment.

In fact, the legislature merely confirmed and strengthened a development that had begun a century and a half before. Since the reign of the founder of the Hussein dynasty (1705–1735), the Bey himself had presided over the sharia council when it was a matter of trying someone for a serious crime, while lesser offences came under the jurisdiction of the *qaid*, the regional governor. Gradually the political rulers had secularized the criminal justice system. The people were happy with this trend because religious justice was costly and its magistrates corrupt.[9] A popular Islam thus developed which left Muslim criminal law completely out of the picture. This was what Fathi Triki called 'customary Islam rooted in the folds of Tunisian society', which is essentially 'a social ethic of mutual aid, hospitality, tolerance, generosity, moderation and reverence'.[10]

In the countryside, peasant customs ignored the severity of sharia law. It was quite common for a young man and woman to run away from their *douar* or region because their families would not let them marry, but usually the families would bow before the *fait accompli*. In the case of a formal complaint, the courts imposed a fine of ten camels on the man if they had already married,[11] and reduced this by half if the girl was unmarried. It was all a long way from death by stoning, or even from sentences of lashing.

The 1861 code continued to recognize this offence (in Article 263) without prescribing severe penalties; the softening of punishment thus had official approval, and continued to do so all the way down to the contemporary decriminalization of elopement except in the case of minors. This was the way of life for the great majority of Tunisians, since at that time only 10 per cent (or, some say, no more than 12–13 per cent) of the population was urbanized.[12] In the towns, prostitution was accepted both by the state and by the population. Dalenda and Abdelhamid Larguèche write: 'Tolerated and even regulated prostitution was an ancient fact … which, in the case of the modern Maghreb, goes back at least to the beginning of the Ottoman period.'[13] Article 281 of the code punished the sale of alcoholic beverages – except in shops specially licensed for the purpose!

In the end, the state remained faithful to Islam, which continued to be the point of reference for the whole population. But it was a popular Islam, different from the one in books. A long evolution, never conceptualized but no less real for that, smoothed the rough edges and toned down the excesses of the sharia. Muslims, whether practising or non-practising, peacefully coexisted with one another and with Jewish and foreign minorities. Bedouin women were not forced to wear the veil, and were thus able to work in the fields and to take part in a (to some extent) mixed social life.

In the city customs were less relaxed, but the severity was not taken too far. In the middle of the nineteenth century, the French consul in Sousse even noted the existence of a few mixed couples, including a Muslim woman living with a Christian in a partnership that the state and the local population seemed to accept.[14] Female adultery was punished with banishment. 'Now that people are no longer drowned for adultery, culpable or overly tender women who would formerly have suffered a harsher fate are sent [to the Kerkena islands] … if their affronted husband lodges a complaint.'[15]

But education, relatively uncommon and wholly traditional, was the one exception to this understanding of Islam on the part of officialdom and the wider population. In the *koutteb* schools there were 1250 *meddebs* who taught boys the alphabet, some elements of Arabic grammar and the recitation of the Koran.[16] The Zituna, which gave an education corresponding to secondary and higher levels, had at most a thousand students. These were intended to become sharia judges, notaries and mosque imams,[17] but the rate of absenteeism was high and, at the end of the nineteenth century, little more than three hundred students actually sat the exam.[18]

Education was purely a matter of studying the Arabic language and the Muslim religion; there was no place for science, mathematics or technical subjects. For the thirty to forty sheikhs who taught at the Zituna,[19] the only history worth narrating was the history of Islam, preferably that of the Prophet and the four 'wise caliphs'. The history of Tunisia before the Islamic occupation was proudly ignored, as was the ancient and modern history of the rest of the universe. Muslim law was understood in the most classical sense, in keeping with the most orthodox theories. It was therefore enough to teach what was seen as the sharia in its original purity. Teachers mentioned the existence of the Mutazilites, for example, but only to say that they were misguided; no attempt was made to impart knowledge of their theories, still less to discuss them. As to Ibn Khaldun or Averroës, they were completely ignored, and so no reference was made to the former's sociological approach or the latter's rationalism. Teaching methods served only to 'fill people's minds'. Long ago, Ibn Khaldun already deplored the decline of education and explained it by the fact that students learned by rote and did not discuss anything.

It did not matter that politics and social customs had undergone considerable evolution: the design, content and personnel of the educational system remained in an ivory tower, remote from any considerations of space and time. Apart from questions of marriage, divorce and inheritance – as these were practised in the towns and judged by sharia courts – Zituna education corresponded to neither the needs nor the reality of Tunisian society. Teachers and students alike were aware that they were developing in a kind of 'unreal world', a world described in books written many centuries before by ulema whose circumstances had little in common with those of nineteenth-century Tunisia.

The divergence was indeed great between real-life Islam and the Islam taught at those schools. The former was the religion of a people who had dropped much of the sharia because of its excessive harshness but had kept the core belief in God and his Prophet, the hope of reaching Paradise after death, a profound humanism and a fine set of values. The experiences of Sufism, based on love of God and one's neighbour, were extremely interesting in this respect. It was an Islam of the innermost heart, resting on deep conviction and communion with God. Sometimes it would involve collective manifestations, but these were always purely voluntary and entirely peaceful.

Hardline school Islam, on the other hand, disregarded the reality of society and rejected any idea of evolution. Normally that kind of divergence is not viable for long: those who receive the hardline education will seek either to influence society by moving it closer to the learned ideal (the approach of fundamentalists at a much later date) or to change the education by bringing it closer to the social reality. The passivity we have been discussing was a consequence of the small number of teachers and students at the time. Later, when education and the possibilities for influencing young people underwent huge expansion, they became the source of major difficulties, since the seeds of fundamentalism had already been sown.

From the very beginning of the movement for a renaissance of Tunisia, the political authorities were aware of the urgent need to reform education. Alongside the creation of the Bardo military college, a number of measures were taken to reform the Zituna: the decree of 21 February 1840, the decree of 1 December 1842, the appointment of a reform commission that operated between April and June 1862, and so on. But these various initiatives ran up against the conservatism of the Zituna and ended in failure.[20]

Later, when the great reformer Khereddine, the true founder of modern Tunisia, was appointed prime minister, he drew the appropriate conclusions from this setback. To be sure, he did not entirely despair of the Zituna since he passed more decrees in 1875 and 1876 to reorganize its teaching work, but in 1875 he also created the modern Sadiki college, which taught science and foreign languages as well as Arabic and religion. This initiative had momentous consequences for the future of the country. Sadiki became the training ground for the Tunisian elite, for the founders and leaders of the independence struggle and subsequently builders of modern Tunisia. The other side of the coin was the split in the training, attitudes and perspectives of young people.

Somewhat schematically, we may say that the Sadikians had Tunisia as their fatherland and the European Enlightenment as their model; while the Zitunians had Medina as their fatherland and the 'wise caliphs' (described in the apologetic literature) as their model. This division became serious when the two educational systems began to expand in the first half of the twentieth century.

In the early years of the century, Sadikians enamoured of liberty and modernity founded the Young Tunisians, a precursor of the national Destour and neo-Destour party.[21] In their paper, *Le Tunisien*, they called for social and economic reforms and criticized colonization in all its forms, at first with moderation but then with ever greater radicalism. In fact, they were always radical in their demand for modernization of the country. They tried to strengthen the activist base by winning over Zituna students, but at the same time criticized them at the level of social and political analysis.

Abdeljalil Zaouche wrote in *Le Tunisien* on 25 February 1909: 'How would it serve twentieth-century Muslims to return to the civilization of their ancestors and remain strangers to scientific progress? Have Italians merely restored Roman civilization, or Greeks been content, as in the past, to give themselves up to the arts and philosophy?'[22] The Zitunians, for their part, characterized the Sadikians as colonized minds imbued with suspect religious beliefs.

The history of Tunisian society in the years before independence was one long series of conflicts and reconciliations between Zitunians and Sadikians. Thus, after the Young Tunisians had demanded the codification of law and the modernization of justice, *Le Tunisien* wrote on 28 February 1910 that the education received by former students of the Zituna was 'too incomplete for them to exercise with authority such important functions as those of a judge'.[23] This struck a blow at both the material and the moral interests of Zitunians, for it tended to block their recruitment to the judiciary and to question the competence of people who thought they had received a sound legal education based on religion. It also hit at their position in society, since they would be deprived of the judicial power of command and the prestige associated with it. This explains the vehemence of their anger directed at the Young Tunisians.

In fact, both sides took up passionate positions. One has only to read some of the articles from March 1910, especially in *Azzohra, Assaweb*,

Morched el Umma and *Le Tunisien*, to appreciate how readily they traded arguments and insults. The debate soon went beyond the particular issue that had triggered it, turning into a fierce *Kulturkampf* apparently between religion and secularism, Francophonia and Arabhood, East and West, but in reality between tradition and modernity. Yet the debates never reached the degree of passion that makes people lose their reason. From the beginning, *Azzohra* preached moderation and played a conciliatory role by stressing the patriotism of the Young Tunisians; it even accepted that there were defects in the Zituna education, despite the respect due to the sheikhs who taught there and were real scholars in their field. Consequently, it became possible to end the invective and to concentrate on discussion of the essential issue. Zitunians once again demanded a reform of syllabuses and teaching methods and, in April 1910, even applauded a speech given in their midst by the leader of the Young Tunisians, Ali Bach Hamba, against whom they had directed such heated invective just a month before.[24] And in May, when the protest movement met with a violent reaction from the colonial authorities, it was Young Tunisian activists who took up the defence of the Zitunians.[25]

This was just one among many similar episodes that punctuated political life in Tunisia, in parallel with the anti-colonial struggle in which both tendencies participated until the achievement of independence.

Independence

After independence, the founders and leaders of the national movement – that is, the modernists – got down to the building of a new state and the division of responsibilities. The modernists first assigned to themselves the leadership of the sectors crucial to national sovereignty: foreign affairs, armed forces, police and national guard. In all these sensitive areas, cadres with a Zituna background were accepted only in subordinate or executive positions. The same was true for the technical sectors (agriculture, industry, public works, communications and health), where young people with a traditional education could not even hold middle-ranking posts of responsibility, not because they were distrusted but because they did not have the necessary competence. In the main, then, the Tunisian state was built without the Zitunians, and as a result many of them continued to bear a powerful grudge. This can be glimpsed in a long interview given by Ghannouchi, leader of the Tunisian Islamists. In his view, 'during those times, everything revolved around the Zituna: traditional handicrafts, Tunisian literature, the whole of Tunisia is the product of the Zituna'.[26] Of course, this account is contrary to the historical facts and shows that the person in question is living in a world of his imagination. He is at least a century behind the times. He forgets that the national movement was founded outside the Zituna, by activists who met with opposition from the Zituna. He forgets that industry had to be rapidly built up alongside handicrafts, and that no Zitunian had been trained for that task. It was not he or people with his kind of education who created modern Tunisia, and his statements show that this still visibly rankles with him. In the three pages of his interview, the word 'alienation' appears four times. All this throws some light on political behaviour and attitudes. Are we talking here of a human problem that was understandable in itself and required a solution? Perhaps. But the leaders of the independence movement concentrated on the social aspect: the unemployment that seriously affected Zitunians. They therefore employed Zitunians on a large scale in sectors such as justice and education, where they were thought to have the necessary minimum of training.

In reality, these two sectors were not considered to be of secondary importance. It was just that the new leaders thought they could simply set broad guidelines and leave the execution of policies up to cadres with a traditional background. Their decision was probably unavoidable – anyway, at the time it seemed to be justified. But it was fraught with serious consequences.

In the case of the justice system, as we have seen, a revolutionary Code of Personal Status was adopted in the first few months after independence. The judges, who nearly all were of a traditional formation, did not take kindly to the code. Of course, they did not place themselves outside the law and they applied the clearest and most important provisions: the abolition of polygamy and marital repudiation, and so on. But, whenever a clause contained an element of ambiguity and needed to be interpreted, they took advantage of the situation to revert to Muslim law. This was the case with divorce, recognition of parentage, custody of children, religious differences in relation to marriage or inheritance, and international disputes. To force their hand, the legislature intervened a number of times to impose modern solutions for particular problems. But, as a whole, Tunisian family law today suffers from an opposition between the modernity of the texts and the traditionalist interpretation that certain judges sometimes give of them.

The same points apply to education. Already in the first two years after independence, a decision was taken to introduce universal education gradually and to adopt the Sadikian system (with a few modifications that did not affect its spirit) at both primary and secondary levels. Arabic was on the timetable, therefore, but the teaching of foreign languages occupied a large place and began as early as primary school. The syllabuses for philosophy, history, geography, civic education and religious education were drawn up in a spirit of modernity and openness to the world. At the same time, the Zituna upper school was gradually wound down, since the many reforms to the system there had never yielded the expected results. All that remained was its higher education function, but the limited prospects that this offered meant that the intake of students became smaller and smaller.

To assist in the spread of mass education, Zitunians were recruited in large numbers both at primary level and as teachers of Arabic and religion in the colleges and lycées. It was thought that, once swallowed up in the mass of teachers, they would be unable to pass on their plans for society to future generations.

However, like the judges who applied the Code of Personal Status by reverting at every opportunity to sharia law, the Zitunian teachers naturally tended to implement the new programmes in a traditionalist spirit. It is true that, in the climate of the times, many of these teachers commented accurately on the texts in the syllabus, most of them by enlightened authors; but others performed their work more grudgingly and took every opportunity to slip in their own views. Thus, pockets of inflexibility and even fanaticism were able to exist and spread in certain educational institutions, encouraged by primary teachers, lycée teachers, inspectors and even administrators. Thanks to the vigilance of the political authorities, this tendency did not become too serious and the system remained generally viable, but it was a rather unstable equilibrium.

The deviation

In the late 1960s the instability in the educational sector was compounded by political instability, as the system based on a single party, a single way of thinking and a personality cult began to run out of steam. Democratic and left-wing protest movements were a rumbling presence on all sides. The Perspectives movement, in particular, so named after an underground paper that appeared between 1962 and 1968, gained new strength. But it was also weakened by internal ideological conflict: a leftist majority around the leadership embraced the Maoism that was then making some headway in Europe, and a minority still wedded to the ideas of progress and democracy was marginalized or forced to leave the group. Despite this diversion, however, the democratic and socialist movement remained influential in the political arena and had an especially strong presence in the university. Thrown into turmoil by the example of France, where the student protests of May 1968 had a contagious effect on the rest of society, the Tunisian political authorities decided to resort to strongarm tactics. Arrests followed by the hundred, torture was used on detainees, and a notorious State Security Court was set up which sentenced several dozen activists to long terms of imprisonment. Already in 1965 Habib Achour, leader of the would-be independent UGTT trade union federation, had been arrested on a false pretext. And a few years later, in 1971, opposition broke out within the single party at its Monastir Congress, which changed the statutes, restored the system of elections to the Political Bureau, and elected a leadership dominated by 'liberals'.

To regain control of the party, the youth and the street, the 'enlightened despot' Bourguiba ensured that despotism would have the upper hand over clear-sightedness. A new party congress, symbolically held in the same town three years later, revoked the decisions of the Monastir Congress, but some ballast had to be thrown overboard to keep happy a rank and file that had to a considerable extent been trained by teachers with a Zituna background. With this in mind, the Higher Council of National Education met in panic on the eve of Monastir II to order a doubling of the number of hours of Islamic education. Already, by administrative fiat, teachers of religious education had been put in charge of civic education as well – a subject entirely outside their field of competence and alien to their ideology. This led to a tripling of their teaching load, which considerably increased their ideological influence over young people.

During this period, from 1970 to 1975, history, geography and philosophy – which had until then been taught in lycées by Tunisians with a modern training or, if necessary, by French volunteers – were meant to be thoroughly Arabized. Foreign volunteers were sent home, and Tunisians incapable of Arabizing their classes in a few weeks were assigned to subordinate functions and replaced with less qualified teachers (ordinary holders of the baccalaureate 'plus 1', etcetera) or former Zitunians who had studied in universities in the East and were more sensitive than Western-trained colleagues to Arabist or Islamist 'identity' issues.

The decision to go for Arabization was entirely legitimate. But if it had not been taken hastily for political reasons, and if the Tunisian university had been charged with rapidly training the necessary teachers, the negative aspects might have been avoided. For, especially in philosophy, the turn involved not only linguistic Arabization but, to a large extent, Arabization and Islamization of the subject matter as well.

The fact is that, for all the subjects in question, teaching content is more important than issues concerning timetable, language or teacher training. And the traditionalist tendency won more and more compromises precisely in the choice of content, the drafting of manuals and the selection of texts to be studied.

In the teaching of philosophy, all non-Muslim thinkers were treated superficially – when they were not simply ignored. The same was true of enlightened Muslim philosophers, whereas a lot of space was given to Ghazali and his school. The old distinction between general and Islamic philosophy disappeared as the latter virtually engulfed the former. Taught as it often was by people without proper training, the whole subject ended up sounding more like theology than philosophy. As to the teaching of French and English, there was no longer any question of using texts by Montesquieu, Rousseau or Locke, but only newspaper articles dealing with various shallow matters. Language was seen as a vehicle for the learning of the sciences, not of foreign cultures. Civic education became a subject without substance, no longer referring to democracy or human rights and still less to the theories underpinning them or the mechanisms for their protection.

Islamic education classes left out in its entirety the renewal movement, from Mohamed Abdu through Jameleddine al-Afghani to Tahar Haddad. There was less and less talk of spirituality and more and more of sharia and politics. Corporal punishment returned to the textbooks, and the most reactionary sharia laws were taught as if the great innovations of the Code of Personal Status had never been introduced. Students learned that a husband may renounce his wife at any moment, as if the whole movement for female emancipation had never happened, and that he may strike her regardless of the law punishing such actions.[27] Turning their back on the Constitution, with its provision for a republican system of government, the new manuals taught that the caliphate was the only legitimate regime, that a Muslim who did not submit to a caliph was to all intents and purposes an infidel, and that democracy should be rejected because it was a Western doctrine alien to our civilization[28] or a system incompatible with Islam.[29] Nor was that all. They taught the obligation to wage *jihad* and the right to reduce prisoners of war to slavery, and even stated that anyone who denied the obligation to pray was an apostate who, like all apostates, should be put to death.[30] Criticism of modern Western philosophers caricatured their positions in a single sentence, describing them as unbelievers (Bertrand Russell), Zionists (Jean-Paul Sartre), and so on, and forbidding Muslims to read their work.[31] Attacking both communism and capitalism, the manuals concluded that Islam was the best social-economic system and thereby made of it not a religion but a form of politics. They also sacralized and idealized in the extreme the history of Islam.

As to the teaching of Arabic literature during this period of deviation, writers forming part of the Tunisian renaissance (Taha Hussein or Kacem Amin, for example) were neglected in favour of less committed authors. Illustrations of grammatical rules or verb conjugations were mostly taken from religious texts, since the drafting of manuals of Arabic language and literature also served the purpose of strengthening political Islam in the minds of pupils.[32] In short, for a period of twenty years, public educational establishments operated as schools for the training of Islamist cadres.

The educational policy adopted and applied in the first half of the 1970s therefore had a clear aim: to inject doses of Arabism and Islamism at school, as a vaccination against the leftist ideas then in vogue at university. Of course, there was never any risk that Tunisia would go over to the communist camp. The widespread introduction of compulsory cooperatives during those years paralysed the economy and caused the population to reject the whole idea; all the more violent would have been their reaction to a Soviet-style statization of the economy. The few hundred students who chanted Maoist slogans were completely isolated from the rest of the population, living in the hothouse atmosphere of the university campus.

What really stuck in the throat was that the students touched the untouchable. Their pamphlets dared to describe Bourguiba as the 'supreme comedian', and their banners proclaimed that 'the only supreme fighter is the people'. That was lese-majesty, the unforgivable crime. In regimes of personal rule, the person of the leader counts more than all the rest. The regime can ally itself with the devil so long as the devil does not criticize the august figure of the president. The Islamists of the time, no more than a small group of traditionalist heirs to the cultural legacy of the ulema, had sufficient intelligence – mixed with a strong dose of opportunism – to play the role of such a respectful 'devil' in relation to the president. Whereas the regime had until then controlled the whole press without exception, it gave the go-ahead in 1972 for the publication of the Islamist paper *Al Maarifa*, and later of *Jawhar al-Islam* and *Al Mujtama*, thinking that since they did not criticize the president or the one-party system they would not present any danger.

To authorize publication of a newspaper or journal is to accept a liberty, to recognize a right. But to foster a far-right opposition while jailing far-left students is to handle political problems with police action and opportunist methods. A democratic debate would have been juster and more effective, but the regime would have none of it. Democratic debate was against its nature. Its chosen strategy, unjust and inappropriate at the time it was adopted, became dangerous for the future when it was extended to education. One cannot touch that sensitive area with impunity. And the doses of Arabization and Islamization injected into syllabuses and textbooks in the early 1970s were starting to bear their bitter fruit by the end of the same decade. Bourguiba, who sometimes showed real brilliance, here committed the worst mistake in the thirty or more years of his rule. He played a clever game of manipulation and lost. In trying to crush a democratic opposition which, despite leftist deviations, posed no threat to society or the state, he brought into being a fundamentalist opposition that had not existed before.

It should be added, however, that this policy certainly exceeded what Bourguiba had intended. In the final years of his rule, exhausted by age and infirmity, he clung to power but was not capable of really governing or of controlling the way in which his decisions were implemented. Zealous underlings went much further down the slippery slope, out of a mixture of demagogy and personal calculation.

A few years of the new educational policies were enough to see the birth of the fundamentalist movement, and a few years later it had grown to a considerable size, especially among university students, at a time when nothing in Tunisia's economic and social situation could account for such a breakthrough. What was happening in education was the only explanation for these major political events.

It might be objected that it was the rise of Khomeini and the Iranian revolution that led to the birth of a fundamentalist movement throughout the Muslim world, and that young people in Tunisia were merely following the general trend. But the objection does not hold water. For, in the 1970s, the Tunisian modernist movement already had deep roots from more than a century of activity and achievement, and traditionalists were marginal in the extreme. The Muslim Brotherhood, which had been around for fifty years in the Middle East, did not exist in Tunisia; the traditionalist fire had burned itself out. All the power of the state was required to rekindle it from the ashes, and the school system was needed to make it grow again.

This analysis of Tunisia obviously cannot be extended to the whole of the Arab world. Each country has its distinctive features. But, if the link is now clear between school syllabuses and the attitudes of young people, we can conclude that throughout the Arab world educational policy has been one of the main factors behind the Islamist wave, and that educational reforms are one of the key elements that may provide a way out of the crisis.

Islamism and education in the Arab countries

In ways that have varied with circumstances, though always under the pressure of traditionalists, all the Arab countries have experienced a manipulation of the educational system due mostly to demagogic policies or a lack of awareness of what was at stake. Or perhaps both. We find here a number of factors reminiscent of those we have already seen at work in Tunisia. In particular, the situation of the Zituna was in every respect comparable to that of Al Azhar in Egypt or the Qarawiyin in Morocco. Egypt's Al Azhar university missed out on modernization because, in a spirit of conservatism, it resisted all the reform initiatives taken by various political authorities between 1805 and 1952.[33]

The fact that this situation persists in most Arab-Muslim countries does not augur well for the future.

Since 1996, the Tunis-based Arab Human Rights Institute has been engaged in a study of 'education and human rights', with a focus on school syllabuses and textbooks in twelve Arab countries that have subscribed to international conventions on human rights. Its national reports show that education contrary to human rights exists in nearly all of these countries, although the frequency and gravity of the conflict varies from country to country. There can be no question here of offering a comparative analysis, still less of drawing up an exhaustive table. But let us simply mention a few revealing samples.

The many years of civil war between Muslims and non-Muslims in Sudan explain, but do not justify, the long passages on *jihad* that have been introduced into school textbooks there, in which an apology for violence is combined with frequent references to sharia law.[34]

In Egyptian textbooks, there is talk of tolerance but also an insistence that Islam is the only true religion.[35] The books invoke the obligation under sharia law to order the doing of good and the avoidance of evil, with the explanation that the struggle against evil can be conducted in word and in deed. This would be a justification, not even very indirect, for the violence that Islamists employ against the state and individuals.[36]

The position of women is always depicted as inferior to that of men; mother is in the kitchen while father is in the library.[37] This is not only a social fact but a religious rule. A Yemeni schoolbook even goes so far as to recall the sharia rule that a woman's submission to God – that is, her Islamic identity – cannot be accepted unless it goes together with submission to her husband. A married woman's prayers will not be received on any day on which her husband is dissatisfied with her. This implies a permanent duty of absolute obedience.[38]

In most Arab countries, it is not only in religious education that one finds an apologetic presentation of the history of Islam. Here, for example, is a passage from the Moroccan book *Rules of the Arabic Language*,[39] which might be translated as follows:

> Haroun ar-Rashid was eloquent, generous, noble and intelligent. He alternated between a pilgrimage to Mecca one year and the waging of holy war the next. He was a man of letters with a lively mind. He knew by heart the noble Koran. He was a great scholar, endowed with a refined aesthetic sense

and a great capacity for proper judgement. He was courageous in supporting the triumph of justice.

But we happen to know that Haroun ar-Rashid, though certainly a great Abbasid caliph, was neither a saint in his private life (he had numerous concubines, and engaged in evenings of heavy drinking …) nor a just ruler (his way of liquidating the Barmaki, for instance, says a lot about his sense of justice). This gives us some idea of the distance between reality and the idealized image in the textbooks.

Moroccan schoolbooks, like their equivalents in other Arab countries, try to justify all the forms of punishment prescribed under sharia law – from one hundred lashes to death by stoning.[40] It is paradoxical that state schools teach old traditions so contrary to the country's legal code and official practice. If they placed the sharia rules in their historical context and offered a critical judgement to explain why the modern legislature had abandoned them, this would help to integrate pupils into their social milieu and to get them to accept modernity without rejecting their original culture. But such is not the case. On the contrary, it is clearly stated that liberty is permitted only on condition that the sharia is not called into question,[41] and that sharia rules remain beyond criticism and define the limits of reason or the critical spirit.[42]

Most of the manuals are meant to ensure that pupils live in an 'Islamic atmosphere'. For instance, in the Moroccan Arabic reader for the sixth year of basic education, which is theoretically a language book and not part of religious education, the subjects of the first six lessons are as follows: (1) Koranic verses; (2) the Prophet's hadiths; (3) 'I am a Muslim'; (4) Islam and consultation; (5) Koranic verses; and (6) the most meritorious way of fasting.[43]

In general, then, the teaching currently practised in Arab-Islamic countries is likely to favour the rise of fundamentalism.[44] It needs to be purged of all assertions contrary to human rights and the foundations of the modern state. With radical reform – what Abdou Filali Ansary calls 'deep adjustments'[45] – the educational systems could in the medium term help to cure society of religious extremism.

Towards a reform of education

At the same time that it prepares young people for university or higher vocational training, the educational system has the purpose of 'training citizens'. For this it is indispensable to spell out ideas and clearly to assert political choices on the thorny issues of identity, language and religion, so that there is no longer any ambiguity about the spirit informing education.

Identity

Man, who is 'by nature a social being' (Ibn Khaldun), needs to feel integrated into society. The sense of belonging to a nation must be neither illusory (which would make it a source of disillusion) nor conflictual (which would make it a source of violence). It must correspond to reality, to the truth.

In the Muslim and especially the Arab world, however, the problem is that for political reasons, pan-Islamic or pan-Arab ideologies have been spread among the public and often at school; they have become a serious source of tension.

We can be certain that Islamic unity is a chimera. It is clearly illusory to hope that countries as different or remote as Afghanistan or Senegal will one day be united in a single polity. The term *Umma*, or community of believers, which used to designate the small number of Muslims grouped around the Prophet in Medina, can no longer have any major political implication. As Mohamed Talbi put it, the frontier of the *Umma* is today drawn 'exclusively as a frontier of people's hearts'.[46] Islam is neither a fatherland nor a nationality. It is a religion, not an identity.

As far as Arab unity is concerned, the Baath Party and Nasser put it on the agenda as a priority to be immediately achieved. Experience has proved otherwise. The Gulf Wars have dispelled the illusions of most, by showing that separate nations exist within the Arab world and have interests of their own which some would call selfish. Those who used to be the most fervent supporters of Arab unity in the Middle East now accept that it is a distant objective and that the main priority today is to achieve cohesion and development within the existing nations or 'mini-nations'.[47]

It is now clear that the project of Arab political unity is extremely difficult to achieve. In any event, it should be neither served nor undermined by educational institutions, whose main quality ought to be political neutrality. A child brought up in Tunisia to feel that he or she belongs to the Tunisian nation will be perfectly capable, should circumstances one day be favourable, of accepting or even working for Arab unity; the acceptance or the action will then be driven by reason rather than passion. Meanwhile, the quality of being Tunisian can be assumed without any sense of frustration.

All over the Arab world, the teaching of history has remained under the influence of a version peddled for more than a thousand years in the religious schools, in which all that existed before the Prophet was the *jahilia* or 'age of ignorance' (a kind of primitive prehistory devoid of interest) and all non-Islamic civilizations were alien and more or less hostile.

Consequently, during the period of deviation Tunisian school-children scarcely learned anything about Hannibal, were ignorant of the work and even the existence of Saint Augustine, and regarded as alien the whole of history before the Islamic conquest (or 'opening', as it was called). The latter was presented in such a triumphalist and emotional manner that the glorious resistance of Kahena and his troops to the Arab invasion was, if not hushed up, then at least shamefully downplayed. As to the later period, the very history of Tunisia was submerged under that of the Islamic empire. Khereddine, the Fundamental Pact, the whole nineteenth-century reform movement: all this was shrouded in ignorance. The distortion of historical truth might not have had any effect on the psychological equilibrium of young people if Tunisia were simply a province of a pan-Islamic or pan-Arab state. But as that is not the case, it meant that children were being formed in the spirit of Arab-Islamic nationality, only to live with a Tunisian nationality outside the school gates. That was a factor leading to frustration and, in extreme cases, to schizophrenia.

This is not at all an anti-Arab or anti-Islamic assertion. Its purpose is simply to avoid a split, to establish a coherent link between school and society. For this to happen, Tunisian schoolchildren must recover their past, 'nationalize' their history, reappropriate the glory of Carthage and the splendour of Tunisia's civilization in the first few centuries after Christ (even if, at the time, it was called the Roman proconsulate). This would lead them not to deprecate their own country, as some young people do who have received an education too tainted by ideology. The Arabic language and Islam would not lose their privileged position. On the contrary, schools should give children a sense of belonging to Arab-Islamic civilization, without erasing their Tunisian personality. Of course, we are speaking here of Tunisia only as an example; the same point applies to all the Muslim countries, which should each try to recover its own history. Moreover, the teaching of religion should be guided by the same spirit.

Religion

We have seen in previous chapters that it is entirely possible to square a new reading of Islam with modern conceptions of law and the state. Such a reconciliation, though not theorized or even explicitly affirmed, constitutes the implicit yet unmistakable foundation of modern states. Various Muslim countries, including Kuwait and Bahrain (though not the other Gulf states) and the Iranian and Sudanese strongholds of militant Islam, hold periodic elections. These are seldom truly democratic because the existence of a regime-backed single or dominant party precludes an honest and regular ballot, but the formal existence of a parliament that supposedly represents the people means that, both officially and in reality, *legislative power has been taken away from the ulema and entrusted to the people's representatives*. This is a major change, a 'big bang'. To ignore it is a dangerous and irresponsible attitude that sows confusion among young people. The main new principle, then, involves popular sovereignty, free legislation by the people's representatives, and independence of the law from the sharia. Even when a law still has a classical Muslim inspiration, it commands acceptance only through the force of law. If it differs from the sharia, this means that part of the sharia has been abrogated. This is true of all the Muslim penal law in most Arab countries. Polygamy is still an option in Morocco or Algeria, for example, because the legislature decided that it should remain possible.

The legislation of the new states stripped the ulema of their power and separated the sphere of social relations from that of religion. If rulers did not have the courage to acknowledge what they were doing, to say aloud what they were thinking and to explain it to the people, this was a sign of their weakness. A continuation of such policies can only weaken them further, but at least they do not confuse young people by teaching them the opposite of what they actually do.

It is always possible to teach children about the sharia in history classes. It can also be taught in courses of religious education, but only if its set of rules is presented as a fact of history, and only if the reasons for the abrogation of these rules are explained as we have explained them above. For all social or juridical issues concerning public or private law, civil or criminal law, personal status or international relations, teachers should be required to teach the theories of enlightened Muslim thinkers who have shown that Islam is perfectly compatible with modernity, and that a revision of the sharia is one of the major challenges of our time. The works of such writers as the Egyptians Rifaa Tahtawi, Mohamed Abdu, Ali Abderrazak and Taha Hussein, or the Tunisians Tahar Haddad, Mohamed Talbi and Abdelmajid Charfi, should have much greater resonance in school textbooks.[48] Their theories should be explained, so that young people are able to square their ideal with reality. Thus in a social context in which Muslim law has been revised, any idea of discrimination between men and women or Muslims and non-Muslims would be criticized and set aside.

On the other hand, on metaphysical questions and all issues concerning the relations of Muslims with God (dogma, prayers, fasting, pilgrimage, etcetera), it would be normal to continue with the teaching of classical Islam. It is also desirable to teach the key values of Islam (love, mutual aid and peace), as well as the values of equality and liberty as these are understood by enlightened modern authors.

Self-knowledge and knowledge of others

Since language is in a way linked to identity, the question of the place of Arabic and foreign languages in education often inflames passions. It is necessary to take some of the heat out of the debate, by clearly spelling out both the privileged position of Arabic as the national language and the important role of foreign languages in opening people's minds to the world.

There are few countries in today's world where at least one foreign language is not taught at school. For developing countries, the teaching of foreign languages is a vital necessity if they are to have access to scientific discoveries and technology. But it is also necessary if people are to be familiar with foreign cultures. The languages of Molière and Shakespeare should be taught, not only as repositories of scientific terminology but as a way of gaining knowledge of other cultures and civilizations.

In the end, whether for identity itself or for aspects of life such as religion and language that are closely bound up with it, the aim should be to train young people to affirm their personality by extending their roots in such a way that they are also largely open to others. The extremes of self-contempt and arrogant self-assertion must be banished, as twin sources of complexes and frustrations. A personality turned in on itself will dream of revenge and violence, while a crushed personality will oscillate between resignation and revolt. To avoid such wrenching distortions, it is necessary to strengthen the general culture of young people and their knowledge of the world. They should have a clear idea (as accurate as possible, neither exaggerated nor demeaned) of their own culture, and form the most accurate possible idea of the whole of world culture.

The philosophical culture of young people should include Islamic philosophy as well as the various foreign schools, from Greek antiquity down to the contemporary world, with all their diversity of views and wealth of debate. Literary culture should be based on study of the great names in ancient and especially modern Arabic literature, as well as the literature of countries overseas.

As to the teaching of history, a crucially important subject, students should know well the history of their own country but also have a clear idea of the great civilizations and major events that have marked the modern and contemporary world. They should therefore have adequate knowledge of the great French Revolution of 1789, the Enlightenment that preceded it, and the evolution of English parliamentarianism.

Finally, the key subject of civic education should regain its independence of religious education.[49] This will enable students to familiarize themselves with the operational rules of a modern state: local and regional government, the separation of powers, the independence of the judiciary, relations between executive and legislature, the principle and forms of democratic elections, the fundamental principle of equality and non-discrimination (especially between men and women), the main individual and collective freedoms, the rights and duties of the citizen, and the evolution of ideas and institutions in the various historical epochs and regions of the world.

Students will thus discover that the only legitimacy worthy of the name is derived from universal suffrage. They will also come to see that human history is in a way the history of the evolution from theocracy to democracy – that is, from a regime that thinks (or anyway says) that it is in possession of absolute truth and is therefore necessarily authoritarian, to a regime that makes the absolute a matter for individual conscience and intervenes only in the domain of the relative (economic and social choices, government administration, etcetera), a domain where challenges are not charged with passion, pluralism can actually work, and peaceful alternation can occur without drama or violence. This is how humanity arrived on 10 December 1948 at the Universal Declaration of Human Rights, a document that ought to be read, explained and commented on in our schools.

This 'direct' teaching of the principles of democracy and human rights is very important, but perhaps their 'indirect' teaching matters even more. It is essential that the texts for the teaching of Arabic, foreign languages or philosophy, as well as for the presentation of historical events and geographical realities, should be selected with these points in mind. No choice in this field is ever innocent; the teaching of the ostensibly most neutral subjects is never neutral. The illustrations chosen for primary textbooks make a considerable impact on schoolchildren. For example, pictures of boys and girls playing together, or of father and mother performing the same tasks, will accustom them to the idea of female emancipation and sexual equality, whereas pictures of a cultivated father and an uneducated mother bound to material chores will make a male-dominated, patriarchal and inevitably misogynist society appear 'the normal thing'.

This pedagogy of sexual equality is necessary not only in syllabuses and manuals but also in everyday life within the educational establishment. From this point of view, mixing is a fundamental principle. At present, most educational institutions in the Arab world are reserved for either boys or girls. It is time to put an end to this apartheid, to dispel any complex of inferiority or superiority on grounds of gender, and to encourage healthier and more natural relations between the boys and girls of today, who are the men and women of tomorrow.

None of this means that the educational establishment should become an ideological centre for brainwashing. On the contrary, in promoting the ideas of liberty, equality, democracy and human rights (ideas that no country formally rejects or dares to reject), schools should lay before their pupils all the theories, all the doctrines. This diversity will teach young people to put in perspective what one or another thinker says: it will help them acquire a critical sense and encourage the development of their own personalities. The sciences should be taught in the same spirit.

The scientific approach

A few remarks should be made here about the methodology and general orientation of science teaching. There is too much of a tendency to teach scientific laws as if they were absolutely indisputable truths that one need only learn to apply. Teachers then think that they are inculcating a scientific spirit and a critical sense whereas sometimes the result is the exact opposite. A pupil who merely learns the content and application of mathematical theorems or natural laws will acquire a certain technical know-how but will always tend to learn obedience rather than the art of reflection. For it is the scientific approach that is the most fruitful aspect of science teaching. This is why it is so interesting to deal with various chapters in the history of the sciences: one discovers that the great scientists and researchers advanced in tentative steps, constantly asking questions and raising doubts, and that scientific truths are often provisional and need to be completed and corrected. This is obviously not a reason to challenge or reject scientific truth, as some reactionary thinkers do, but it is a reason to keep scientific knowledge in perspective. The laws of mechanics defined by Isaac Newton, together with numerous other discoveries, were the basis for the prodigious development of science that humanity has known in the last two centuries. Yet Einstein came along and challenged those laws in the early twentieth century, showing not that they were false but that their field of application was limited and that, to understand cosmic phenomena, for instance, we must turn to the laws of general relativity.

A genuinely scientific approach therefore combines solid knowledge with a spirit of ongoing research, that is, with creative doubt. This truly scientific, truly critical spirit can be acquired neither solely through an apprenticeship in mathematics, nor through a teaching of physics so formal that secondary school pupils and higher students are more concerned to solve equations than to grasp the physical elements that are their object. That kind of extreme abstraction ends up being against nature, since physics, as the name suggests, is precisely the science of reality.

So, a reform of the educational system should not seek only to modify the syllabuses in literary studies or the human and social sciences; it should also change teaching methods in the so-called exact sciences, so that young people really understand the nature of physical, chemical and biological phenomena. Moreover, these sciences should be taught in their totality – that is, without bracketing off problems that are considered so sensitive as to be embarrassing. Taboo theories such as the big bang or the evolution of species, including the human species, should be properly tackled and explained. This approach to science teaching greatly displeases the fundamentalists. They have no difficulty taking on board mathematical abstractions or their technical applications, and they readily accept (do they have a choice?) curative medicines, air transport or the use of computers to perform calculations, yet they dismiss the scientific approach that led to these developments. They appreciate the certainty of mathematics but reject the finely shaded thinking that underlies the social and human sciences.

Fundamentalists look, for example, at the Islamic law that fourteen centuries ago prescribed amputation of a thief's hand, and they think it is as certain as two plus two equals four. To say that the rule corresponded to the historical circumstances of the time, and that it could and should be revised today, is to introduce a disturbing element of doubt, to suggest an approach that appals them and a sense of nuance contrary to their rigid and closed mental structures. Fundamentalist ideas can seduce only young people with a theological training or science students who have learned to solve equations in the manner of a computer. But a robot, though very useful, cannot think, is ignorant of the scientific approach and knows only how to act out what it has been programmed to do.

To support their claim to modernism or open-mindedness, some fundamentalist leaders point to the computer scientists or engineers in their ranks, and indeed inexperienced observers have been led astray by the sight of people with a medieval mind working on a computer. Similarly, the relative success of the fundamentalist current in science and engineering faculties, more than in law or literature, may seem surprising when one knows that the students in question are bearers of an archaic ideology.

In this connection, Séverine Labat's thoroughly researched study of Algerian fundamentalists – what we might call an 'anatomy and physio-logy of fundamentalism' – shows that the main founders and leaders of the Islamic Salvation Front (FIS) got their primary and secondary education at traditional *kouttebs* or *medresas* or from the ulema.[50] This proves the direct relationship between how a child is educated and how he or she behaves as an adult. Labat describes the career path and specialist studies of each of the fifteen members of the first leadership (*shura*) council of the FIS; there were 5 shopkeepers, 3 teachers of religious education, 3 engineers, 2 science teachers, 1 maths teacher and 1 primary school teacher.[51] This means that they had either attended nothing more than elementary school or received a further religious or scientific education. In the last case, we are surely talking of an early specialization: that is, a lack of general culture and the mere learning of a technique making it possible to use a machine, which indicates neither an open mind nor a genuinely scientific orientation.

To avoid such defects, specialization should not be contemplated until the end of middle school, two years before the baccalaureate examination. This would allow time to give future engineers, doctors or scientists a kind of cultural 'minimum wage' concerning the evolution of knowledge over the last few centuries, as well as some familiarity with the major political, economic and social events and the great ideological debates of that period and, therefore, the essential elements for an understanding of contemporary issues. This opening up to ideas and the wider world should continue for future scientists and technologists, and to this end post-secondary specialization should not exclude the teaching of general culture and languages up to baccalaureate level.

This conclusion applies with special force to Third World countries, where the family and local milieux do not play an extensive role in filling the gaps in general culture left by school.

Quantity and quality

Ideally, after the period of compulsory education, all young people (the majority) who wish to do so would go on to lycée and sit the baccalaureate. However, that is not the best option. For until the nation has enough financial resources and enough trained teachers to give every child a good education, it is a more serious failing to sacrifice quality than to limit the quantitative supply. There are several reasons why this is so.

First, a major quantitative leap in the numbers receiving secondary education, and then inevitably higher education, would today mean that many classes were taken by inadequately trained teachers, that much technical material and laboratory equipment was in short supply or obsolete, that the aim of enabling a wider cultural formation for schoolchildren and students was given up – in short, that countries with limited means were condemned to have a surfeit of young graduates who lacked the competence and general culture that their diplomas were supposed to indicate.

Next, if there was a decline in the general standard of secondary education, there would necessarily ensue a decline in the standard of higher education. The possibility of a chain reaction has already been demonstrated in a number of Arab–Muslim countries over the past few decades.

Some argue that the educational base should be enlarged to foster the training of an elite. But on the contrary, the training of an elite requires a sound base, as large as possible but above all solid. Elite training is a key goal because a people without an elite is a people without guides and without a future. The word *elite* should here be taken in the broad sense, to include thinkers in the humanities and sciences, creative workers, competent and efficient managers, and so on.

Finally, the awarding of undeserved diplomas has deleterious effects on both the individual and society. For the individual, it gives the illusion of a competence that is not really there and inevitably leads to a rude awakening; he or she will in the end be unhappier than an uneducated peasant who has never cherished unrealizable dreams. For society, the effect is graver still. Frustrated people integrate poorly into their social milieu, becoming perpetual malcontents who are tempted to act in ways that destabilize the country and hinder its march towards progress. They will tend to have chimerical visions and to accept and propagate the most regressive ideas.

Ignorance among the peasantry is an evil that it is relatively easy to combat. Evening literacy classes and an initiation into the techniques of modern agriculture or industry are sufficient, since those who enrol for the courses in question enthusiastically follow them to overcome a lack of knowledge of which they are usually well aware. Often, moreover, they suffer this ignorance with the modesty of 'simple folk'. Things become infinitely more complicated in the case of 'meta-ignorance', where the holder of a worthless degree, for example, is ignorant of his very ignorance.

Cultural underdevelopment is incomparably more dangerous than straightforward ignorance, for ignorant people are modest and, though their needs are legitimate, they do not have great pretensions. The undercultured, on the other hand, think they know everything, and when there are many of them, they think they can run the whole show. In 'backward' societies – that is, societies at an underdeveloped level – the revolt of the undercultured is based on ignorance and therefore results in an aggravation of the backwardness.

The 'people's furnaces' experiment attempted by Mao Zedong in China in the late 1950s, when peasants had to do the work of technicians and engineers, involved huge waste. The Cultural Revolution, a few years later, was even worse. Red Guards – actually teenagers heated to boiling point – were urged to hit out at academics, engineers and managers, or at least to send them off to work in the fields. The whole thing was a grave injustice, coupled with an economic, social and cultural catastrophe.

The Iranian Revolution was led by mullahs, some of whom knew the whole of classical Islam – and, in particular, every real or imaginary detail of the life of Ali, the fourth caliph – but next to nothing apart from that. Worse still, some who thought themselves knowledgeable because they had vaguely heard of a certain Rousseau and his social contract, or of a certain Montesquieu and his separation of powers, had a ready answer to all such 'atheistic theories invented by the Great Satan, the West'.[52]

In both cases, the outcome was the dragooning of intellectuals, a major brain drain and progress towards greater underdevelopment. The 'people's furnaces' theory and the Cultural Revolution eventually fizzled out, since, being human theories, they could be combated by other men and women. But the Iranian Revolution keeps going, a little less intensely than before, because it is based on religion and is therefore incomparably more difficult to combat.

A militant fundamentalist, even if he has learned to solve mathematical equations or to use a computer, has an extremely limited general culture – which is why degrees on the cheap and early specialization at school should be banned.

For all these reasons, it is greatly desirable to have quite dense syllabuses and demanding examinations that will ensure a high educational level at primary and secondary school. A lot of space should also be set aside there for cultural activities, with clubs devoted to theatre, cinema, painting, dancing, and so on that will allow students to use their leisure time in ways that expand their horizons.

An ambitious reform of the kind suggested above presupposes that teachers will be motivated to make it work. In France, in the late nineteenth and early twentieth centuries, teachers known as the 'hussars of the Republic' were able to change public opinion in the space of one generation, from a monarchist majority to a virtual republican consensus. We should not forget that the National Assembly elected in 1870 had a large monarchist majority. But in 1875, after circumstances had prevented the restoration of the monarchy, republicans managed to assemble a majority of one for the establishment of the Third Republic. The ensuing turnaround in public opinion owed a great deal to the professional cohesion of schoolteachers, to the clarity of their ideological choices, to their militant spirit[53] and to their conviction that only the school system could make equality possible and give the best students, whatever their social origin, access to the top positions in society.

In Arab-Muslim countries, teachers do not have the same 'cohesion' or the same training. Thanks to various (sometimes ambivalent) ideological orientations, the teachers as a whole at primary and secondary schools are capable of the best as well as the worst. A number of tendencies exist within them. The current that feels itself to be supported by the government is able to command acceptance for its positions. A radical reform can succeed if teachers feel that the new educational policy involves clear choices and a firm will on the part of the whole state hierarchy, especially its top echelons, and that the government expects the educational system to make a decisive contribution to the modernization of society – in other words, that the system has been charged with a political mission of the highest importance (the word *political* being understood in its worthiest sense). It is therefore absolutely necessary that governments should come out loud and clear for modernization through education, and that they should implement it with the greatest vigilance and an unbending resolve.

The law of 28 July 1991 (formally amended in 2002), which initiated the reform of the Tunisian educational system, followed the broad guidelines that have just been described.

For all the Arab-Islamic countries, cultural policy is just as important as education. We need to develop our own culture and, at the same time, to open ourselves wide to the culture of others. This is the business of intellectuals and all creative workers. But, insofar as the state largely controls the media in most Muslim countries, there is also a degree of government responsibility.

The distorting idealization and sacralization of Islamic history has had a number of harmful effects, and today's soaps or Ramadan programmes on mostly state-owned channels aggravate the phenomenon instead of encouraging a more critical reading. We now know that the policy of flirting with Islamism to cut the ground from under the feet of the Islamists has always ended up playing into their hands. Cultural policy must be geared to complete freedom of creation, greater encouragement of creative workers, and greater openness to world culture.

Conclusion

In this book we have examined Koranic verses and elements of the Prophet's *sunna* which clearly show that Islam is a religion not a politics, a question of conscience not of belonging, an act of faith not of force.

We have noted many crucial historical events that amply demonstrate that the Islamic empire, from its founder Abu Bakr down to Atatürk and the abolition of the caliphate in 1924, was essentially a profane rather than a religious creation.

We have looked at the theories of Kassem Amin, Tahar Haddad and Ali Abderrazak, who took up and used ideas originally put forward by the Mutazilites, Averroës and the rationalists. Those theories may enable Muslims in the third millennium to combine their religion with fully committed modernism in a life of peace and harmony – the peace of a clear conscience as well as social and religious peace.

The tragic problem for our societies is that, instead of being the basis for a social and political consensus, instead of being the object of systematic education and consistent political discourse, these elements and theories are both under attack from fundamentalists and lacking in defensive resources. They are defended neither by governments – most of which are too fragile and devoid of democratic legitimacy – nor by intellectuals and democrats – who lack the necessary freedom of speech and action. As a result, we have nations of distraught believers who, since independence, no longer know to which saint they should dedicate themselves.

Rulers who live in modernity and teach tradition are maintaining an unstable equilibrium, an unworkable system. They are writing explosion into the genes of society. The few economic and social improvements, where they exist at all, are in this respect only calming devices that postpone the hard decisions without pulling up the evil by the roots. But they do create some scope for a policy change that might allow young people to be brought up in the spirit of the new times. As long as the rulers do not commit themselves to change, however, a new equilibrium cannot be established; they will go on rigging elections, banning opposition parties, jailing malcontents and torturing rebels. Human rights activists, on the rare occasions when they can speak out, will remain torn between the need to denounce the danger that fundamentalists represent for tomorrow and the need to condemn the human rights violations to which fundamentalists are exposed today.

Peace and harmony will prevail among individuals and among nations when we have clearly separated politics from religion and taught our children the principles underlying that separation.

Notes

Introduction

1. The French edition of this work was first published in 1998. For the English edition, the author has made some slight modifications to take account of the most important events in the intervening years.

2. In 1807 Napoleon convoked a supreme Jewish council, or Sanhedrin, which agreed formally to abandon polygamy (no longer practised for centuries) and accepted that civil marriage and divorce should come prior to, and take precedence over, marriage and repudiation according to Mosaic law.

3. See Mohamed Bayram V, *Analytic Bibliography*, by M. Ben Abdeljalil and K. Omran (in Arabic), Tunis: Beit el Hikma, 1989, p. 291.

4. See D. Shayegan, *Le Regard mutilé. Schizophrénie culturelle; pays traditionels face à la modernité*, Paris: Albin Michel, 1989 (published in English as *Cultural Schizophrenia: Islamic Societies Confronting the West*, Syracuse, NY: Syracuse University Press, 1997); H. Sharabi, *Neopatriarchy: a Theory of Distorted Change in Arab Society*, New York: Oxford University Press, 1988.

5. The decision to abolish the religious courts was implemented gradually, and it was 1974 before it took full effect.

6. See S. A. Abou Sahlieh, *Non-musulman en pays d'islam*, Fribourg: Éditions universitaires, 1979.

7. On the role of Middle Eastern teachers, see B. Stora, 'Désespoir social', *Jeune Afrique* 1881, p. 13.

8. *Le Monde*, 13 October 1994.

9. J.-P. Péroncel-Hugoz, *Le Radeau de Mahomet*, Paris: Documents-Lieux communs, 1983, p. 71.

10. A. Abderrazak, *Islam and the Foundations of Power* (in Arabic), Beirut: Entreprise arabe pour les études et la publication, 1972, p. 109.

11. See the Tunisian daily *La Presse*, 7 August 1993.

12. *Le Nouvel Observateur*, 23–29 October 1997, p. 23.

13. The Tunisian Constitution has been amended several times, but the changes have no bearing on the issues with which we are concerned here.

14. See A. Filali-Ansary, *L'Islam est-il hostile à la laïcité?* Casablanca: Le Fennec, 1997.

Chapter 1 • Islamic Fundamentalism

1. *Libération* (Paris), 26 February 1996, p. 8; and *La Presse* (Tunis), 26 December 1995, p. 1. Already in 1995, the Egyptian Human Rights Organization counted 963 killed, including 333 during the last ten months of 1995, and pointed out that fundamentalists were assuming the greatest responsibility for the murders. See *Lettre de la FIDH* (International Federation for Human Rights) No. 16, December 1995– January 1996, p. 10 (in Arabic). The Egyptian government, for its part, declared at a press conference on 11 June 1997 that, between 1993 and 1997, the police seized from fundamentalists a total of 6,020 automatic

rifles, 627 rocket launchers, 48,000 assorted rifles, and 10,000 revolvers. *La Presse* (Tunis), 12 June 1997, p. 9.

2. See the motion drafted by 158 British MPs, in *Le Monde*, 9–10 June 1985, p. 3.

3. *Le Monde*, 30 June 1995, p. 13.

4. M. L. Bouguerra, *Le Maghreb* (an independent paper published in Tunisia), No. 70, 7 June 1985.

5. Amnesty International Bulletin, April 1986.

6. 'Les Islamistes soudanais saluent les auteurs de l'attentat contre le Président égyptien', *Le Monde*, 7 July 1995, p. 5.

7. On the ill-treatment of foreign wives, see B. Mahmoody, *Not Without My Daughter*, New York: St Martin's Press, 1987; S. Fayad, *Clameurs*, Paris: Denoël, 1994. On stoning see F. Sahenjam, *La Femme lapidée*, Paris: Livre de Poche, 1992. See S. Zeghidour, 'L'Islam et la loi des hommes: la femme infidèle', *Le Nouvel Observateur*, 25–31 October 1990, p. 76.

8. A fatwa is a religious judgement which, emanating from a highly placed figure, can have the force of law.

9. UN Commission on Human Rights, *Report of the Special Rapporteur on the Implementation of the Declaration on the Elimination of All Forms of Intolerance and of Discrimination Based on Religion and Belief*, UN Doc. E/CN.4/1996/95/ Addendum: *Report on the Mission of the Special Rapporteur to the Islamic Republic of Iran* (9 February 1996); see especially sections 64 and 69.

10. Ibid., section 63.

11. Ibid., section 43.

12. The countries of the Mashriq use numerals of Indian origin that are described as Arabic numerals, whereas the West uses numerals that it describes as 'Arabic' but which are known in the East as 'European'.

13. J.-P. Péroncel-Hugoz, *Le Monde*, 9–10 June 1985, p. 2.

14. F. F. Charfi, in the journal *Alliage* (France) No. 22, 1995, p. 7.

15. On Khereddine, see M. Smida, *Khéreddine, ministre réformateur, 1873–1877*, Tunis: Maison tunisienne de l'édition, 1971; and J. S. Van Kriken, *Khéreddine et la Tunisie 1850–1881*, Leiden: Brill, 1988. Originally entitled (in Arabic) *The Surest Path To Know the State of Nations*, Khereddine's book was republished in French translation as *Essai sur les réformes nécessaires aux états musulmans*, Paris: Edisud, 1987.

16. On this whole question, see N. Sraïëb, *Le Collège Sadiki de Tunis, 1875–1956*, Paris: CNRS, 1994.

17. For a recent bilingual (Arabic and French) edition, see A. Thaalbi, *L'Esprit libéral du Coran*, Tunis: Dar El Gharb El Islami, 1985.

18. T. Haddad, *Notre femme dans la charia et dans la société*, Tunis: Maison tunisienne de l'édition, 1972.

19. See A. Dor'i, *The Life of Tahar Haddad* (in Arabic), Tunis: Maison tunisienne de l'édition, 1975.

20. See the thesis of A. E. Aribi, presented at the faculty of literature, University of Tunis.

21. B. Harmassi, *État et société au Maghreb*, Paris: Anthropos, 1975, p. 133. See also *Sraïëb*, pp. 296-7.

22. See the French translation of this petition in *Rawafid* (published by the Higher Institute for the History of the National Movement, Tunis), No. 2, 1996, pp. 93–7.

23. Tlili Ajili, 'Les conservateurs et les mouvements réformistes en Tunisie entre 1896 et 1914', *Rawafid* No. 2, 1996, p. 61.

24. A. Kraïem, 'Le premier procès d'Abdelaziz Thaalbi (juillet 1904)', *Revue d'histoire maghrébienne*, No. 41-42, June 1986, p. 112. See also B. Abdelkafi, *Essabah* (a Tunisian daily paper),

4 April 1963.

25. M. S. Mrad, *Le Deuil sur la femme de Haddad*.

26. M. T. Ben Achour, *Scientific Critique of the Book 'Islam and the Foundations of Power'* (in Arabic), Tunis, 1925.

27. Ajili, p. 71.

28. C. Benattar, 'Souvenirs du Palais', *Le Petit Matin* (Tunis), 31 August 1935, p. 3; Kraïem, p. 104; Benattar, in *Le Petit Matin*, 1 September 1945.

29. Ibid.

30. Kraïem, p. 110.

31. In this connection, see L. L. Al Ghoul, *L'Islam des confréries et les changements sociaux à l'époque coloniale 1881–1934*, Faculté des sciences humaines et sociales de Tunis, 1990, p. 138. On the Issawa, see Kraïem, p. 107.

32. See the letter of 25 July 1904 that the delegate to France's Résidence Générale in Tunisia addressed to the Ministry of Foreign Affairs, in *Wathaïq*, No. 19, 1993, p. 37.

33. Kraïem, p. 106.

34. *Wathaïq*, No. 13, 1990, p. 26; and Benattar, *Le Petit Matin*, 31 August 1935, p. 3.

35. Benattar, *Le Petit Matin*, 31 August 1935, p.3.

36. *La Dépêche tunisienne*, 24 July 1904.

37. Benattar, in *Le Petit Matin*, 1 September 1935.

38. Ajili, pp. 64–6.

39. Ibid., p. 67.

40. Ibid., p. 67 , n. 84.

41. 'Rapport au Quai d'Orsay par le Résident général de France', in *Wathaïq*, No.1.

42. This is what Abdelmajid Charfi calls the *mohadana* of the Zituna sheikhs; see R. Mellouli, *Modernité et progrès*, Tunis: Débat d'idées, p. 51. In their clandestine newspaper *Ennokta*, which they produced in 1954 at the civilian prison in Tunis, patriotic activists wrote of clerics under the heading 'The enemies are among us'. See L. Adda, 'Ennokta', *Rawafid*, No. 2, 1996, p. 5.

43. H. Abdessamad, 'La résistance face à la question de la réforme de l'enseignement zitounien (1930–1933)', in *Les Mouvements politiques et sociaux dans la Tunisie des années 1930*, Actes du 3e séminaire sur l'histoire du mouvement national, Tunis: CNUDST, 1987, p. 805.

44. On all these aspects, see the issue of the *Financial Times* quoted in the USIS bulletin of 11 May 1996.

45. See P. Balta, *L'Islam*, Paris: Le Monde éditions, 1997, p. 168.

46. See B. Philip, *Le Monde*, 27 March 1996.

47. *Le Monde*, 21 March 1997, p. 4. See also *Sawasiah* (the Arabic bulletin of the Cairo Institute for Human Rights), No. 12, September 1996.

48. 'Les intégristes afghans ont libéré deux Français', *Le Monde*, 21 March 1997.

49. Quoted (and here retranslated) from *Jeune Afrique*, No. 1871, 13–19 November 1996, p. 50.

50. R. Essaïd, *Hasan al-Banna, When, How, Why?* (in Arabic), Cairo: Madbuli, 1997, p. 89.

51. *The Maghreb* (in Arabic), No. 81, 10 December 1983, p. 58.

52. *Realities* (in Arabic), No. 37, 13 July 1984, pp. 9–10.

53. S. Jourchi, in the review *Al-Majallah*, No. 227, and *Erraï*, No. 302, p. 12.

54. *15–21* (Arabic-language Tunisian magazine), No. 10.

55. Ibid.

56. Ibid.

57. Israel did the same with Hamas as a means of weakening Al Fatah. The consequences are well known.

58. A. Harmassi, *Le mouvement islamiste* (in Arabic), Tunis: Beyram Linnachr, 1985, pp. 111, 113.

59. See the article by Ghannouchi, 'What Is the West?' (Arabic), *Al Maarifa*, No. 10, November 1978.

60. See, for example, *Al Maarifa*, No. 10, p. 8.

61. Harmassi, particularly p. 102.

62. See *Al Maarifa*, No. 3, 1972, p. 20.

63. Ibid., No. 4, p. 2.

64. Ibid., No. 7, p. 47.

65. One finds Sayid Kotb's name throughout the collected issues of *Al Maarifa*. Mawdudi, a Pakistani doctrinarian, is one of the most fanatical ideologists of fundamentalism. He supported the bloody regime of Zia ul-Haq in return for its use of corporal punishment and its collaboration with the American security services against the Communist regime in Afghanistan. See H. Manaa, 'Fundamentalism and violence in Arab and Islamic society', *Arab Human Rights Review* (Arabic), 1996, No. 3, p. 55.

66. The Arabic term *jahilia* can mean both 'ignorance' and 'the pre-Islamic era' – a fact that already expresses a whole vision, a whole programme.

67. S. Kotb, *Route Markers* (in Arabic), Cairo: Dar Echchorouk, pp. 127–9. See N. H. Abu Zeid, *Critique of Religious Discourse* (Arabic), Cairo: Sina, 1992, p. 48.

68. S. Mawdudi, *A Short History of the Islamic Revivalist Movement*, Lahore: Islamic Publications, 1979, p. 30. See also Abu Zeid, p. 32.

69. Kotb, p. 81. See Abu Zeid, pp. 64–5.

70. Ibid.

71. Kotb, p. 136.

72. B. Ghalioun, *Islam et politique, la modernité trahie*, Paris: La Découverte, 1997.

73. *The Koran*, translated by N. J. Dawood, Harmondsworth: Penguin, rev. edn 1999, p. 108.

74. See A. Filali Ansary, 'Entre foi profonde et lucidité assumée', a commentary on Fazlur Rahman's *Islam and Modernity* (Chicago, 1982), in *Prologues* (Casablanca), No. 10, 1997, p. 6.

75. See Balta, p. 174.

Chapter 2 • Islam and Law

1. Interview by Z. Krichen in Arabic, summarized by H. Redissie in French, in *Maghreb* No. 147, 14 April 1989, pp. 20–1.

2. See verse 3 of sura 4 ('Women') and verse 6 of sura 23 ('The Believers'): *Koran*, translated by N. J. Dawood, Harmondsworth: Penguin, rev. edn 1999, pp. 366–84 and 220–25.

3. D. and A. Larguèche, *Marginales en terre d'islam*, Tunis: Cérès Productions, 1992, pp. 85–112.

4. *The Koran*, verse 256 of sura 2 ('The Cow').

5. *The Koran*, p. 87.

6. Mohamed Talbi, *Islam et dialogue*, Tunis: MTI, 1972. An English translation appeared in New Delhi under the title *Islam and the Modern Age*.

7. R. Caspar, 'Entre les déclarations universelles des droits de l'homme et le statut de la dhimma', in *3e rencontre islamo-chrétienne,* Tunis: CERES, 1982.

8. Ibid.

9. N. H. Abu Zeid, *Critique of Religious Discourse* (in Arabic), Cairo: Sina, 1992, p. 99.

10. Let us mention, as one example among a thousand, the thirteenth-century theologian Ibn Taymya who is often invoked by today's fundamentalists. In his *fatwa* on the matter, he says

that since Egypt was conquered by arms 'the Imam may destroy churches there or refuse to allow them to be built'. See B. O'Keefe, *Islamochristiana*, Rome, 1996, p. 53–78.

11. C. Lévi-Strauss, *Tristes Tropiques*, Harmondsworth: Penguin, 1976, p. 376.

12. See S. A. A. Abu Sahlieh, *Non-musulmans en pays d'islam*, Fribourg: Editions universitaires, 1979.

13. *The Koran*, pp. 94, 155.

14. J. Daniel, *Dieu est-il fanatique? Essai sur une religieuse incapacité de croire*, Paris: Arléa (dist. Le Seuil), 1996.

15. S. A. A. Abu Sahlieh, 'Le délit d'apostasie aujourd'hui et ses conséquences en droit arabe et musulman', *La Revue de l'Institut pontifical des études arabes et islamiques, Islamochristiana*, Rome, No. 20, 1994, p. 95.

16. Ibn Khaldoun, *Prolégomènes*, chapter on the *fiqh* and its prescriptions.

17. See A. Charfi, *Islam and Modernity* (in Arabic), Tunis: MTE, 1990, p. 129.

18. R. Daghfous, *Le Yéman islamique des origines jusqu'à l'avènement des dynasties autonomes*, Tunis: Faculty of Social Sciences, 1995, vol. 1, p. 363 ; *Histoire de Tabari*, Beirut: Dar el kotob el ilmya, 1988, vol. 3, p.330.

19. The concept *fijmaa* was later developed to signify the consensus among ulema.

20. See Charfi, pp. 129, 293; the report on the Islamic–Christian meeting in Tunis in 1985, in *Islamochristiana* No. 9; M. Talbi, *Islamochristiana*, No. 11, pp. 99–113 ; H. Enneifar, *Islamochristiana*, No. 13, pp. 1-10; Amel Grami, *The Problem of Apostasy in Islamic Thought* (thesis in Arabic), Faculty of Literature, Tunis, 1993, and *Freedom of Conscience in Islam*, Casablanca, 1997.

21. The peculiarities of the Libyan regime make it difficult to classify. Although the General People's Congress combats the fundamentalists, it has recently ordered collective punishment of tribes containing one religious extremist – and uses the sharia law on apostasy to justify it! See the Tunisian daily *La Presse*, 10 March 1997, p. 8.

22. See the record of the moving but also disgusting 'dialogue' between the judges and the condemned men in Khartoum prison on 19 January 1985, in *Droits de l'homme arabe*, Cairo, No. 10.

23. *Al Ahram* (Cairo), 14 April 1976; Sudan News Agency, 18 January 1985. On this whole issue, see Abu Sahlieh, *Islamochristiana*, No. 2, p. 99.

24. *Realities* (Tunis, in Arabic), No. 610, 1–8 August 1997, p. 14.

25. Abu Sahlieh, p. 101.

26. A. Annaïm, *On the Evolution of Islamic Legislation*, with an introduction by Hussein Ahmed, Cairo: Sina, 1994, p. 20.

27. The main of these works by Nasr Hamed Abu Zeid, all in Arabic and published by Sina in Cairo, are: *A Critique of Religious Discourse*; *Text, Authority, Truth*; *The Rationalist Method in Koranic Commentary*; and *The Meaning of the Text*.

28. The punishment of death by stoning is all the more horrific because of the way in which it is carried out. In fact, the ulema have specified all the details to ensure the maximum suffering; in line with these, Article 104 of the current Iranian penal code prescribes that 'the stones used to inflict death must not be so large that the condemned person dies as soon as the first or second stone is thrown'. See *Lettre de la Fédération internationale des droits de l'homme*, special issue on Iran, 27 March–3 April 1997, p. 9.

29. The terms 'married man' and 'married woman' are here used to translate the Arabic *sheikh* and *sheikha*, which literally mean 'persons of a mature age'. With a little prompting, these words may suggest the quality of no longer being single – and that is how the ulema (to whom we owe the verse) have always interpreted it.

30. *Le Koran*, translated by Sadok Mazigh, Paris: Éditions du Jaguar, 1985.

31. See N. H. Abu Zeid, *Text, Authority, Truth*, p. 137.

32. *The Koran*, pp. 62, 83, 246.

33. See the *Report by the Independent Expert on the Conditions in Somalia*, Mohamed Charfi, UN Economic and Social Council, Doct. ECN.4/1996/14 Add. 1, 10 April 1996.

34. http://www.humanrights.harvard.edu/documents/regionaldocs/ cairo_dec.htm. See H. Zouari, *La Déclaration du Caire de 1990 sur les droits de l'homme en islam*, memoir of the DEA, Faculté des Sciences juridiques, politiques, et sociales, Tunis, 1996. On the whole issue of human rights and Islam, see S.A.A. Abou Sahlieh, *Les Musulmans face aux droits de l'homme*, Bochum: Winkler, 1994.

35. On this point, see Annaïm, p. 48.

36. Abu Zeid, *Critique of Religious Discourse*, p. 94.

37. See Ibn Khaldun's *Prolégomènes*, Beirut: Maison du livre arabe, 5th edn., p. 441.

38. Ibid., p. 444.

39. See Abdelmajid Charfi's *Islam and modernity*, pp. 287–88.

40. In the journal *El Manar*, Cairo, 1906; see A. Charfi, p. 115.

41. S. Ghrab, 'Brève histoire du pouvoir en Islam', in *Pluralisme et laïcité*, GRIC/Bayard, Paris: Centurion, 1996, p. 69.

42. In the case of a mother, her share is equal to that of the father.

43. *The Koran*, p. 27.

44. The percentage shares may total more than 100, for example, in cases where a woman names as legatees her father, her mother, her husband and her two daughters. The son's share might be less than the daughter's, for example if a woman names as legatees her father, her mother, her husband and a single offspring: the share of the latter is larger in the case of a daughter than of a son.

45. See M. Morand, *Études de droit musulman algérien*, Algiers, 1910, pp. 70–71.

46. Fustel de Coulanges, *La Cité antique*, Paris: Hachette, 1930.

47. Plato, *The Laws*, VIII, 849; Aristotle, *Politics*, VII, 5, 7.

48. On this whole matter, see Batiffol and Lagarde, *Droit international et privé*, Nos. 9ff.

49. *The Koran*, p. 41.

50. See my course at the Academy of International Law: 'L'influence de la religion sur le droit international privé des pays musulmans', *Recueil des cours de l'Académie*, Vol. 203, 1987, pp. 325 and especially 347.

51. Centenary brochure of the Bank of Tunisia, 1884–1984.

52. *The Koran*, p. 259.

53. See M. S. Ashmawi, *Riba and Interest in Islam* (in Arabic), Cairo: Sina, 1988, p. 43.

54. In the Gulf countries, which respect other elements of sharia law, interest-bearing loans are part of the banking system.

55. On the developments that followed, see M. Charfi, *Introduction à l'étude du droit*, 3rd edn, Tunis: Cérès, 1997, pp. 59ff.; and, in Arabic, M. Charfi and A. Mezghanni, *Introduction to the Study of Law*, Tunis: CNP, 1993, pp. 215ff.

56. M. El Shakankiri, 'Loi divine, loi humaine et droit dans l'histoire juridique de l'islam', *Revue internationale de droit comparé*, 1981, p. 767 and especially p. 778.

57. See A. El Fassi, *Self-Criticism* (in Arabic), 2nd edn, p. 224.

58. Averroës, *Discours décisif*, Paris: Garnier-Flammarion, 1996, p. 120.

59. A rare pearl of an exception was Najmeddine Tufi, who died in 715 of the Hegira. He argued that the general interest could and should take precedence over the text – but it is no accident that he never founded a school.

60. See M. El Khodari, *A History of Islamic Legislation* (in Arabic), Beirut, 1967, p. 278; and J. Shacht, 'Classicisme, traditionalisme et ankylose dans la loi religieuse de l'islam', in

Classicisme et déclin dans l'histoire de l'islam, 2nd edn, Paris: Maisonneuve et Larose, 1977.

61. A. Amin, 'The leaders of Islam in the modern age', in *Islamic Encyclopedia* (in Arabic), Beirut: Maison du livre arabe, p. 7.
62. Of course, polygamy also exists in a number of non-Muslim African tribes, but even there it is doomed to disappear as it lacks a religious foundation and is unable to withstand the assaults of modernity.
63. *The Koran*, p. 60.
64. Y. Ben Achour, 'Islam et constitution', *Revue tunisienne de droit*, 1974, p. 121.
65. H. Jaït, *Personnalité et devenir arabo-islamiques*, p. 142. See M. Camau's commentary in *Pouvoir et institutions au Maghreb*, Tunis: CERES, 1974, p. 121.
66. On this point, see Annaïm, p. 96.
67. See ibid., p. 94.
68. Tahar Hadad's book *Our Woman in the Sharia and in Society* (in Arabic), which first appeared in Tunis in 1929 and has been through several editions since then, gave rise to major controversy. See M. Charfi, *Introduction à l'étude du droit*, pp. 95ff.
69. Charles Verlindin, *L'Esclavage dans l'Europe médiévale*, vol. 1, Bruges, 1995, and vol. 2, Ghent, 1979.
70. See, in particular, 9:60, 2:177 and 90:11, 12 and 13.
71. Mohamed Talbi's works are many and various. Perhaps the most important is *Iyal Allah* (God's Children), subtitled *De nouvelles idées sur les rapports du musulman avec les autres et avec lui-même*, Tunis: Cérès, 1992. The main ideas in this book are taken up again in another work, *Plaidoyer pour un islam moderne*, Tunis (Cérès), Casablanca (Le Fennec) and Paris (Desclée de Brouwer), 1998.
72. The verse is so difficult to grasp in all its nuances that the French translator of the Koran, Sadok Mazigh, felt obliged to add a note concerning the word 'trust' (*dépôt*) that it surely referred to 'the spirit', implying 'consciousness, judgement, free choice, submission to the supreme will: everything that constitutes both man in his perfection and the true believer'. See *Le Koran*.
73. The most important of Taha's works is *The Second Message in Islam* (in Arabic).
74. See C. E. Renard, 'À la mémoire de M. M. Taha', *Prologues: Revue maghrébine du livre* (Casablanca), No. 10, Summer 1997, pp. 14–20.
75. Annaïm, p. 86.
76. M. Hamidullah, 'Le musulman dans le milieu occidental et son retour au pays d'origine', in Jacques Berque, ed., *État, normes et valeurs dans l'islam contemporain*, Paris: Payot, 1966, pp. 192–209.
77. Similarly, when the Koran says in chapter 2, verse 185: 'Whoever of you sees with his eyes the new moon let him fast in that month' (in Blachère's French translation), it is addressing the tribes of Arabia which had no precise calendar and adopted lunar months beginning from the moment when they 'saw with their eyes' the crescent of the new moon. In consequence of respect for age-old practices and a literal interpretation of the sacred texts, the Muslim world still suffers from the impreciseness of its calendar. People know the feast days or the beginning and end of the month of Ramadan only a few hours in advance – as if it were still impossible for Muslims to calculate the days and hours of the conjunction of the sun and moon, while 'others' are able to send space probes around Jupiter or Saturn.
78. S. Ghrab, p. 74.
79. H. Jaït, pp. 58, 59.
80. Annaïm, p.55.
85 S. Ghrab, pp. 69 and especially 74.

Chapter 3 • Islam and the State

1. A. Charfi, *Islam et modernité*, Tunis: MTE, 1990, p. 214.
2. See S. J. El Azm, *Courrier international*, 30 July–5 February 1997, p. 34.
3. The GIA communiqué is dated 26 August 1994; see *Le Monde*, 28-29 August 1994. The caliph was killed a few days later. See P. Balta, *L'Islam*, Paris: Le Monde editions, 1997, p. 48.
4. Balta, p. 174.
5. See Isaac Deutscher, *Stalin*, Harmondsworth: Penguin, 1968, Chapter 12: 'The Generalissimo'.
6. See *The Koran*, 6:133, 6:165, 7:69, 7:74, 7:129, 10:14, 10:73, 11:57, 25:55 (twice), 27:62, 35:39 and 57:7.
7. For this interpretation of the verse, see M. F. Othman, *Foundations of Arab Political Thought* (in Arabic), Beirut, 1979.
8. *Le Koran*, French translation by S. Mazigh, Paris: Éditions du Jaguar, 1985, 3:20. A similar point is made at 5:92, 5:99, 13:40, 14:52, 16:35, 24:54, 29:18, 42:48 and 64:12.
9. See *The Koran*, translated by N. J. Dawood, Harmondsworth: Penguin, rev. edn 1999, 2:19, 7:188, 11:2, 17:105, 25:56, 33:45, 34:28, 35:24, 41:4 and 48:8.
10. See also, 7:184, 7:188, 11:2, 11:12, 15:89, 22:49, 26:115, 28:46, 29:50, 32:3, 34:44, 34:46, 35:24, 35:37, 35:42, 38:70, 46:9, 51:50, 51:51, 53:56, 67:8, 67:9, 67:26, 2:119, 17:105, 25:1, 25:56, 33:45, 34:28, 35:34, 41:4, 48:8 and 74:36.
11. Cf. 17:15, 27:92 and 39:41.
12. See the edition of Ali Abderrazak's *Islam and the Foundation of Power*, published in Beirut in 1978 and with an introduction by M. Hakki.
13. M. Hakki, ibid., p. 5.
14. See S. Kotb, *Commentary on the Koran*, vol. 8, Beirut, 1971, p. 566; and M. T. Ben Achour, *Commentary on the Koran* (in Arabic), Tunis: Maison Tuisienne de l'édition, vol. 30, p. 307.
15. See Tabari's commentary on the Koran, reissued in Beirut in 1992, p. 557.
16. See Ibn Kathir's commentary on the Koran, reissued in Beirut in 1992, p. 539.
17. On the writings of classical authors concerning the theory of *jihad*, see A. Morabia, *Le Gihad dans l'islam mediéval*, Paris: Albin Michel, 1993.
18. See, for example, the White House communiqué on 2 February 1996.
19. A. Charfi, 'La sécularisation dans les sociétés arabo-musulmanes modernes', in *Pluralisme et laïcité*, published by the Groupe de recherches islamo-chrétien, Paris: Bayard-Centurion, 1996, p. 28.
20. See S. Ghrab, 'Brève histoire des pouvoirs en Islam', in *Pluralisme et laïcité*, pp. 69 and esp. 74; M. S. Ashmawi, *The Islamic Caliphate* (in Arabic), Cairo: Sina, 2nd edn, 1992, p. 102; *The History of Tabari* (in Arabic), Beirut: Maison des livres scientifiques, vol. 2, p. 244; on the defeat of Saad, see Ashmawi, pp.99, 116.
21. Ashmawi, p. 102.
22. Ibid.
23. Daghfous, p. 316.
24. On this question, see I. Choufani, ed., *La Guerre des apostats*, Beirut: Trésors éternels, 1995, and the review in *Riwak arabi* No. 1, pp. 109ff.
25. Those who find this judgement too severe might like to reflect on the reasons why Khalid ibn al-Walid killed Malek Ben Nouera, a Muslim accused of apostasy, whose wife happened to be too beautiful. See *The History of Tamari* (in Arabic), Beirut, 1988, vol. 2, p. 274. He abused her that very evening, treating with disdain the suffering of a woman who had just lost her husband and the revulsion she must have felt for his murderer. It is true

that, according to sharia law, the wives of conquered men become slaves on a par with
mere things. Today, the GIA 'militants' in Algeria attack villages and kill their inhabitants
on the grounds of apostasy, sometimes kidnapping their women and collectively abusing
them as war booty. Still today, many streets in Muslim towns bear the name of ibn al-
Walid and historians present him as a great leader; his legendary exploits are part of the collective memory. Muslim peoples have been deluded by the embellishment and sacralization of their history.

26. Ashmawi, p. 112.
27. H. Jaït, *La Grande Discorde*, Paris: Gallimard, 1989, pp. 81, 82.
28. Ibid.
29. Ibid.
30. Ashmawi, p. 119.
31. Harun ar-Rashid had no fewer than two thousand concubines, while al-Mutawakkil had
    four thousand. See Ashmawi, p. 183.
32. Ibid.
33. Ibid., p. 243.
34. See Abderrazak's *The Foundations of Islamic Power*, 1972 edn, edited by Mohamed Amara,
    Beirut, p. 128.
35. M. N. Farhat, 'Le fondamentalisme et les droits de l'homme', *Revue arabe des droits de
    l'homme*, 1997, No. 4, p. 131. See also M. A. Jabri, *La Raison politique arabe*, Casablanca,
    1990, p. 251.
36. Its title is *The Juridical Regime in the Sultanate*.
37. M. Talbi, in *Jeune Afrique* No. 1892, 9–15 April 1997, p. 81.
38. Ashmawi, p. 23.
39. H. Jaït, *La Grande Discorde*, p. 155.
40. Ibid.
41. See M. Arkoun, *L'Islam, morale et politique*, Paris: Desclée et Brouwer, 1986, pp. 159–60.
42. Abdu Filali Ansari, In the introduction to the French edition of A. Abderrazak, *L'Islam et
    les fondements du pouvoir*, Paris: Le Fennec/La Découverte, 1994, p. 22.
43. *La Bible de Jérusalem*, Paris: Éditions du Cerf, 1973, 'Le Livre de Josué', p. 259.
44. 'Ancien Testament', Traduction œcuménique de *La Bible*, Paris: Éditions du Cerf, 1975, p.
    421.
45. A. Finkielkraut, *L'Humanité perdue, essai sur le XXe siècle*, Paris: Le Seuil, 1996, p. 22.
46. See E. Karabélias, 'Apostasie et dissidence religieuse à Byzance de Justinien 1er jusqu'à
    l'invasion arabe', *Islamochristiana* No. 20, Rome, 1994, p. 41.
47. R. Etchegaray, 'Culture chrétienne et droits de l'homme, du rejet à l'engagement', in
    Culture chrétienne et droits de l'homme, Brussels: *Fédération internationale des universités
    catholiques*, 1991, p. 8.
48. Ibid., pp. 12, 13.
49. B. El Nadi and A. Rifaat, *Le Courrier de l'UNESCO*, January 1996, p. 9.
50. M. Verwilghen, preface to *Culture chrétienne et droits de l'homme*, p. x.
51. In fact, the fundamentalist approach is the same in all religions. Myra Daridan writes that
    'the Islamist arguments are found almost word for word among certain Christians as well as
    certain Orthodox Jews' who consider that 'religion is a single whole to be taken as such'.
    Un islam du cœur, Paris: Cerf, 1997, p. 67.
52. J. Gaudemet, *Revue de droit canonique*, Paris: Dalloz, 1984, pp. 81ff.
53. A. Peyrefitte, *La Société de confiance*, Paris: Odile Jacob, 1995, p. 69.
54. Ibid., p. 75.
55. Chapter 35:IV of the Catechizm, quoted by Peyrefitte, p. 98.

56. *Traité de l'usure*, 1776.

57. Peyrefitte, p. 117.

58. Ibid., p. 182.

59. M. Villey, *La Pensée juridique moderne*, Paris: Dalloz, 1976, p. 280.

60. P. Petit, *Encyclopedia universalis*, Paris: Encyclopaedia universalis de France, 1988, vol. 5, p. 386.

61. A. Mezghani and S. Laghmani, *Studies on Modernity and Law* (in Arabic), Tunis: Sud Édition, p.170.

62. Ibid., p. 77.

63. In H. Boularès's work *L'Islam, la peur et l'espérance*, Paris: J.-C. Lattès, 1983, p. 157. Chapter VIII has the title 'The impossibility of secularism'. (Published in English as *Islam: The Fear and the Hope* by Zed Books, London and New Jersey, 1990).

64. Secondary funding may come from collections or the product of public habous.

65. H. Ennifar, 'État et religion dans le débat actuel, islamisme ou voie moyenne', in *Pluralisme et laïcité*, p. 205.

66. See Banjul, 'La nouvelle Mecque de l'islamisme', *Jeune Afrique* No. 1882, 29 January–4 February 1997.

67. *L'Express*, 30 October 2003.

Chapter 4 • Education and Modernity

1. *Le Nouvel Observateur*, 20–26 February 1997, p. 7; *L'Express*, 9 November 1995.

2. *La Presse* (Tunis), 12 December 1995.

3. J. Eisenberg, 'Des rabbins, des prophètes et des fous', *Le Monde*, 29 November 1995, p. 17.

4. A. Tuilier, *Histoire de l'Université de Paris et de Sorbonne*, Paris: Nouvelle Librairie de France, Paris, 1994, p. 31.

5. Ibid., pp. 132–6.

6. Ibid., pp. 45, 339.

7. B. Boiteveau, 'À propos des gardiens de l'Islam', *Correspondance* (Tunis) No. 46, June 1997, p. 5.

8. Ibid., p. 3.

9. J. Ben Tahar, *Crimes and Punishments* (in Arabic), Tunis: Mannouba Faculty of Letters, 1995, p. 26.

10. F. Triki, *La Stratégie d'identité*, Paris: Arcantères, 1998, p. 90.

11. Ben Tahar, p. 142.

12. J. Abdelkafi, *La Politique d'aménagement du territoire et de planification urbaine*, Tunis: ITES, 1995, p. 189. The higher estimate is found in A. Nouschi, 'Observations sur les villes dans le Maghreb précolonial', *Les Cahiers de la Méditerranée* No. 23, December 1981, p. 3.

13. D. and E. Larguèche, *Marginales en terre d'islam*, Tunis: CERES Productions, 1992, p. 19.

14. E. Pélissier, *Description de la Régence de Tunis*, 1st edn, Paris, 1853; reissued Tunis: Bouslama, 1980, pp. 337ff.

15. Ibid., p. 108. In the Middle Ages, adultery by a Muslim woman with a non-Muslim man had carried the death penalty, but stoning was replaced with drowning as the method of execution. It was known as the 'sack and sea' punishment.

16. B. L. Azaiez, *Tels syndicalistes, tels syndicats*, Steac: Imp. Tunis-Carthage, 1980, p. 1.

17. Pélissier, p. 51.

18. M. El Aziz Ben Achour, *The Zituna Mosque* (in Arabic), Tunis: Ceres, 1991, pp. 109, 110.

19. Ben Achour, p. 105; Pélissier, p. 51.

20. M. El Aziz Ben Achour, 'Enseignement et tradition: la Zitouna', in *Itinéraire du savoir en*

Tunisie, Paris: Alif-CNRS, p. 130; and N. Sraïeb, *Le Collège Sadiki de Tunis*, Tunis: Alif.

21. Out of the nine leaders of the Young Tunisians's newspaper *Le Tunisien*, eight had had a modern education and the ninth was none other than Abdelaziz Thaalbi, whose conflictual relations with the Zituna have been mentioned before. See B. Harmassi, *État et société au Maghreb*, Paris: Éditions Anthropos, 1975, p. 123, n. 15.

22. Quoted in Harmassi, p. 123.

23. See A. Ben Miled and M. Driss, *Abdelaziz Thaalbi et le mouvement Jeunes Tunisiens*, Tunis, 1991, p. 114.

24. On this whole episode, see T. Ayadi, *Mouvement réformiste et mouvements populaires à Tunis (1906–1912)*, Tunis: Faculty of Literature and Humanities, series *History*, vol. XXX, 1986, pp. 129–36.

25. Ben Miled and Driss, p. 117.

26. F. Burgat, *L'Islamisme en face*, Paris: La Découverte, 1994, pp. 49ff.

27. See the Manual of Islamic Education, 4th year of secondary school, 1988 edition.

28. Manual of Islamic Education, 5th year of secondary school, 1988 edition, p. 39. Previous editions contained the same points on different pages.

29. Ibid., p. 73.

30. Ibid., pp. 124–39, 170.

31. See the whole of the Manual of Islamic Education, 6th year of secondary school, 1988 edition.

32. One example among many is the 1988 edition of the Arabic reader for the 4th year of primary school. Its illustration of generosity is a financial contribution to the building of a mosque (p. 116), and, of mutual aid, the pooling of efforts to build another mosque (p. 14). It teaches the conjugation of verbs by referring to the obligation to pray (p. 24), to God (pp. 129, 163) or to the duty to go on a pilgrimage (pp. 104, 106). Similar evidence could be adduced from nearly all other Muslim countries.

33. See M. Zeghal, *Gardiens de l'islam. Les oulémas d'Al Azhar dans l'Égypte contemporaine*, Paris: Presses de sciences politiques, 1996, pp. 59–60.

34. See, in particular: Islamic Education, 3rd year, middle schools, pp. 8, 15, 37 and 40; and idem, 5th year, pp. 83ff.

35. Islamic Education, 2nd year, middle schools, p. 40.

36. Institut arabe des droits humains, Rapport sur l'Égypte, p. 39. For a critical look at Egyptian school books, see N. H. Abu Zeid, *A Critique of Religious Discourse* (in Arabic), Cairo: Sina, 1992, p. 104.

37. Egyptian Reader, 1st year of primary school, pp. 28, 30.

38. Islamic Education, 3rd year, middle schools, p. 37.

39. Elementary School, 8th year, p. 175.

40. Islamic Education, 2nd year of secondary school, 1996 edn., pp. 85ff.

41. Islamic Education, 9th year of elementary school, 1996 edn., p. 65.

42. Moroccan textbook: *Islamic Thought and Philosophy* (in Arabic), 1996.

43. We could fill dozens of pages with examples of this kind from the Moroccan *Language Lessons* (in Arabic), a manual for the fifth year of elementary school which is in fact a book of grammar. After the statement of each grammatical rule, it gives an illustration that has clearly not been taken at random: the suffering of the early Muslims persecuted at Mecca (p. 3), more events in Mecca (p. 38), the need to be a good Muslim (p. 41), the conduct of Omar, the second caliph (p. 59), Muslims and science through history (p. 78), the conduct of the Prophet (p. 84), Muslim Andalusia (p. 85), Baghdad in the age of the Abbasids (p. 91), a prayer (p. 103), Ramadan, the month of fasting (p. 136), Muslims obey the Koran (p. 139), the Prophet (p. 140), and so on.

44. For a critique of the teaching of history in Algeria, see 'Comment on enseigne l'histoire en Algérie', record of the conference on *The Teaching of History*, 26-27 February 1992, Oran: Centre de recherches en anthropologie sociale et culturelle, 1995.

45. Abdou Filali Ansary, 'Entre foi profonde et lucidité assumée', in *Prologues* (Casablanca), No. 10, 1997, p. 6.

46. Mohamed Talbi, 'Une communauté de communautés', *Islamochristiana* (Rome), No. 4, p. 11.

47. M. J. Al Ansari, 'The structure of Arab political culture and political behaviour' (in Arabic), *Al Muntada*, organ of the Club of Arab Thought (Amman), No. 126, March 1996.

48. In a memorandum on religious education in Tunisia, submitted in 1995 to the Pontifical Institute for Arab and Islamic Studies in Rome, Michel Guillaud notes that the 145 authors studied in this field included 111 contemporaries, 6 from the nineteenth century and only 28 from longer ago.

49. A special department has been created at the Faculty of Humanities and Social Science in Tunis, whose diploma in civic education is now required to teach this important subject in secondary schools.

50. Séverine Labat, *L'Islamisme algérien*, Paris: Le Seuil, 1995, p. 126.

51. Ibid., p. 138.

52. These points refer to the majority of Iranian mullahs and Sunni ulema, but there are certainly exceptions which, if they continue to grow as they have in recent times, could evidently change some of the terms of the problem.

53. J. Ozouf and M. Ozouf, *La République des instituteurs*, Paris: Gallimard-Le Seuil, 1992; and J. Ozouf, *Nous les maîtres d'écoles*, Paris: Folio-Histoire, 1993.

Index

Abbas, Ibn, 49
Abbasids, 7, 84, 94
Abdelkader, Sidi, 25
Abderrahman, Omar, 15, 53
Abderrazak, Ali, 11, 25, 107, 118, 137, 156, 166
Abdu, Mohamed, 24, 87, 89-90, 92, 147, 156
Abedelaziz, Omar ben, 115
abrogation, 156; idea of, 108
Abu Bakr, 49-50, 116-17, 125, 166
Abu Ghraib prison, 2
Abu Zeid, Nasr Hamed, divorce proceedings, 53-4
Achour, Habib, 146
Adam, biblical, 104-6
adultery, stoning death, 56-9, 79
Afghani, Jameleddine al, 92, 147
Afghanistan, 2, 153; sovereignty entitlement, 109; Taliban rule, 29; US fundamentalist arming, 28
Aflak, Michael, 7
Aisha, 114
Al Azhar University, Egypt, 5, 8, 11, 25, 52-3, 87-8, 102, 137, 150
Al Hadhira, newspaper, 23
Al Hallaj, execution of, 51
Al-Mutawakkil, Caliphate, 86
Algeria, 33; elections 1991, 9, 19, 100; intellectuals, 36; Islamists, 14-15, 160; polygamy, 155; teachers, 137
Algerian Islamic Salvation Front (FIS), 9, 36, 160-1; programme, 104
Ali, Mohamed, 136
Amichai, Yehuda, 135
Amin, Kacem, 4, 148, 166
Amir, Yigal, 135
Amnesty International, 14
Amor, Abdelfattah, 18
Ansary, Abdou Filali, 152
apostasy, 48, 51-2, 138, 148; accusations of, 112; Christian death penalty, 119; divorce ruling, 53-4; Islamic death penalty for, 50,
56, 58, 67, 95, 103;'economic', 113
Aquinas, Thomas, 21, 122, 136
Arab world; astronomers, 118; civilization, 12; language, 156, 158; law, 75; literature, 157; pre-Islamic, 94, science, 80; tribal, 93; unity idea, 11, 153-4
Arab Human Rights Institute, 151
Arabization, 113; education, 147
arbitration, Arabia practice, 106
Aristotle, 79; Christian condemnation, 136; *Politics*, 116, 122
Arius, 124
Armed Islamic group, Algeria (GIA), 9, 11, 33, 104
Atatürk, Kemal, 41, 90, 102, 133, 166
Auda, Abdelkader, 30
audiovisual communications, 64
authoritarianism, 12, 34, 157; Islamic cover, 51
Averroës (Ibn Rushd), 21, 86, 118, 136, 140, 166
Avicenna, 118

Baath Party, 6, 153
Baghdad, fall of 1258, 87
Bahais, Iranian persecution, 47
Bahrain, 155
Bali, terrorist attack, 109
Bank of Tunisia, 82
banking system, Muslim countries, 4, Europe, 82; Islam, 81-2
Banna, Hasan al, 29
Bar Ilan, religious university Tel Aviv, 135
Bassu war, 60
Bayram, Mohamed, 4, 136
Bedouin society, 69, Maghreb, 49
Belhaj, Ali, 19
Ben Bedis, ulema, 102
Ben Bella, Ahmed, 9
Ben Jedid, Chadli, 9, 53
Blum, Léon, 47
Bouhajeb, Ali 136

180

abolition, 89; public liberty violations, 9–
10; religious teaching, 155; slavery
abolition, 4; State Security court, 146
Tunisian Code of Obligations and
Contracts, 81
Turabi, Hassan al, 17, 19, 30, 52, 95
Turkey: corrupt political class, 134;
polygamy abolition, 90; Rafah party, 132;
religious teaching, 132; secular constitution; Tanzimat reforms, 102

Ubada, Saad ibn, 112
ulema, 3, 51, 74–6, 80, 83–4, 117; colonial
subservience, 90; Egyptian political
pressure, 107; law-making, 84–5; role of,
73; science abandonment, 13
umma, 126, 153
United Nations, 2, 18
United States of America (USA), 11, 46;
fundamentalist arming, 28; war on
Afghanistan, 2
Universal Declaration of Human Rights, 3,
59, 63, 158
universal suffrage, 77, 157
urbanisation, 68
usury, 82; avoidance, 82
Uthman, Caliph, 25

Valladolid, royal commission meeting, 119
veil, the, 5, 7, 22, 44
vengeance, 60
Verlindin, Charles, 94
violence, 130; fundamentalist legitimization,
16; monotheistic religions, 120

Wafd political party, 11
Walid, Khalid ibn al, 113
waqf, 74
war booty, Koran on, 100
Weber, Max, 123
West, the, 36; hatred for, 30–1
women, anti-feminism, 67–8; Bedouin, 5,
139; emancipation, 10; inequality, 42–4;
inheritance law, 72; Islamist role for, 31;
liberation movement, 8; right to vote, 3
World Trade centre, first attack on, 15;
9/11 attack on, 1–2, 28, 109

Yemen, textbooks, 151
Young Tunisians party, 142–3
Young Turks, 20, 90

Zaghlul, Saad, 11
zaket, 94, 113
Zalloum, Abdelkadim, 33
Zanj, popular revolt, 51
Zaouche, Abdeljalil, 142
Zeid, Abu, 92
Zeroual, Liamine, 14
Zina, 77–8
Zionism, 31, 36
Zituna religious university, Tunisia, 5, 21–2,
25–6, 52, 83, 87, 102, 137, 140, 143, 150;
elite, 24, 27; graduate teacher employ-
ment, 145; judicial power, 142; reform
failure, 141
Zohr, Ibn, 118